BERLITZ®

KU-015-699

JAPANESE
for travellers

By the staff of Berlitz Guides

How best to use this phrase book

● We suggest that you start with the **Guide to pronunciation** (pp. 8–9), then go on to **Some basic expressions** (pp. 10–15). This gives you not only a minimum vocabulary, but also helps you get used to pronouncing the language.

● Consult the **Contents** pages (3–5) for the section you need. In each chapter you'll find travel facts, hints and useful information. Simple phrases are followed by a list of words applicable to the situation.

● Separate, detailed contents lists are included at the beginning of the extensive **Eating out** and **Shopping guide** sections (Menus, p. 44, Shops and services, p. 97).

● If you want to find out how to say something in Japanese, your fastest look-up is via the **Dictionary** section (pp. 163–189). This not only gives you the word, but is also cross-referenced to its use in a phrase on a specific page.

● If you wish to learn more about constructing sentences, check the **Basic grammar** (pp. 158–162).

● Note the **colour margins** are indexed in Japanese and English to help both listener and speaker. And, in addition, there is also an **index in Japanese** for the use of your listener.

● Throughout the book, this symbol ☛ suggests phrases your listener can use to answer you. If you still can't understand, hand this phrase book to the Japanese-speaker to encourage pointing to an appropriate answer. The English translation for you is just alongside the Japanese.

Revised edition – 2nd printing 1988
Printed in Hungary

Contents

A few words about the language	6

Guide to pronunciation	8

Some basic expressions	10

Arrival — 16

16	Passport control	19	Where…?
16	Customs	19	Hotel reservation
18	Baggage—Porters	20	Car hire (rental)
18	Changing money	21	Taxi

Hotel—Accommodation — 22

23	Checking in—Reception	29	Difficulties
26	Registration—Hotel staff	30	Laundry—Dry cleaner's
27	General requirements	31	Hairdresser—Barber
28	The bath	32	Checking out
28	Telephone—Post (mail)	32	Camping—Public lodgings

Eating out — 33

33	Where to eat	52	Game and poultry
34	What to eat	53	Rice—Noodles
36	How to eat	54	Vegetables—Tofu
37	Japanese cuisine	55	Seasoning—Spices
38	Finding the restaurant	56	Fruit
39	Reservation	57	Dessert
40	Asking and ordering	58	Drinks
42	Breakfast	58	Beer—Sake
44	What's on the menu?	59	Wine
45	Starters (Appetizers)	60	Other alcoholic drinks
46	Salad—Soup—Egg dishes	60	Nonalcoholic drinks
47	Fish and seafood	61	Tea—The tea ceremony
49	Sushi—Sashimi—Tempura	62	The bill (check)
50	Meat	63	Complaints
52	Chicken	64	Snacks—Picnic

4

Travelling around 65

65	Plane	75	Boat service
66	Train	76	Car
68	Inquiries	77	Asking the way
70	Tickets	78	Parking
70	Reservation	79	Breakdown—Road
71	On the train		assistance
72	Baggage—Porters	79	Accident—Police
73	Underground (subway)	80	Road signs
74	Bus—Tram (streetcar)	80	Bicycle hire (rental)

Sightseeing 81

82	Where...?	85	Who—What—When?
83	Admission	85	Religious services
84	Special interests	86	Countryside

Relaxing 87

87	Theatre—Concert—Cinema	89	Nightclubs—Discos
88	The Japanese theatre	90	Geisha
89	Tickets	91	Sports

Making friends 93

93	Introductions	95	The weather
95	Invitations	96	Dating

Shopping guide 97

98	Shops and services	118	Electrical appliances—
100	General expressions		Hi-fi equipment
104	Bookshop—Newsstand—	120	Grocery
	Stationer's	121	Jeweller's—Watch-
106	Chemist's (drugstore)		maker's
110	Clothing	123	Optician
111	Clothes and accessories	124	Photography
112	Size	126	Tobacconist's
115	Fabrics	127	Souvenirs
116	Shoes	128	Records—Cassettes
117	Department store	128	Toys

Your money: banks—currency 129

| 130 | At the bank | 131 | Business terms |

At the post office 132

| 133 | Telegrams | 134 | Telephoning |

Doctor 136

136	General	142	Prescription—Treatment
137	Parts of the body		ment
138	Accidents—Injury	143	Fee
139	Illness	143	Hospital
140	Women's section	144	Dentist

Reference section 145

145	Countries	153	Public holidays
146	Numbers	153	Greetings
149	Year and age		and wishes
149	Seasons	154	Signs and notices
149	Months	155	Emergency
150	Days	155	Lost property
151	What time is it?	156	Conversion tables

Basic Grammar 158

Dictionary and index (English-Japanese) 163

Japanese index 190

Map of Japan 192

Acknowledgments
We are particularly grateful to Keiko Ito and Hiromi Chino for their help in the preparation of this book, and to Dr. T.J.A. Bennett for his advice concerning the phonetic transcription. We also wish to thank Anne-Marie Golaz and David Pulman for their assistance.

THE LANGUAGE

日本語について

A few words about the language

Learn only a smattering of the language and your trip to the Land of the Rising Sun will be even more enjoyable. The Japanese will more than just appreciate your efforts to communicate in their language – they will be astonished that you even try.

Japanese can be simple and direct but more often it is complex and subtle (in this book we have kept to basics). Apart from a confusing similarity of script, it bears no resemblance to Chinese or any other Asiatic language and isn't even remotely related to English. Where Japanese comes from not even language scholars know for sure. Japan, its people, customs and above all its language, were almost totally isolated for over 2000 years until the late nineteenth century. With a vocabulary and sentence structure all its own, the language reflects the whole Japanese way of thinking. In a word, it is unique.

Yet a lot of foreign words have sneaked into Japanese, particularly in this century. From *disco* to *cocoa,* from *monorail* to *manager,* you will come across many an imported English word. Sometimes, however, they are pronounced so differently that you may not recognize them at first hearing. And you may have to pronounce them both the Japanese and the English ways before you are understood. Such 'loan words' are written in *katakana* (see next page).

Japanese characters

Traditionally, Japanese is written from top to bottom starting in the upper right-hand corner. But it's also written horizontally and from left to right (as in this book). Basically the Japanese script you will be looking at is a mixture of three different systems called *kanji, hiragana* and *katakana.*

GRAMMAR, see page 158

Kanji

Kanji, adopted from the Chinese, are the basic ideograms, each character representing one word.

山 mountain	川 river	水 water	火 fire
太 陽 sun	月 moon	星 star	大 地 earth

Hiragana

Hiragana characters are used for words of Japanese origin and often also for particles (which designate subject or object) and endings or words spelled in *kanji. Hiragana* and *katakana* scripts represent individual syllables.

あ a	か ka	さ sa	た ta	な na	は ha	ま ma	や ya	ら ra	わ wa
い i	き ki	し shi	ち thi	に ni	ひ hi	み mi		り ri	
う u	く ku	す su	つ tsu	ぬ nu	ふ fu	む mu	ゆ yu	る ru	
え e	け ke	せ se	て te	ね ne	へ he	め me		れ re	
お o	こ ko	そ so	と to	の no	ほ ho	も mo	よ yo	ろ ro	を (w)o
				ん n					

Katakana

Katakana is often used for writing English and other foreign words and names – a kind of shorthand system.

ア a	カ ka	サ sa	タ ta	ナ na	ハ ha	マ ma	ヤ ya	ラ ra	ワ wa
イ i	キ ki	シ shi	チ chi	ニ ni	ヒ hi	ミ mi		リ ri	
ウ u	ク ku	ス su	ツ tsu	ヌ nu	フ fu	ム mu	ユ yu	ル ru	
エ e	ケ ke	セ se	テ te	ネ ne	ヘ he	メ me		レ re	
オ o	コ ko	ソ so	ト to	ノ no	ホ ho	モ mo	ヨ yo	ロ ro	ヲ (w)o
				ン n					

日本語について

Guide to pronunciation

As a minimum vocabulary for your trip, we have selected a number of basic words and phrases under the title "Some basic expressions" (pages 10–15).

An outline of the sounds of Japanese

If you follow carefully the indications supplied below, you will have no difficulty in reading the transliterations in such a way as to make yourself understood. (This book also contains the Japanese script. If, despite your efforts, your listener doesn't seem to understand you, then show him or her the book and indicate what you mean to say.)

Japanese is composed less of vowels and consonants than of syllables, consisting of a consonant and a vowel. All syllables are pronounced with almost equal force; there is no strong stress, except for emphasis.

A transliteration is a representation of the sounds of the language in the Latin (our) alphabet, as opposed to the traditional Japanese alphabet. It can be read quite easily once a few rules have been mastered. We have decided to use a transliteration based on the Hepburn Romanisation, as this is the most helpful of the systems in use at present.

Vowels

Letter	Approximate pronunciation
a	as in car, but shorter and pronounced further forward in the mouth
e	as in ten
i	as in police, but shorter

発音

| o | as in gone, but with lips slightly more rounded |
| u | as in put, but with lips not rounded |

1) Vowels carrying a bar (ā, ē, ī, ō, ū) should be pronounced long. The long sound of **i** is also written **ii**. The length of vowels in Japanese is important; you should clearly distinguish short from long vowels, as this difference can change the meaning of a word, e.g., **obasan** means aunt and **obāsan** means grandmother.

2) If two vowels appear together, e.g., **ai, ie,** they should be pronounced separately; each vowel keeps its normal sound. However, **ei** is often pronounced like **ē**.

3) Between voiceless consonants (k, p, s, t, h) or after a voiceless consonant at the end of a phrase, **i** and **u** are generally whispered, or not pronounced at all, e.g. **mimasu** becomes **mimas** and **imashita** becomes **imashta.**

Consonants

These are pronounced approximately as in English with the following exceptions:

g	as in go when at the beginning of a word; everywhere else (including in the particle ga) it is often pronounced like ng in ring
n	as in no; but when it is at the end of a word or syllable, more like ng in ring, although it is not incorrect, even then, to pronounce it as in no
r	pronounced with the tongue more or less in the position for l (there is no separate l in Japanese), but the tongue does not touch the front of the mouth, nor is the sound "rolled"
s	always as in see
w	the lips are not rounded but left slack

Double consonants should be pronounced "long", i.e., hold the sound for a moment. The doubling of a consonant is important, it can change the meaning of a word.

Some basic expressions

Yes.	はい。	hai
No.	いいえ。	iie
Please.	どうぞ／お願いします。	dōzo/o-negaishimasu
Thank you.	ありがとうございます。	arigatō gozaimasu
Thank you very much.	どうもありがとうございます。	dōmo arigatō gozaimasu
That's all right/You're welcome.	どういたしまして。	dō itashimashite

Greetings あいさつ

Good morning.	お早うございます。	ohayō gozaimasu
Good afternoon.	今日は。	konnichiwa
Good evening.	今晩は。	konbanwa
Good night.	お休みなさい。	oyasumi nasai
Good-bye.	さようなら。	sayōnara
See you later.	では又後程。	dewa mata nochihodo
This is Mr./Mrs./Miss* ...	こちらは…さんです。	kochira wa ... san desu
How do you do? (Pleased to meet you.)	はじめまして。	hajime mashite
How are you?	お元気ですか。	ogenki desu ka
Very well, thanks. And you?	はい、ありがとうございます。貴方は。	hai arigatō gozaimasu. anata wa
Fine.	元気です。	genki desu

---

* According to Japanese practice, the surname comes first. You should use the suffix -san (Mr., Mrs. or Miss) after the family name. This means that if you meet someone called Horiba Iwao you should address him as "Horibasan".

Sorry? (I didn't understand that.)	すみません。	sumimasen
Excuse me. (May I get past?)	すみません。	sumimasen
Sorry!	ごめんなさい。	gomennasai

Questions 質問

Where?	どこ	doko
How?	どうやって/どれ位	dōyatte/dorekurai
When?	いつ	itsu
What?	何	nani
Why?	何故/どうして	naze/dōshite
Who?	誰	dare
Which?	どちら/どれ	dochira/dore
Where is ...?	…はどこですか。	... wa doko desu ka
Where are ...?	…はどこですか。	... wa doko desu ka
Where can I find/ get ...?	…はどこにありますか。	... wa doko ni arimasuka
How far?	どれ位の距離ですか。	dorekurai no kyori desu ka
How long?	どれ位の時間ですか。	dorekurai no jikan desu ka
How much/ How many?	どれほど、〔いくら〕/いくってすか。	dorehodo [ikura]/ikutsu desu ka
How much does this cost?	これはいくらですか。	kore wa ikura desu ka
When does ... open/ close?	…はいつ開きますか/いつ締りますか。	... wa itsu aki masu ka/ itsu shimari masu ka
What do you call this/that in Japanese?	これ/あれは日本語で何と言いますか。	kore/are wa nihongo de nanto īmasu ka
What does this/that mean?	これ/あれはどう言う意味ですか。	kore/are wa dōyū imi desu ka

Do you speak ...? …を話しますか。

Do you speak English?	英語を話しますか。	eigo o hanashimasu ka

Does anyone here speak English?	ここに誰か英語を話す人がいますか。	koko ni dareka eigo o hanasu hito ga imasu ka
I don't speak (much) Japanese.	日本語を（あまり）話しません。	nihongo o (amari) hanashimasen
Could you speak more slowly?	もう一度ゆっくり話して下さいますか。	motto yukkuri hanashite kudasai masu ka
Could you repeat that?	もう一度言って下さいますか。	mō ichido itte kudasai masu ka
Please write it down.	それを書いて下さい。	sore o kaite kudasai
Can you translate this?	これを訳して下さいますか。	kore o yakushite kudasaimasu ka
Please point to the ... in the book.	この本の中で、その…を指さして下さい。	kono hon no naka de sono ... o yubisashite kudasai
word/phrase/ sentence	単語/言いまわし/文	tango/ii mawashi/bun
Just a moment.	ちょっと待って下さい。	chotto matte kudasai
I'll see if I can find it in this book.	この本の中にあるかどうか見てみましょう。	kono hon no naka ni arukadōka mitemimashō
I understand.	わかりました。	wakarimashita
I don't understand.	わかりません。	wakarimasen
Do you understand?	おわかりですか。	o-wakari desu ka

Can you help me? 手伝って下さいますか。

Can I have ...?	…を下さいますか。	... o kudasaimasu ka
Can we have ...?	…を下さいますか。	... o kudasaimasu ka
Can you show me ...?	…を見せて下さいますか。	... o misete kudasaimasu ka
I can't.	出来ません。	dekimasen
Can you tell me ...?	…を教えて下さいますか。	... o oshiete kudasaimasu ka
Can you help me?	手伝って下さいますか。	tetsudatte kudasai masu ka
Can you direct me to ...?	…はどこにありますか。	... wa doko ni arimasu ka

I'd like ...   …が欲しい

I'd like/We'd like ...	…が欲しいのですが。	... ga hoshii no desu ga
I'd like to see ...	…が見たいのですが。	... ga mitai no desu ga
We'd like to eat/drink ...	…が食べ/飲みたいのですが。	... ga tabe/nomi tai no desu ga
What do you want?	何がよろしいでしょうか。	nani ga yoroshii deshō ka
I want/We want ...	…が欲しいのですが。	... ga hoshii no desu ga
I want to buy ...	…が買いたいのですが。	... ga kaitai no desu ga
We want to go to ...	…へ行きたいのですが。	... e ikitai no desu ga
I/We need ...	…が要るんですが。	... ga irun desu ga
I'm looking for ...	…を探しています。	... o sagashite imasu
Give me ..., please.	…を下さい。	... o kudasai
Give it to me, please.	それを下さい。	sore o kudasai
Bring me ...	…を持って来て下さい。	... o mottekite kudasai
Bring it to me.	それを持って来て下さい。	sore o mottekite kudasai
Show me ...	…を見せて下さい。	... o misete kudasai
Show it to me.	それを見せて下さい。	sore o misete kudasai
It's important.	大切です。	taisetsu desu
It's urgent.	急用です。	kyūyō desu

I'm ...   私は…

I'm hungry.	お腹がすきました。	onaka ga suki mashita
I'm thirsty.	喉がかわきました。	nodo ga kawaki mashita
I'm tired.	疲れました。	tsukare mashita
I'm lost.	道に迷いました。	michi ni mayoi mashita
I'm ill.	病気です。	byōki desu
I'm fine.	元気です。	genki desu

It is/There is ...   …があります。

It is ...	…です。	... desu
Is it ...?	…ですか。	... desu ka

It isn't ...	…ではありません。	... dewa arimasen
Here it is.	はい、ここにあります。	hai koko ni arimasu
Here they are.	はい、ここにあります。	hai koko ni arimasu
There it is.	はい、あそこにあります。	hai asoko ni arimasu
There they are.	はい、あそこにあります。	hai asoko ni arimasu
There is/There are ...	…があります。	... ga arimasu
Is there/Are there ...?	…がありますか。	... ga arimasu ka
There isn't/aren't ...	…はありません。	... wa arimasen
There isn't/aren't any.	全然ありません。	zenzen arimasen

It's ... …です。

big/small	大きい/小さい	ōkii/chīsai
quick/slow	速い/遅い	hayai/osoi
hot/cold	熱い/冷たい	atsui/tsumetai
hot/cold (weather)	暑い/寒い	atsui/samui
full/empty	いっぱい/から	ippai/kara
easy/difficult	易しい/難しい	yasashii/muzukashii
heavy/light	重い/軽い	omoi/karui
open/shut	開いている/締っている	aiteiru/shimatteiru
right/wrong	正しい/間違い	tadashii/machigai
old/new	古い/新しい	furui/atarashii
old/young	年とっている/若い	toshitotteiru/wakai
next/last	次の/最後の	tsugi no/saigo no
beautiful/ugly	美しい/みにくい	utsukushii/minikui
free (vacant)/occupied	空き/使用中	aki/shiyōchū
good/bad	良い/悪い	yoi/warui
better/worse	より良い/より悪い	yori yoi/yori warui
early/late	早い/遅い	hayai/osoi
cheap/expensive	安い/高い	yasui/takai
near/far	近い/遠い	chikai/tōi
here/there	ここ/あそこ	koko/asoko

Quantities 量

a little/a lot	少し/沢山	sukoshi/takusan
few/a few	ほとんどない/少し	hotondo nai/sukoshi
much, many	沢山 (の)	takusan (no)
more/less	もっと多く/もっと少なく	motto ōku/motto sukunaku

more than/less than	より（もっと）多く/より（もっと）少なく	yori (motto) ōku/yori (motto) sukunaku
enough/too	じゅうぶん/過ぎ	jūbun/sugi
some/any	少し/どれか一つ	sukoshi/doreka hitotsu

A few more useful words　その他の役に立つ言葉

at	に	ni
on	の上（に）	no ue (ni)
in	の中（に）	no naka (ni)
to	へ	e
after	の後	no ato
before	の前	no mae
for	のために/の代りに	no tame ni/no kawari ni
from	から	kara
with	と共に	to tomo ni
without	なしで	nashide
through	を通して	o tōshite
towards	に（向って）	ni (mukatte)
until	までに	made ni
during	の間	no aida
next to	の隣に	no tonari ni
behind	後	ushiro
between	の間	no aida
since	以来	irai
above	の真上に	no maue ni
below	下に	shita ni
under	の下に	no shita ni
inside	の中に	no naka ni
outside	の外に	no soto ni
up	上（に）	ue (ni)
upstairs	階上	kaijō
down	下（に）	shita (ni)
downstairs	階下	kaika

and	と	to
or	あるいは	aruiwa
not	ない	nai
never	決して…ない	kesshite ... nai
nothing	何もない	nani mo nai
none	ひとつもない	hitotsu mo nai
very	大変	taihen
too (also)	も又	mo mata
yet	まだ	mada
soon	すぐに	sugu ni
now	今	ima
then (after that)	その時/それから	sonotoki/sorekara
perhaps	たぶん	tabun
only	だけ	dake

Arrival

Passport control　入国審査

To enter Japan, you will need a valid passport, and you'll
have to fill in an embarkation/disembarkation card.

Here's my ...	これが私の…です。	kore ga watashi no ... desu
passport	パスポート	pasupōto
embarkation/disembarkation card	出国/入国カード	shutsu koku/nyū koku kādo
I'll be staying ...	…滞在の予定です。	... taizai no yotei desu
a few days	二、三日	ni-san nichi
a week	一週間	isshū-kan
two weeks	二週間	ni-shū-kan
a month	一ケ月	ikkagetsu
I don't know yet.	まだ分かりません。	mada wakarimasen
I'm here ...	…来ました。	... kimashita
on business	仕事で	shigoto de
on holiday	休暇で	kyūka de
on a sightseeing tour	観光で	kankō de
I'm a tourist.	私は観光客です。	watashi wa kankō kyaku desu
I'm just passing through.	ちょっと立ち寄るだけです。	chotto tachiyoru dake desu

If things become difficult:

I'm sorry, I don't understand.	ごめんなさい。分かりません。	gomen nasai, wakarimasen
Does anyone here speak ...?	ここに誰か…を話す人がいますか。	koko ni dareka ... o hanasu hito ga imasu ka
English	英語	eigo
French	フランス語	furansugo
German	ドイツ語	doitsugo

税 関
(zeikan)
CUSTOMS

The goods you import should be declared orally or in writing, but Japan has now adopted the customs clearance system of spot-checking practised in many countries. There are three exits: green (nothing to declare), red (something to declare) and white (for non-residents).

The following chart shows the main duty-free items you may take into Japan:

Cigarettes	Cigars	Tobacco	Spirits	Wine
400 or	100 or	500 g.	3 bottles of ¾ l. each	

I have nothing to declare.	申告する物は何もありません。	shinkoku suru mono wa nani mo arimasen
I have ...	…持っています。	... motte imasu
400 cigarettes a bottle of whisky a bottle of wine	たばこを400本 ウィスキーを一本 ワインを一本	tabako o yonhyappon uisukī o ippon waīn o ippon
Must I pay duty on this?	税金を払わなくてはいけませんか。	zeikin o harawanakutewa ikemasen ka
How much?	いくらですか。	ikura desu ka
It's for my personal use.	それは私が使う物です。	sore wa watashi ga tsukau mono desu
It's not new.	新品ではありません。	shinpin de wa arimasen
It's a gift.	贈物です。	okurimono desu
Where is the customs office?	税関事務所はどこですか。	zeikan jimusho wa doko desu ka

税金を払わなくてはいけませんよ。	You'll have to pay duty on this.
あそこの窓口で払って下さい。	Please pay at the office over there.
荷物はもっとありますか。	Have you any more luggage?

Baggage—Porter　手荷物-ポーター（赤帽）

If you are lucky enough to find a porter, you can ask him to take your luggage to customs for you. Otherwise you'll find luggage trolleys for the use of the passengers.

Where is/are ...?	…はどこですか。	... wa doko desu ka
luggage claim	手荷物受取	tenimotsu uketori
luggage trolleys (carts)	手荷物用カート	tenimotsu yō kāto
Porter!	ポーター/赤帽さん。	pōtā/akabō san
Please take my bag/ luggage/suitcase.	私のバッグ/荷物/スーツケースを持って下さい。	watashino baggu/nimotsu/ sūtsu kēsu o motte kudasai
That's mine.	それは私のです。	sore wa watashi no desu
Take this luggage to the ...	この荷物を…へ持って行って下さい。	kono nimotsu o ... e motte itte kudasai
bus	バス	basu
luggage lockers	荷物用ロッカー	nimotsu yō rokkā
taxi	タクシー	takushī
How much is that?	それはいくらですか。	sore wa ikura desu ka
I can't find my luggage.	私の荷物が見つかりません。	watashi no nimotsu ga mitsukari masen

Changing money　両替

Foreign currency and traveller's cheques (checks) can be exchanged or cashed only at authorized exchange offices. Most hotel exchange counters stay open in the evening, and the airport bank is open from 7 a.m. to 10 p.m.

Where can I change money?	どこでお金を両替出来ますか。	doko de o-kane o ryōgae deki masu ka
I want to change some ...	…を両替したいのですが。	... o ryōgae shitai no desu ga
traveller's cheques	トラベラーチェック	toraberā chekku
dollars	ドル	doru
pounds	ポンド	pondo
What is the exchange rate?	交換レートはいくらですか。	kōkan rēto wa ikura desu ka

BANK—CURRENCY, see page 129

Where ...? …どこですか。

Where is the ...?	…はどこですか。	... wa doko desu ka
booking office	予約窓口	yoyaku madoguchi
tourist information centre	観光案内所	kankō annaijo
How do I get to ...?	…にはどう行ったらいいでしょうか。	... ni wa dō ittara iideshō ka
Is there a(n) ... into town?	市内への…はありますか。	shinai eno ... wa arimasu ka
airport bus	空港バス	kūkō basu
city bus	市バス	shi basu
coach	直通バス	chokutsū basu
train	電車	densha
Where does it leave from?	どこから出ますか。	doko kara demasu ka
Where can I buy a ticket?	切符はどこで買えますか。	kippu wa doko de kaemasu ka
Where can I get a taxi?	タクシーはどこで乗れますか。	takushī wa doko de nore masu ka

Hotel reservation ホテル予約

If you haven't booked in advance, the Japan Travel Bureau (交通公社 —kōtsūkōsha) can help you.

Do you have a hotel guide?	ホテルガイドはありますか。	hoteru gaido wa arimasu ka
Can you reserve a room for me ...?	…一部屋予約したいのですが。	... hito heya yoyaku shitai no desu ga
at a hotel/Japanese-style inn/guest house	ホテル/旅館/民宿に	hoteru/ryokan/minshuku ni
a single room	シングルルーム	shinguru rūmu
a double room	ダブルルーム	daburu rūmu
in the centre	中心地	chūshin chi
near ...	…の近く	... no chikaku
not too expensive	余り高くない	amari takakunai
Where is the hotel?	そのホテルはどこですか。	sono hoteru wa doko desu ka
Do you have a street map?	詳しい地図はありますか。	kuwashii chizu wa arimasu ka

HOTEL/ACCOMMODATION, see page 22

Car hire (rental) レンタカー

There are car hire firms in all major cities. Except for holders of U.S. and Canadian driving licences, an International Driving Permit is necessary.

Note: In Japan, you drive on the left-hand side of the road and overtake on the right. Most traffic signs are written in Japanese characters only.

I'd like to hire (rent) a car.	車を借りたいのですが。	kuruma o karitai nodesu ga
small	小型	kogata
medium-sized	中型	chūgata
large	大型	ōgata
automatic	オートマチック	ōtomachikku
I'd like it for a day/ a week.	一日/一週間借りたいの ですが。	ichi-nichi/isshū kan karitai nodesu ga
Are there any week-end arrangements?	週末特別料金があります か。	shūmatsu tokubetsu ryōkin ga arimasu ka
Do you have any special rates?	特別料金はありますか。	tokubetsu ryōkin wa arimasu ka
What's the charge ...?	…料金はいくらですか。	... ryōkin wa ikuradesu ka
per day/week per kilometre	一日/一週間の キロメートルあたりの	ichi-nichi/isshū kan no kiromētoru atari no
Is mileage included?	走行距離計算ですか。	sōkō kyōri kēsan desu ka
I want to leave the car in ...	…で車を乗り捨てたいの ですが。	... de kuruma o norisutetai no desu ga
I'd like a car with a driver.	運転手付の車が欲しいの ですが。	untenshu tsuki no kuruma ga hoshii no desu ga
I want full insurance.	保険は全部入りたいので すが。	hoken wa zenbu hairitai no desu ga
What's the deposit?	保証金はいくらですか。	hoshōkin wa ikura desu ka
I've a credit card.	クレジットカードを持っ ています。	kurejitto kādo o motte imasu
Here's my driving licence.	これが私の運転免許証で す。	kore ga watashi no unten-menkyo shō desu

到着

CAR, see page 76

Taxi タクシー

Taxis are readily available at hotels, stations and airports, and can usually be flagged down at street corners. If the lamp behind the windscreen is red, saying *kusha,* the taxi is free; a green light means that it is occupied. As few taxi drivers speak English, it is wise to have your destination written down on a piece of paper.

Where can I get a taxi?	どこでタクシーに乗れますか。	doko de takushī ni noremasu ka
Get me a taxi, please.	タクシーを呼んで下さい。	takushī o yonde kudasai
What's the fare to ...?	…までいくらですか。	... made ikura desu ka
Take me to ...	…に連れて行って下さい。	... ni tsurete itte kudasai
this address	この住所	kono jūsho
the airport	空港	kūkō
the city air terminal	シティーエアーターミナル	shitī eā tāminaru
the ... Hotel	…ホテル	... hoteru
the town centre	中心街	chūshin gai
Go straight ahead.	まっすぐに行って下さい。	massugu ni itte kudasai
Turn ... at the next corner.	次の曲り角を…曲って下さい。	tsugi no magarikado o ... magatte kudasai
left/right	左へ/右へ	hidari e/migi e
Drive more slowly, please.	もう少しゆっくり運転して下さい。	mōsukoshi yukkuri unten shite kudasai
Stop here, please.	ここで止って下さい。	koko de tomatte kudasai
I'm in a hurry.	急いでいます。	isoide imasu
Could you wait for me?	待っていて下さいますか。	matte ite kudasai masu ka

Note: It is prudent to have the taxi driver confirm that he knows the way to the destination, as he may not indicate of his own accord that he doesn't ...

Do you know the way?	道を御存知ですか。	michi o go-zonji desu ka
It's near ...	…の近くです。	... no chikaku desu

Hotel—Other accommodation

You can choose between two totally different types of hotel: Western- or Japanese-style. The range within each of these categories runs from basic and cheap, to de luxe and expensive.

Western-style 洋式

ホテル
(hoteru)

Hotel. These are comparable to modern hotels in Europe or the United States and range from luxury class to modest. They offer conventional Western-style facilities and cuisine, although Japanese food is also available. Rates are on a "per room, per day" basis and can be reduced under certain circumstances (off-season, long-stay, etc.).

ビジネスホテル
(bisiness hoteru)

Business hotel. The rooms are small, often with no room service. But they are clean and comfortable, usually located near the city centre.

Japanese-style 和式

旅館
(ryokan)

Japanese-style hotel. These are similar to ordinary Japanese houses except that they are much larger, with a minimum of 11 guest rooms. You will also receive personal service and attention akin to the hospitality of a Japanese family. Room prices include breakfast and dinner; the rate is reduced if meals are omitted, but this should be decided before you check in.

Some *ryokans* have facilities for handling Western visitors, such as individual bathrooms and Western-style washrooms. They can also prepare simple Western-style meals. The majority of the *ryokans*, however, are not geared to catering to Western guests. For this reason, staying in one of the simpler *ryokans* may be an exciting way to spend your days in Japan, in the real Japanese way.

民宿 (minshuku)	Guest house. These are often found in holiday resorts, and the guest is treated as a member of the family, enjoying a homely and informal atmosphere. The overnight charge includes two meals, often featuring regional specialities. The guest is expected to lay out his bedding *(futon)* at night and roll it up and stow it away again the next morning.	
宿坊 (shukubo)	If you have a particular interest in Buddhism, you can stay in a Japanese temple and join in the monks' daily life.	

In this section, we are mainly concerned with the smaller and middle-class hotels and inns. You'll have no language difficulties in the luxury and first-class hotels where at least some of the staff has been trained to speak English.

Checking in—Reception チェックイン-フロント

My name is ...	私の名前は…です。	watashi no namae wa ... desu
I've a reservation.	予約してあります。	yoyaku shite arimasu
Here's the confirmation.	これが確認書です。	kore ga kakuninsho desu
I don't have a reservation.	予約してありません。	yoyaku shite arimasen
Do you have any vacancies?	空いた部屋はありますか。	aita heya wa arimasu ka
I'd like ...	…が欲しいのですが。	... ga hoshii no desu ga
a single room	シングルルーム	shinguru rūmu
a double room	ダブルルーム	daburu rūmu
a room ...	…部屋	... heya
with twin beds	ツインベッドの	tsuin beddo no
with a double bed	ダブルベッドの	daburu beddo no
with a bath	バス付の	basu tsuki no
with a shower	シャワー付の	shawā tsuki no
with a balcony	バルコニー付の	barukonī tsuki no
with a view	景色の良い	keshiki no yoi
We'd like a room ...	…部屋がいいのですが。	... heya ga ii no desu ga
at the front	表側の	omote gawa no
at the back	裏側の	ura gawa no
facing the mountains/ the sea/the street	山に/海に/通りに面した	yama ni/umi ni/tōri ni menshita

CHECKING OUT, see page 32

ホテル

It must be quiet.	静かな部屋をお願いします。	shizukana heya o o-negai shimasu
Is there (a) ...?	…はありますか。	... wa arimasu ka
air conditioning	冷房装置	reibō sōchi
heating	暖房装置	danbō sōchi
hot water	お湯	o-yu
laundry service	洗濯サービス	sentaku sābisu
private toilet	個人用手洗	kojin yō tearai
radio/television in the room	部屋にラジオ/テレビ	heya ni rajio/terebi
room service	ルームサービス	rūmu sābisu
sauna	サウナ	sauna
swimming pool	プール	pūru
Could you put a cot/ en extra bed in the room?	簡易ベッド/もう一つ別のベッドを部屋に入れて下さいますか。	kan-i beddo/mō hitotsu betsu no beddo o heya ni irete kudasai

How much? いくらですか。

What's the price ...?	…の値段はいくらですか。	... no nedan wa ıkura desu ka
per night	一泊	i-ppaku
per week	一週間	isshū kan
excluding meals	食事抜き	shokuji nuki
for full board (A.P.)	三食付き	san-shoku tsuki
for half board (M.A.P.)	朝食と夕食付き	chōshoku to yūshoku tsuki
Does that include ...?	…は含まれていますか。	... wa fukumarete imasu ka
breakfast	朝食	chōshoku
meals	食事	shokuji
service	サービス	sābisu
Is there any reduction for children?	子供の割引はありますか。	kodomo no waribiki wa arimasu ka
Do you charge for the baby?	乳児も勘定に入りますか。	nyūji mo kanjō ni hairi masu ka
That's too expensive.	高すぎます。	taka sugimasu
Haven't you anything cheaper?	もっと安いのはありませんか。	motto yasui no wa arimasen ka

NUMBERS, see page 146

ホテル

How long? 何日？

We'll be staying ...	…滞在します。	... taizai shimasu
overnight only	一晩だけ	hitoban dake
a few days	二・三日	ni-san nichi
a week (at least)	（少なくとも）一週間	(sukunaku tomo) isshū kan
I don't know yet.	まだわかりません。	mada wakarimasen

Decision 部屋を決める

May I see the room?	部屋を見せて頂けますか。	heya o misete itadake masu ka
That's fine. I'll take it.	いいですね。この部屋にします。	ii desu ne. kono heja ni shimasu
No. I don't like it.	気に入りません。	kiniirimasen
It's ...	…ます。	... masu
too small	小さすぎ	chīsa sugi
too dark	暗すぎ	kura sugi
too noisy	うるさすぎ	urusa sugi
Can you give me ...?	…が欲しいのですが。	... ga hoshii no desu ga
a different room	違う部屋	chigau heya
a room with a bath/ with a better view	バス付の/もっと良い景色の部屋	basu tsuki no/motto yoi keshiki no heya
Do you have anything ...?	…部屋はありますか。	... heya wa arimasu ka
better	もっと良い	motto yoi
bigger	もっと大きい	motto ōkii
cheaper	もっと安い	motto yasui
quieter	もっと静かな	motto shizukana
higher up	もっと上の階の	motto ueno kai no
lower down	もっと下の階の	motto shita no kai no

パスポートを見せて下さい。	May I see your passport?
このカードに記入して頂けますか。	Would you mind filling in this registration form?
ここにサインして下さい。	Sign here, please.
どの位御滞在になりますか。	How long will you be staying?

HOTEL

Registration 登録

Upon arrival at a hotel you'll be asked to fill in a registration form; it's almost certain to carry an English translation. However, if you stay in a *ryokan,* especially in the country, the form may only be in Japanese.

I can't read Japanese.	日本語は読めません。	nihongo wa yomemasen
What does this mean?	これはどういう意味ですか。	kore wa dōyū imi desu ka

姓/名	Name/First name
現住所	Home address
国籍/職業	Nationality/Profession
生年月日/出生地	Date of birth/Place of birth
身分証明書/パスポート	Identity documents/Passport number
到着日	Date of arrival
次の目的地	Further destination
署名（サイン）	Signature

What's my room number?	私の部屋番号は何番ですか。	watashi no heya bangō wa nanban desu ka
Will you have my luggage sent up?	私の荷物を上げて下さいますか。	watashi no nimotsu o agete kudasaimasu ka
Where can I park my car?	車はどこに駐車出来ますか。	kuruma wa doko ni chūsha dekimasu ka

Hotel staff ホテルスタッフ

hall porter	ホールポーター	hōru pōtā
maid	メイド	meido
manager	支配人	shihainin
page (bellboy)	ボーイ	bōi
porter	ポーター	pōtā
receptionist	フロント	furonto gakari
switchboard operator	交換手	kōkanshu

General requirements 一般的な表現、質問

I want to leave this in your safe.	これを金庫に預けておきたいのですが。	kore o kinko ni azukete okitai no desu ga
The key to room ..., please.	…室の鍵をお願いします。	... shitsu no kagi o o-negai shimasu
Will you wake me at ..., please?	…時に起こして下さいますか。	... ji ni okoshite kudasai masu ka
May we have breakfast in our room?	部屋で朝食がとれますか。	heya de chōshoku ga tore masu ka
What's the voltage here?*	ここの電圧は何ボルトですか。	koko no den-atsu wa nan boruto desu ka
Do you have an adaptor?*	アダプターはありますか。	adaputā wa arimasu ka
Where's the socket (outlet) for the shaver?	電気カミソリのソケットはどこですか。	denki kamisori no soketto wa doko desu ka
May I have a/an some ...?	…が欲しいのですが。	... ga hoshii no desu ga
ashtray	灰皿	haizara
bath towel	バスタオル	basutaoru
extra blanket	もう一枚毛布	mō ichimai mōfu
envelopes	封筒	fūtō
(more) hangers	(もっと) ハンガー	(motto) hangā
hot-water bottle	湯タンポ	yutanpo
ice cubes	氷	kōri
needle and thread	針と糸	hari to ito
extra pillow	もう一つ枕	mō hitotsu makura
reading-lamp	スタンド	sutando
soap	石けん	sekken
writing paper	便箋	binsen
Can you find me a ...?	…を見つけて来て下さいますか。	... o mitsukete kite kudasai masu ka
babysitter	ベビーシッター	bebī shittā
secretary	秘書	hisho
typewriter	タイプライター	taipuraitā

---

* The current is 100 volts throughout Japan, with 50 cycles in the east and Tokyo, and 60 cycles in western Japan. American-style sockets are used, with flat-pin plugs. Large hotels have 110 and 220 volt outlets for shavers, hair dryers, etc.

ホテル

BREAKFAST, see page 42

Where can I make photocopies?	コピーはどこでとれますか。	kopī wa doko de tore masu ka
Where's the ...?	…はどこですか。	... wa doko desu ka
bathroom	風呂場	furoba
dining room	食堂	shokudō
emergency exit	非常口	hijō guchi
hairdresser's (men's/women's)	理髪室/美容室	rihatsushitsu/biyōshitsu
lift (elevator)	エレベーター	erebētā
Where are the toilets?	お手洗はどこですか。	o-tearai wa doko desu ka

Note: Japanese-style toilets are level with the floor and have no seats; you have to squat, facing the flushing handle. Plastic slippers are provided at the entrance.

The bath 風呂

If you stay in a *ryokan* in the country, there may only be a communal bathroom at your disposal. If so, there will either be separate facilities for men and women, or separate bathing times. The Japanese regard bathing as a form of relaxation, while the serious washing is done before getting into the bath. You will find basins and taps along the walls, and you should use these to rinse, soap, scrub and wash yourself down. When you are clean step into the steaming hot bath and relax. Don't pull the plug out at the end, the water will still be clean and other people will follow you.

Where is the bath?	風呂はどこですか。	furo wa doko desu ka
Can I take a bath?	お風呂に入れますか。	o-furo ni haire masu ka

Telephone—Post (mail) 電話-郵便

Can you get me Kyoto 1234567?	京都123 4567をお願いします。	kyōto ichi-ni-san yon-go-roku-nana o o-negai shimasu
How much are my telephone charges?	電話料金はいくらですか。	denwa ryōkin wa ikura desu ka
Do you have stamps?	切手はありますか。	kitte wa arimasu ka

POST OFFICE AND TELEPHONE, see page 132

ホテル

Would you post (mail) this for me, please?	これを郵送して頂けますか。	kore o yūsōshite itadakemasu ka
Are there any letters for me?	私あての手紙はありますか。	watashi ate no tegami wa arimasu ka
I'd like to send this parcel.	この小包を送りたいのですが。	kono kozutsumi o okuritai no desu ga
Are there any messages for me?	私あての言付けがありますか。	watashi ate no kotozuke ga arimasu ka

In a *ryokan* or a *minshuku* it's polite to let the receptionist know when you go out.

I'm going out.	出かけて来ます。	dekakete kimasu
I'll be back ...	…戻ります。	... modori masu
in 2 hours	2時間程で	2 jikan hodo de
in the evening	晩には	ban ni wa

Difficulties 困り事

| The ... doesn't work. | …が動きません。 | ... ga ugokimasen |

air conditioner	冷房装置	reibō sōchi
fan	扇風機	senpūki
heating	暖房装置	danbō sōchi
light	電灯	dentō
radio	ラジオ	rajio
television	テレビ	terebi

The tap (faucet) is dripping.	蛇口が漏れます。	jaguchi ga more masu
There's no hot water.	お湯が出ません。	o-yu ga demasen
The wash basin is blocked.	洗面台がつまっています。	senmendai ga tsumatte imasu
The window is jammed.	窓が動きません。	mado ga ugokimasen
The curtains are stuck.	カーテンが動きません。	kāten ga ugokimasen
The bulb is burned out.	電球が切れています。	denkyū ga kirete imasu
My room has not been prepared.	部屋の用意がしてありません。	heya no yōi ga shite arimasen

The ... is broken.	…がこわれています。	... ga kowarete imasu
blind	ブラインド	buraindo
lamp	ランプ	ranpu
plug	差し込み	sashikomi
shutter	よろい戸	yoroido
switch	スイッチ	suitchi
Can you get it repaired?	直して頂けますか。	naoshite itadakemasu ka

Laundry — Dry cleaner's　洗濯-ドライクリーニング

I want these clothes ...	この服…下さい。	konofuku ... kudasai
cleaned	をクリーニングして	o kurīningu shite
ironed	にアイロンをかけて	ni airon o kakete
pressed	をプレスして	o puresu shite
washed	を洗って	o aratte
When will they be ready?	いつ出来上がりますか。	itsu deki agari masu ka
I need them ...	…いります。	... iri masu
tonight/tomorrow before (Friday)	今夜/明日 (金曜日)までに	kon-ya/asu (kin-yōbi) made ni
Can you ... this?	これを…頂けますか。	kore o ... itadakemasu ka
mend	繕って	tsukurotte
patch	つぎあてして	tsugiate shite
stitch	かがって	kagatte
Can you sew on this button?	このボタンを付けて頂けますか。	kono botan o tsukete itadakemasu ka
Can you get this stain out?	このしみはとれますか。	kono shimi wa toremasu ka
Is my laundry ready?	私の洗濯物は出来ていますか。	watashi no sentaku mono wa dekite imasu ka
This isn't mine.	これは私のではありません。	kore wa watashi no dewa arimasen
There's something missing.	足りないものがあります。	tarinai mono ga arimasu
There's a hole in this.	これに穴があいています。	kore ni ana ga aiteimasu

Hairdresser—Barber 理髪室-床屋

Japanese hairdressers are renowned for their excellent service.

Is there a ... in the hotel?	ホテルの中に…はありますか。	hoteru no nakani ... wa arimasu ka
barber/hairdresser	床屋/理髪室	tokoya/rihatsushitsu
beauty salon	美容室	biyōshitsu
Can I make an appointment for (Thursday).	(木曜日)に予約出来ますか。	(mokuyōbi) ni yoyaku dekimasu ka
I want a shampoo and set.	シャンプーセットをお願いします。	shanpū setto o o-negai shimasu
A haircut, please.	カットをお願いします。	katto o o-negai shimasu
bleach	ブリーチ	burīchi
blow-dry	ブロー	burō
colour rinse	カラーリンス	karā rinsu
dye	ヘアダイ	hea dai
permanent wave	パーマ	pāma
I'd like setting lotion/some hairspray.	セットローション/ヘアスプレーをお願いします。	setto rōshon/hea supurē o o-negai shimasu
Do you have a colour chart?	カラー見本がありますか。	karā mihon ga arimasu ka
Not too short.	余り短かくしないで下さい。	amari mijikaku shinaide kudasai
A little more off the ...	…をもう少し刈って下さい。	... o mōsukoshi katte kudasai
back/neck	うしろ/襟首	ushiro/erikubi
sides/top	両側/てっぺん	ryōgawa/teppen
I'd like a shave.	ひげをそって下さい。	hige o sotte kudasai
Trim my ..., please.	…をととのえて下さい。	... o totonoete kudasai
beard	あごひげ	ago hige
moustache	口ひげ	kuchi hige
sideboards (sideburns)	頬ひげ	hoo hige
I'd like a/some ...	…をお願いします。	... o o-negai shimau
face pack	パック	pakku
manicure	マニキュア	manikyua
scalp massage	頭部のマッサージ	tōbu no massāji

DAYS OF THE WEEK, see page 150

Checking out　チェックアウト

The bill, please.	お勘定、お願いします。	o-kanjō o-negai shimasu
I'm leaving ...	…たちます。	... tachimasu
early in the morning	早朝	sōchō
around noon	お昼頃	o-hiru goro
at once	すぐに	sugu ni
Please have my bill ready.	勘定書を用意しておいて下さい。	kanjō gaki o yōi shiteoite kudasai
Can I pay by credit card?	クレジットカードで支払えますか。	kurejitto kādo de shiharae masu ka
Would you send someone to bring down our luggage?	荷物を降ろすのに誰かよこして下さいますか。	nimotsu o orosu noni dareka yokoshite kudasai masu ka
Can you keep my luggage until ...?	…まで私の荷物を預かっていただけますか。	... made watashi no nimotsu o azukatte itadakemasu ka
this afternoon	午後	gogo
this evening	今晩	kon ban

Camping—Public lodgings　キャンプ-国民宿舎

Camping is not very popular in Japan, though there is a limited number of camp sites throughout the country.

The government-sponsored *kokumin shukusha* (public lodges) in the countryside are primarily designed for the Japanese, but welcome foreign tourists as well. Lodging includes two meals. The same applies to *kokumin kyuka mura* (public holiday villages, offering recreational facilities). Reservations should be made through the Japan Travel Bureau.

Is there a camp site near here?	この近くにキャンプ場がありますか。	kono chikaku ni kyanpujō ga arimasu ka
We'd like to stay in a ...	…に泊りたいのですが。	... ni tomaritai no desu ga
holiday village	休暇村	kyūka mura
public lodge	国民宿舎	kokumin shukusha
youth hostel	ユースホステル	yūsu hosuteru

TIPPING, see inside back-cover

ホテル

Eating out

Wherever you are in Japan, a delicious meal is never far away. The Japanese like to dine out, and they also like to entertain in restaurants. As a result the country has such a variety of restaurants that virtually any craving can be satisfied. The following pages explain the different kinds of establishments and what you can expect to eat in them.

Where to eat どこで食べるか

バー (bā)	Bar. Drinks and snacks served. Most bars have hostesses, and you'll have to pay for their drinks, too.
ビヤガーデン (biyagāden)	Beer garden. Beer and snacks served in rooftop gardens.
喫茶店 (kissaten)	Coffee shop. These are very common throughout Japan. Coffee, soft drinks and snacks are served. Most coffee shops have music.
飲み屋 (nomiya)	*Sake* bar specializing in the famed Japanese rice wine, also serves beer, appetizers and Japanese-style snacks.
レストラン (resutoran)	Restaurant. These fall into three categories: international Western cuisine; Japanese; and Western-style, influenced by Japanese cuisine.
料理屋 (ryōriya)	Specializes in Japanese-style food only. Basically, *ryoriya* can be divided into two categories: the *ozashiki* (private room) restaurant where the meal is served in your own Japanese-style room, and the counter restaurant where your dish will be prepared in front of you. However, some *ryoriya* will combine these two types or even have tables and chairs.
小料理屋 (koryōri-ya)	Small restaurant serving traditional Japanese food.

MENU, see page 44

外食

炉端焼き (robatayaki)	Japanese country-style pub-restaurant. They serve fish, meat and vegetables grilled over an inset hearth *(ro)* in front of the guests.
スナックバー (sunakku bā)	Snack bar with a good choice of drinks; in Tokyo, many of them are open all night.
屋台 (yatai)	Street stalls (pushcarts), serving roasted sweet potatoes, noodles, soup, stew or barbecued food. Very popular, they open in the evening till late at night.

Many establishments have a mindboggling display of dishes in the window, representing an accurate reproduction of each dish on the menu. Naturally this simplifies ordering as you can take the waiter outside and point.

What to eat   何を食べるか

Many eating places are named after their speciality: *sushi-ya, yakitori-ya, okonomiyaki-ya,* etc. So when choosing a restaurant you should first decide what you feel like eating. Here's a list and short description of some typical Japanese dishes.

串揚げ (kushiage)	Deep-fried skewered food; it includes chicken and pork as well as seasonal vegetables and seafood.
おでん (oden)	Fish stew: cuttle fish, hard-boiled eggs, radish, kelp, seaweed, turnips, rice dumplings and other ingredients are slowly simmered for a long time in a broth. You often get this from the *yatai* street vendors.
お好み焼き (okonomiyaki)	Japanese-style pancake which you prepare with a spatula on a hot griddle with an egg batter and either shrimps or meat, and chopped vegetables. This cheap do-it-yourself meal is very popular with students.
ラーメン (rāmen)	Chinese noodles served in a chicken or pork broth.
さしみ (sashimi)	Raw fish sliced into small bite-sized pieces of varying shapes, served with various condiments (see page 49). *Sashimi* is usually served as part of a larger meal.

しゃぶしゃぶ (shabu-shabu)	Thinly-sliced beef cooked with vegetables in a broth. It is often a do-it-yourself meal—the waitress will show you how to do it.
そば/うどん (soba/udon)	Very popular noodle dish, served hot or cold (see page 53). *Omori,* or extra helping, is available for those with a large appetite.
すき焼き (sukiyaki)	Thin slices of tender fillet of beef and vegetables sautéed in front of you over a gas or charcoal fire (see page 52).
すし (sushi)	Slightly vinegared rice with raw fish and vegetables, served in different shapes and forms. In *sushi* bars, you either sit at a table with a plate of assorted fish and seafood, or, which is more fun, up at the counter where you can choose the fish you fancy and watch the cook's dexterity as he slices it up. (See also page 49).
天ぷら (tempura)	Various kinds of fresh seafood and vegetables, coated in a batter of egg and flour, and quickly deep-fried. In a *tempura* restaurant the chef will cook the meal right in front of you. (See also page 49).
うなぎ (unagi)	Eel, usually grilled.
焼き鳥 (yakitori)	Pieces of chicken barbecued on small wooden skewers with onions and green peppers. Not really a full meal but they are very good snacks with *sake* or beer. In a *yakitori-ya* you'll often also find dishes using different meat, fish or vegetables.
寄せ鍋 (yosenabe)	Thick soup of chicken, shellfish, prawns, bean curd and vegetables. A cosy "family" meal: you sit around the *nabe* (pot) in the middle of the table and help yourself.

To find out more about the ingredients and other dishes, look under "Fish and Seafood", "Meat", "Vegetables", etc. (see page 44).

When you're not trying Japanese food you can turn to the familiar fast-food favourites that are found in most large cities. Or go to one of the many excellent restaurants serving exclusively Western food; most nationalities can be found.

MENU, see page 44

How to eat どうやって食べるか

The Japanese, like the Chinese, eat with chopsticks. They were introduced into Japan from China in the 5th century together with the Chinese ideograms or characters.

How to use chopsticks can be briefly explained as follows: you hold the upper stick between your thumb and first two fingers, while you keep the lower stick stationary with your third finger or both your second and third fingers; and you hold the sticks with one third above the hand and two thirds below.

In Japanese restaurants, you'll usually be brought a pair of wooden half-split chopsticks in a paper envelope, which can easily be split into two for use. In Japanese homes, however, re-usable sticks of various materials are used.

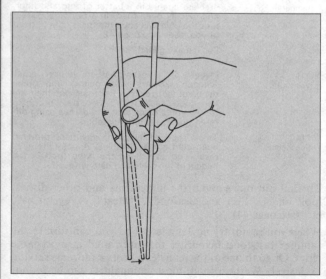

When eating your soup, take the pieces of food from it with your chopsticks and drink the broth directly from the bowl, as there'll be no spoon. Make all the noise you like, it's expected. Slurping is especially good with noodles, say the Japanese.

In Japanese-style restaurants or Japanese homes, you don't sit on chairs, around a high table as you do in the West. Instead you squat down on the *tatami* (straw mat floor). This is known as *zashiki* seating, and is great fun, especially when dining in a large group. The Japanese sit with their legs folded or kneeling, but visitors should make themselves comfortable any way that is possible, even stretching their legs under the low table.

Remember to take off your shoes before stepping on the *tatami* mat. If you need to leave the *tatami* area for any reason, you'll probably find that the restaurateur has provided slippers.

Japanese cuisine 日本料理

Centuries ago, while Europeans were still gnawing on pieces of meat, with cutlery a luxury only for the ruling classes, the Japanese had long been eating orchestrated meals designed to please the palate as well as the eye. Other considerations were the method of serving—neat and elegant—and the dishes used. Unlike in European cuisine where utensils are chosen to match each other, the Japanese chose dishes that would complement the food being served. The ingredients and methods of cooking also differ from those used in the West as the Japanese believe that one should be able to taste the natural flavours of the food, and seasonings should be used only to enhance and not disguise these.

Some of the food, raw and cooked, may be strange to the Western palate, but it is eminently edible, nourishing and, once you've got the hang of it, absolutely delicious.

外食

As a general rule you'll notice that the cooked food is served warm rather than hot, and the Japanese do not feel it loses its flavour if you let it get cold while sampling something else, since many dishes are served simultaneously.

Enjoy the traditional start to each meal with an *oshibori* – not an exotic appetizer but a refreshing hot or cold towel for your hands and face.

Meal times 食事の時間

Lunch (昼食 —*chūshoku*): from noon to 2 p.m.

Dinner (夕食 —*yūshoku*): from 6 p.m. to 9 p.m.

Hungry? お腹がすきましたか。

I'm hungry/I'm thirsty.	お腹がすきました/のどがかわきました。	onaka ga sukimashita/nodo ga kawakimashita
I'd like something to eat/drink.	何か食べたい/飲みたいのですが。	nanika tabetai/nomitai no desu ga
Can you recommend a good restaurant?	おいしいレストランを教えて頂けますか。	oishii resutoran o oshiete itadakemasu ka
I'd like to go to a ...	…に行きたいのですが。	... ni ikitai no desu ga
tempura restaurant	てんぷら料理の店	tenpura ryōri no mise
self-service restaurant	セルフサービスのレストラン	serufu sābisu no resutoran
snack bar	スナックバー	sunakku bā
vegetarian restaurant	菜食料理の店	saishoku ryōri no mise
Which is the best *sushi* restaurant?	どの寿司屋が一番おいしいですか。	dono sushiya ga ichiban oishii desu ka
Are there any inexpensive restaurants around here?	この近くに安いレストランはありますか。	kono chikaku ni yasui resutoran wa arimasu ka
Is there a ... restaurant in town?	この町に…料理の店はありますか。	kono machi ni ... ryōri no mise wa arimasu ka
Chinese	中国	chūgoku
French	フランス	furansu
Indian	インド	indo
Italian	イタリア	itaria
Korean	韓国	kankoku

If you feel like dining out in one of the many fine restaurants in the large cities ask your hotel receptionist to reserve a table for you—or try it yourself:

Please reserve me a table at ... restaurant.	…レストランにテーブルを予約して下さい。	… resutoran ni tēburu o yoyakushite kudasai
I'd like to reserve a table ...	…テーブルを予約したいのですが。	… tēburu o yoyakushitai no desu ga
for 4 people	4人用の	4 nin yō no
at 8 o'clock	8時に	8 ji ni

In a great number of Japanese restaurants both *tatami* (or *zashiki*) and table seating are available.

| We'd like to sit at a table/in a *zashiki*. | テーブル/座敷がいいのですが。 | tēburu/zashiki ga ii no desu ga |

And if you go directly to the restaurant:

I'd like a table for 4.	4人用のテーブルをお願いしたいのですが。	4 nin yō no tēburu o o-negai shitai no desu ga
Could we have a table ...?	…テーブルがいいのですが。	… tēburu ga ii no desu ga
in the corner	隅の	sumi no
by the window	窓際の	mado giwa no
on the terrace	テラスの	terasu no
in a nonsmoking area	禁煙コーナーの	kin-en kōnā no
We'd like to sit at the counter.	カウンターの席に座りたいのですが。	kauntā no seki ni suwaritai no desu ga

いらっしゃいませ。	Welcome.
何がよろしいでしょうか。	What would you like?
これなどよろしいと思います。	I recommend this.
お飲物は何になさいますか。	What would you like to drink?
私どもには…はございません。	We haven't got ...
…はいかがでしょうか。	Would you like ...?

Asking and ordering　注文する

Many restaurants simplify the problem of ordering by displaying replicas of the available dishes on plates in the window—customers need only point to order.

(Waiter/Waitress), please.	（ウエイターさん/ウエイトレスさん）、お願いします。	(ueitāsan/ueitoresusan) o-negai shimasu
May I have the menu, please?	メニューをいただけますか。	menyū o itadake masu ka
Do you have a menu in English?	英語のメニューはありますか。	eigo no menyū wa arimasu ka
What do you recommend?	お勧め料理は何ですか。	o-susume ryōri wa nandesu ka
I'd like this.	これをお願いします。	kore o o-negai shimasu
Do you have a set menu/local dishes?	定食/郷土料理はありますか。	teishoku/kyōdo ryōri wa arimasu ka
What is the price of the set menu?	定食はいくらですか。	teishoku wa ikura desu ka
I'd like to eat (some) . . .	…をいただきます。	. . . o itadakimasu
chicken	とり	tori
fish	魚	sakana
game	野鳥獣の肉	yachōjū no niku
meat	肉	niku
beef	牛肉	gyūniku
pork	豚肉	butaniku
veal	仔牛肉	koushiniku
noodles	めん類	men rui
rice	ごはん	gohan
seafood	魚介類	gyokai rui
soup	スープ	sūpu
vegetables	野菜類	yasai rui
Is it served . . .?	…ですか。	. . . desu ka
raw/cooked	生/調理したもの	nama/chōrishita mono
hot/cold	熱い/冷たい	atsui/tsumetai
Is it very spicy/ salty?	非常に香辛料/塩がきいていますか。	hijō ni kōshinryō/shio ga kiite imasu ka
I'm in a hurry.	急いでいるんですが。	isoide irundesu ga
Do you have anything ready quickly?	何か早く出来るものはありますか。	nani ka hayaku dekiru mono wa arimasu ka

I'd like to drink ...	…をいただきます。	... o itadakimasu
beer	ビール	bīru
sake	酒	sake
(Japanese) tea	(日本) 茶	(nihon) cha
water	水	mizu
wine	ワイン	wain

Could we have a/an/some ..., please?	…をいただけますか。	... o itadakemasu ka
ashtray	灰皿	haizara
chopsticks	はし	hashi
cup	コップ	koppu
fork	フォーク	fōku
glass	グラス/コップ	gurasu/koppu
knife	ナイフ	naifu
napkin (serviette)	ナプキン	napukin
plate	皿	sara
spoon	スプーン	supūn

May I have some ...?	…をいただけますか。	... o itadake masu ka
bread	パン	pan
butter	バター	batā
lemon	レモン	remon
oil	オイル	oiru
pepper	胡椒	koshō
salt	塩	shio
soy sauce	しょう油	shōyu
sugar	さとう	satō
vinegar	酢	su

Some useful expressions for dieters and special requirements:

I'm on a low-salt diet.	私は塩分をひかえているんですが。	watashi wa enbun o hikaete irundesu ga
I mustn't eat food containing flour/sugar.	小麦粉/砂糖の入ったものは食べられません。	komugiko/satō no haitta mono wa taberaremasen
I must avoid fatty dishes.	脂肪分の多い料理は避けなければなりません。	shibōbun no ōi ryōri wa sakenakeraba narimasen
Do you have (a) ... for diabetics?	糖尿病の人のための…はありますか。	tōnyōbyō no hito no tame no ... wa arimasu ka
cakes	ケーキ	kēki
fruit juice	フルーツジュース	furūtsu jūsu
special menu	特別メニュー	tokubetsu menyū

外食

Can I have an arti-ficial sweetener?	ダイエットシュガーをいただけますか。	daietto sugā o itadake masu ka
I'm a vegetarian.	私は菜食主義です。	watashi wa saishoku-shugi sha desu
Do you have vege-tarian dishes?	菜食主義者用の料理はありますか。	saishokushugi sha yō no ryōri wa arimasu ka
Could I have ... instead of meat?	お肉の代りに…をいただけますか。	o-niku no kawari ni ... o itadakemasu ka

In Japanese restaurants, especially when seated at the counter, it's not unusual to order some more dishes after your first order.

I'd like to start with ...	まず…を頂きたいのですが。	mazu ... o itadakitai no desu ga
I'll have ... next.	それから…を下さい。	sorekara ... o kudasai
I'll order more later.	後でまた注文します。	ato de mata chūmon shimasu
May I have more ...?	もう少し…を頂けますか。	mō sukoshi ... o itadake masu ka
Just a small portion.	ほんの少しだけ。	hon no sukoshi dake
Nothing more, thanks.	これでもう結構です。	kore de mō kekko desu

If it's a bit late you could inquire:

| When do you stop serving? | ラストオーダーはいつですか。 | rasutoōdā wa itsu desu ka |

Breakfast 朝食

If you stay in a Japanese-style hotel *(ryokan),* you will automatically be served the standard Japanese breakfast consisting of a bowl of rice, soy bean soup, seaweed, raw eggs, etc. If this does not appeal to you, you may order a Western-style breakfast the night before. In cheaper *ryokans* or in *ryokans* in the country, however, it is not advisable to do so, as they may not know how to prepare a Western-style breakfast.

At Western-style hotels you'll have no problem. They provide Continental, English or American breakfasts.

外食

As a change from your hotel dining room you can also go to a *kissaten* (coffee house), where they have the "morning service" before 10 a.m., a Western-style breakfast for the price of the coffee.

I'd like a ... breakfast, please.	…朝食をいただきたいのですが。	... chōshoku o itadakitai no desu ga
Japanese-style	和風の	wafū no
Western-style	洋風の	yōfū no

I'll have a/an/some ...	…を下さい。	... o kudasai
bacon and eggs	ベーコンエッグ	bēkon eggu
boiled egg	ゆで卵	yude tamago
soft	半じゅく	hanjuku
hard	固ゆで	kata yude
bread	パン	pan
butter	バター	batā
(hot) chocolate	(熱い) ココア	(atsui) kokoa
cereal	セレアル	serearu
coffee	コヒー	kōhī
black/with milk	ブラック/ミルク	burakku/miruku
decaffeinated	カフェイン抜き	kafein nuki
eggs	卵	tamago
fried eggs	目玉焼	medama yaki
scrambled eggs	いり卵	iri tamago
fruit juice	フルーツジュース	furūtsu jūsu
grapefruit	グレープフルーツ	gurēpu furūtsu
orange	オレンジ	orenji
ham and eggs	ハムエッグ	hamu eggu
honey	蜂蜜	hachimitsu
jam	ジャム	jamu
marmalade	マーマレード	māmarēdo
milk	ミルク	miruku
cold/hot	冷たい/熱い	tsumetai/atsui
rolls	ロールパン	rōru pan
tea	紅茶	kōcha
with milk	ミルク入り	miruku iri
with lemon	レモン入り	remon iri
toast	トースト	tōsuto
yoghourt	ヨーグルト	yōguruto

May I have some ...?	…を頂けますか。	... o itadake masu ka
pepper	胡椒	koshō
salt	塩	shio
sugar	砂糖	satō
water	水	mizu
hot water	お湯	o-yu

外食

What's on the menu? メニューに何がありますか。

Under the headings below you'll find a list of dishes and ingredients in Japanese with their English equivalent. When ordering your meal, the best way to use this guide is to show the waiter the food lists and let him point to what is available. Use pages 38–40 for ordering in general.

| What's this? | これは何ですか。 | kore wa nan desu ka |
| What's in it? | 中に何が入っていますか。 | nakani nani ga haitte imasu ka |

45	Starters (Appetizers)	前菜、オードブル	zensai, ōdoburu
46	Salad	サラダ	sarada
46	Soup	スープ	sūpu
46	Egg dishes	卵料理	tamogoryōri
47	Fish and seafood	魚介類	gyokairui
49	Sushi—Sashimi—Tempura	すし—さしみ—天ぷら	sushi—sashimi—tenpura
50	Meat	肉	niku
52	Sukiyaki	すき焼き	sukiyaki
52	Chicken	とり	tori
52	Game	猟鳥獣類	ryōchōjūrui
53	Rice	ごはん類	gohanrui
53	Noodles	めん類	menrui
54	Vegetables	野菜	yasai
55	Tofu	豆腐	tōfu
55	Seasoning—Spices	調味料—スパイス	chōmiryō—supaisu
56	Fruit	果物	kudamono
57	Dessert	デザート	dezāto
58	Drinks	飲物	nomimono
61	Tea	茶	cha
64	Snacks—Picnic	スナック—ピクニック	sunakku—pikunikku

BREAKFAST, see page 42

外食

Starters (Appetizers) 前菜

I'd like an appetizer.	オードブルをお願いします。	ōdōburu o o-negai shimasu
What do you recommend?	おすすめ料理は何ですか。	o-susume ryōri wa nan desu ka
アスパラガス	asuparagasu	asparagus
アンチョビー	anchobi	anchovies
伊勢えび	ise-ebi	lobster
いわし	iwashi	sardines
オードブル盛り合せ	ōdōburu moriawase	assorted appetizers
オリーブ	orību	olives
かき	kaki	oysters
かたつむり	katatsumuri	snails
かに	kani	crabmeat
キャビア	kyabia	caviar
車えび	kuruma-ebi	prawns
小えび	ko-ebi	shrimps
魚の卵	sakana no tamago	roe
さけ	sake	salmon
さば	saba	mackerel
サラダ	sarada	salad
サラミ	sarami	salami
スモークサーモン	sumōku sāmon	smoked salmon
セロリー	serori	celery
ソーセージ	sōsēji	sausage
チーズ	chīzu	cheese*
にしん	nishin	herring
生の／くん製の	nama no/kunsei no	raw/smoked
はまぐり	hamaguri	clams
ハム	hamu	ham
ピーマン	pīman	sweet peppers
まぐろ	maguro	tunny fish (tuna)
マッシュルーム	masshurūmu	mushrooms
メロン	meron	melon
ラディシュ	radisshu	radishes

おつまみ (o-tsumami)
savouries that accompany drinks, such as nuts, salted crackers, dried shredded cuttlefish, etc.

つきだし (tsukidashi)
cocktail snacks similar to *o-tsumami*, but a little more substantial, and available only in Japanese restaurants

---

* Though cheese is now available in Japan (at least a few kinds), it's not an authentic part of Japanese cuisine. Of course you'll find cheese in foreign restaurants.

Salad サラダ

Salad isn't a part of traditional Japanese cuisine. Pickled vegetables (see page 54) are a more authentic equivalent. However, you can order salads in Western-style restaurants.

What salads do you have?	どんなサラダがあります か。	don-na sarada ga arimasu ka

Soup スープ

In a Japanese meal, there are two kinds of soup, *misoshiru* (thick) and *suimono* (clear) which are eaten simultaneously with the main course (boiled rice and other items).

I'd like some soup.	スープをお願いします。	sūpu o o-negai shimasu
What do you recommend?	何かおいしいスープがあ りますか。	nanika oishii sūpu ga arimasu ka
チキンスープ	chikin sūpu	chicken soup
はまぐりのスープ	hamaguri no sūpu	clam soup
トマトスープ	tomato sūpu	tomato soup

みそ汁 (miso-shiro)	soy-bean paste soup with vegetables and *tofu* (white soy-bean curd). The ingredients vary slightly depending on whether the soup is served for breakfast, lunch or dinner.
吸物 (suimono)	clear soup of fish or chicken with vegetables, seasoned with soy sauce and sweet rice wine.

Egg dishes—Omelets 卵料理-オムレツ

There are no specific egg dishes or omelets in authentic Japanese cuisine, although eggs are very frequently used as ingredients. Omelet (called *omuretsu* in Japanese) is a Western import and is found in Western-style restaurants.

I'd like an omelet.	オムレツをお願いします。	omuretsu o o-negai shimasu

卵豆腐 (tamagodōfu)	a square, steamed-egg pudding, served cold
卵焼 (tamagoyaki)	eggs fried in layers, mixed with soy sauce, sugar and sweet rice wine
茶碗蒸 (chawan mushi)	a kind of egg custard containing mushrooms, shrimps, chicken or fish paste

外食

Fish and seafood　魚介類

As an island nation, Japan has developed, over the centuries, a variety of seafood specialities unlike any found in the rest of the world.

| I'd like some fish. | 魚を頂きたいのですが。 | sakana o itadakitai no desu ga |
| What kinds of seafood do you have? | どんな魚介類があります か。 | donna gyokai rui ga arimasu ka |

あおやぎ	aoyagi	round clams
あじ	aji	pompano
あなご	anago	conger eel
あゆ	ayu	Japanese trout
あわび	awabi	abalone
アンチョビ	anchobi	anchovies
いか	ika	cuttlefish
いくら	ikura	salmon roe
伊勢エビ	ise-ebi	lobster
いわし	iwashi	sardines
うなぎ	unagi	eel
うに	uni	sea urchins
おひょう	ohyō	halibut
かき	kaki	oysters
かずのこ	kazunoko	herring roe
かに	kani	crab
かつお	katsuo	bonito
かます	kamasu	pike
かわめんたい	kawa mentai	burbot
かれい	karei	turbot
きす	kisu	sillago
こい	koi	carp
小えび	ko-ebi	shrimps
こはだ	kohada	gizzard shad
車えび	kuruma-ebi	prawns
さけ	sake	salmon
さば	saba	mackerel
ざりがに	zarigani	crayfish
舌平目	shitabirame	sole
しらうお	shirauo	whitebait
しゃこ	shako	squilla
すずき	suzuki	sea bass
鯛	tai	sea bream
たこ	tako	octopus
たら	tara	cod
たらこ	tarako	cod roe
どじょう	dojō	loach
にしん	nishin	herring

はまぐり	hamaguri	clams
はまち	hamachi	yellowtail
平目	hirame	flounder
ほうぼう	hōbō	gurnet
はたて貝	hotate-gai	scallops
ぼら	bora	mullet
まかじき	makajiki	swordfish
まぐろ	maguro	tunny (tuna)
ます	masu	trout

The most typical way of preparing fish is "salt-broiling" *(shio-yaki)*: the fish is sprinkled with salt and grilled until the skin becomes crisp. Other methods of preparation:

baked	天火で焼いた	tenpi de yaita
broiled	直火で焼いた	jikabi de yaita
deep-fried (in batter)	天ぷらにした	tenpura ni shita
deep-fried (plain)	から揚げした	karaage shita
fried	油で揚げた	abura de ageta
grilled	直火で焼いた	jikabi de yaita
marinated	漬汁に漬けた	tsukejiru ni tsuketa
poached	軽くゆてた	karuku yudeta
raw	生の	nama no
smoked	くんせいにした	kunsei ni shiba
steamed	蒸した	mushita

かれいの唐揚 (karei no karaage)	fried turbot
鯛の塩焼 (tai no shio yaki)	salt-broiled sea bream
さばのみそ煮 (saba no misoni)	stewed mackerel with soy-bean paste
うなぎ丼ぶり (unagi-donburi)	charcoal-broiled eel served on rice

Cooking at the table:

| 魚すき (uosuki) | Japanese-style soup with fish, shellfish, vegetables and mushrooms |
| かきなべ (kaki nabe) | oyster soup, also called *dotenabe* |

Sushi—Sashimi—Tempura　すし-さしみ-天ぷら

These are the most commonly-found Japanese seafood dishes:

Sushi, basically, is rice with fish and vegetables. It's delicately seasoned with vinegar, salt, sugar and sweet rice wine and served in many different shapes and forms. Raw fish and vegetables are placed in the middle, mixed in or put on top of the rice.

にぎりずし (nigiri-zushi)	rice patty topped with slices of cooked egg and various raw seafoods (tunny, swordfish, abalone, clam, shrimps, sea bream, octopus, etc.), flavoured with grated horseradish, and served with soy sauce
巻きずし (maki-zushi)	tiny roll of vinegary rice wrapped up in paperlike seaweed. Usually, there are raw fish and vegetables in the middle of the roll.

Sashimi consists of little bite-sized pieces of fresh raw fish (mostly tunny) which are served with soy sauce and *wasabi,* very powerful green horseradish. White rice accompanies *sashimi,* and *sake* is usually drunk with it.

ふぐさし (fugusashi)	very thinly-sliced raw globefish
かつおのたたき (katsuo no tataki)	sliced bonito, very lightly grilled, raw in the centre
あじのたたき (aji no tataki)	raw, minced pompano mixed with finely-chopped green onions and ginger
こいのあらい (koi no arai)	sliced raw carp, served with a *miso* (soy-bean paste), vinegar and sugar sauce

Tempura: various kinds of fresh seafood (shrimps, prawns) and vegetables (green pepper, carrots, aubergines, mushrooms, sliced lotus root) are coated in a batter of egg and flour and quickly deep-fried in sesame or pure vegetable oil. These morsels are then dipped in a *ten-tsuyu* sauce of sweet rice wine, fish broth and soy sauce. Add grated Japanese radish with pimiento powder or grated fresh ginger. Served with a bowl of rice and a small dish of pickled vegetables.

Meat 肉類

Originally the Japanese weren't meat-eating people. Largely because of the Buddhist influence, meat was never part of the Japanese diet until introduced by Westerners about a century ago. This explains why there's only a limited choice of Japanese meat dishes. However Kobe beef and Matsuzaka beef are among the best varieties of beef in the world—but it's very expensive. The most commonly-found meat dishes are made with beef and pork.

What kinds of meat have you got?	どんな肉がありますか。	don-na niku ga arimasu ka
I'd like some ...	…をお願いします。	... o o-negai shimasu
beef	牛肉	gyūniku
lamb	子羊の肉	kohitsuji no niku
mutton	マトン	maton
pork	豚肉	butaniku
veal	子牛肉	koushiniku
あばら肉	abaraniku	T-bone/rib steak
オックステール	okkusutēru	oxtail
カツレツ	katsuretsu	escalope
肩の肉	kata no niku	shoulder
肝臓	kanzō	liver
牛肉	gyūniku	beef
首	kubi	neck (best end)
鞍下肉	kurashitaniku	saddle
子牛	koushi	veal
子牛の脳味噌	koushi no nōmiso	calf's brains
子牛の膵蔵	koushi no suizō	veal sweetbreads
子牛のロース肉	koushi no rōsuniku	veal cutlets
子羊	kohitsuji	lamb
子羊の骨付あばら肉	kohitsuji no honetsuki abaraniku	lamb chops
サーロイン	sāroin	sirloin
舌	shita	tongue
シチュー肉	shichū niku	stew
シャトーブリアン	chatōburian	chateaubriand
腎臓	jinzō	kidney
ステーキ	sutēki	steak
ソーセージ	sōsēji	sausage
トルヌドー	torunudo	tournedos
肉だんご	niku dango	rissoles
ハム	hamu	ham
冷肉盛り合わせ	reiniku moriawase	cold cuts

外食

ビフテキ	bifuteki	beefsteak
豚肉	butaniku	pork
豚の骨付あばら肉	buta no honetsuki abaraniku	pork chops
ベーコン	bēkon	bacon
ヒレ肉	hireniku	fillet
骨付あばら肉	honetsuki abaraniku	chop/cutlet
マトン	maton	mutton
胸肉	mune niku	breast
もつ	motsu	tripe
もも肉	momoniku	leg
ローストビーフ	rōsuto bīfu	roast beef
ローストポーク	rōsuto pōku	roast pork

baked	天火で焼いた	tenpi de yaita
barbecued	バーベキューした	bābekyūshita
boiled	ゆでた	yudeta
braised	とろ火で煮た	torobi de nita
broiled	焼いた	yaita
en casserole	土鍋で煮た	donabe de nita
fried	揚げた	ageta
grilled	焼いた	yaita
roasted	ローストした	rōsutoshita
stewed	シチューにした	shichūnishita
stuffed	詰め物をした	tsumemono o shita
underdone (rare)	生焼き／レアー	nama yake/reā
medium	普通／ミディアム	futsū/midiamu
well-done	良く焼く／ウェルダン	yoku yaku/werudan

Specialities 日本独特の料理

かつ丼 (katsu-don)	deep-fried pork cutlet (like *ton katsu*), cooked in egg and onion and served on a bed of rice
串かつ (kushi katsu)	skewered cutlet
しゃぶしゃぶ (shabu shabu)	thinly-sliced beef cooked with vegetables in broth and eaten with a sesame/miso sauce
じんぎすかん (jingisukan)	marinated mutton grilled at the table with vegetables
とんかつ (ton katsu)	breaded, deep-fried pork cutlet
焼肉 (yakiniku)	thinly-sliced beef or pork marinated and then grilled

外食

And finally, probably the best-known Japanese meat dish:

すき焼き (sukiyaki)	Thin slices of tender beef, leeks, bean curd cubes, thin noodles and burdock are cooked in an iron pan on the table in front of you. The ingredients are simmered in an aromatic mixture of soy sauce, *mirin* (sweet *sake*) and water, with a little sugar. You receive a small side bowl containing a whipped raw egg into which you dip the *sukiyaki* morsels for cooling just before eating. Using chopsticks, help yourself to whatever you like from the iron pan.	

Chicken とり

I'd like some chicken.	とりをいただきたいのですが。	tori o itadakitai no desu ga

とり	tori	chicken
手羽	teba	wing
もも	momo	leg
ささ身	sasami	breast
レバー	rebā	liver
ハツ	hatsu	heart
皮	kawa	skin
砂ぎも	suna-gimo	gizzard

焼き鳥 (yakitori)	pieces of chicken (whitemeat, leg, heart, gizzard, etc.) and vegetables threaded onto bamboo skewers dipped into a specially-prepared sweet soy sauce before being grilled
鳥の水炊き (tori no mizutaki)	chicken boiled in stock, often with mushrooms and other vegetables, at the table

Game and poultry 猟鳥獣類と家禽類

I'd like some game.	猟鳥をお願いします。	ryōchō o o-negai shimasu

あひる	ahiru	duck
あひるの子	ahiru no ko	duckling
いのしし	inoshishi	wild boar
うずら	uzura	quail
がちょう	gacho	goose
きじ	kiji	pheasant
すずめ	suzume	sparrow
はと	hato	pigeon
ひなばと	hinabato	squab
七面鳥	shichimencho	turkey

外食

Rice　ごはん類

In a Japanese meal rice *(gohan)* is served separately, in a bowl, and it's usual to raise the bowl when eating. The rice is not cooked till it's dry, but left slightly sticky. On a Western-style menu rice is usually called *raisu*.

Here are a few specialities:

お茶漬け (ochazuke)	boiled rice soaked with broth or green tea, garnished with grilled salmon, cod roe, pickles and pickled plums
おにぎり (onigiri)	round or triangular rice ball, sprinkled with sesame seeds or covered with dried seaweed, usually filled with fish (salmon, cod) or spicy vegetables; very popular for picnics
雑炊 (zōsui)	boiled rice, mixed with vegetables, seafood or eggs, seasoned with soy sauce and served in a large bowl
丼物 (donburi-mono)	deep-fried prawns and vegetables or egg with chicken served on rice in a large bowl

Noodles　めん類

Noodle dishes are very popular, as they make a delicious and filling simple meal. It's all right to make slurping noises while eating them—the extra intake of oxygen is said to add to the taste.

そば／うどん (soba/udon)	noodles served with a sprinkling of shredded pork, beef, chicken or egg with leeks and mushrooms in a bowl of fish stock. *Soba* are buckwheat noodles, and *udon,* slightly thicker, are made of wheat flour. They may also be served cold with a dip of soy sauce, freshly-chopped onions, ginger and minced horseradish.
ラーメン (rāmen)	Chinese noodles in a broth served hot or chilled
そうめん (sōmen)	very thin white wheat flour noodles, usually served chilled, with vegetables (cucumber, tomato), and eaten with a soy sauce, grated ginger and minced green onion dip

Vegetables 野菜

Which vegetables do you recommend?	おすすめの野菜がありますか。	o-susume no yasai ga arimasu ka
I'd prefer some salad.	私はサラダにします。	watashi wa sarada ni shimasu

赤キャベツ	akakyabetsu	red cabbage
アスパラガス	asuparagasu	asparagus
いんげん豆	ingenmame	kidney beans
えんどう豆	endōmame	peas
かぼちゃ	kabocha	pumpkin
カリフラワー	karifurawā	cauliflower
キャベツ	kyabetsu	cabbage
きゅうり	kyūri	cucumber
ぎんなん	gin nan	gingko nut
莢いんげん	sayaingen	French (green) beans
しし唐	shishitō	spicy green pepper
じゃがいも	jagaimo	potatoes
セロリ	serori	celery
そら豆	soramame	broad beans
だいこん	daikon	white radishes
玉ねぎ	tamanegi	onions
てんさい	tensai	beet(root)
とうもろこし	tōmorokoshi	sweet corn (corn)
トマト	tomato	tomatoes
長かぼちゃ	nagakabocha	courgette (zucchini)
なす	nasu	aubergines (eggplant)
にんじん	ninjin	carrots
ねぎ	negi	leeks
はくさい	hakusai	chinese cabbage
ピーマン	pīman	sweet peppers
ブロッコリ	brokkori	broccoli
ほうれん草	hōrensō	spinach
マッシュルーム	masshurūmu	mushrooms
芽キャベツ	mekyabetsu	Brussels sprouts
ラディシュ	radisshu	radishes
れんこん	renkon	lotus
レンズ豆	renzumame	lentils

おひたし (ohitashi)	boiled green vegetables served with soy sauce and dried bonito shavings or sesame seeds
漬物 (tsukemono)	Japanese pickles. These are vegetables pickled in salt, bran, rice and *miso* or *sake*, and usually served as a side dish.

Tofu 豆腐

Tofu is normally eaten on its own with soy sauce or *miso* (see below), or included in other dishes (*nabe-mono, shabu-shabu,* soups, etc.). It's a pale soy-bean curd made from the liquid remaining after the beans have been boiled, which is coagulated with bittern and pressed into a mould.

揚げ出し (age-dashi)	lightly fried plain *tofu*
田楽 (dengaku)	slices of *tofu* on bamboo skewers, grilled over a charcoal fire, served with *miso*
湯豆腐 (yudōfu)	cubes of boiled *tofu* served hot with soy sauce and minced green onions, grated ginger, red pepper and dried bonito flakes

Seasoning—Spices 調味料-スパイス

味の素	aji no moto	monosodium glutamate
あさつき	asatsuki	minced green onions
大根おろし	daikon oroshi	grated Japanese radish
ごま	goma	sesame
のり	nori	seaweed
もみじおろし	momijioroshi	red pepper
味醂	mirin	sweet rice wine
しょうが	shoga	ginger
しょう油	shōyu	soy sauce
唐辛子	togarashi	hot red pepper
にんにく	ninniku	garlic

木の芽 (konome)	Japanese pepper leaves used for flavour and decoration
さんしょう (sanshō)	pepper made from the nuts and leaves of the toothache tree
花がつお (hanagatsuo)	fine shavings of dried bonito
味噌 (miso)	fermented soy-bean or rice paste, usually slightly brown
七味唐辛子 (shichimi tōgarashi)	"seven spices" (various peppers, seaweed, Japanese lemon, etc.)
わかめ (wakame)	soft seaweed, often an ingredient found in *miso* soup

Fruit 果物

The quality of fresh fruit in Japan is high, as can be the price; so check before you order.

Do you have fresh fruit?	新鮮な果物がありますか。	shinsen na kudamono ga arimasu ka
I'd like a fresh fruit cocktail.	新鮮な果物のサラダをお願いします。	shinsen na kudamono no sarada o o-negai shimasu
アーモンド	āmondo	almonds
あんず	anzu	apricots
いちご	ichigo	strawberries
いちじく	ichijiku	figs
オレンジ	orenji	oranges
かき	kaki	persimmon
カシューナッツ	kashū nattsu	cashew nuts
キーウイ	kīui	kiwi-fruit
木いちご／ラズベリー	kiichigo/razuberī	raspberries
くり	kuri	chestnuts
くるみ	kurumi	walnuts
グレープフルーツ	gurēpu furūtsu	grapefruit
くろすぐり	kurosuguri	blackcurrants
やしの実	yashi no mi	coconut
さくらんぼ	sakuranbo	cherries
すぐり	suguri	gooseberries
すいか	suika	watermelon
なし	nashi	pear
なつめやし	natsumeyashi	dates
ネクタリン	nekutarin	nectarine
パイナップル	painappuru	pineapple
バナナ	banana	banana
パパイヤ	papaiya	papaya
ピーナッツ	pīnattsu	peanuts
ぶどう	budō	grapes
プラム	puramu	plums
ヘーゼルナッツ	hēzerunattsu	hazelnuts
干しすもも	hoshi sumomo	prunes
干ぶどう	hoshi budō	raisins
マンゴ	mango	mango
みかん	mikan	tangerine
メロン	meron	melon
もも	momo	peach
りんご	ringo	apple
レモン	remon	lemon

Dessert デザート

Dessert is not a typical part of the Japanese meal. Called *dezāto*, it was introduced by Westerners about a century ago.

I'd like a dessert, please.	デザートをお願いします。	dezāto o o-negai shimasu
Just a small portion.	ほんの少しだけ。	hon-no sukoshi dake
I don't want anything too sweet.	甘すぎるものは欲しくありません。	amasugiru mono wa hoshiku arimasen

アイスクリーム	aisukurīmu	ice cream
アイスクリームコーヒー	aisukurīmu kōhī	iced coffee with ice cream
ホイップクリーム	hoippu kurīmu	whipped cream
ケーキ	kēki	cake
汁粉	shiru-ko	sweet redbean-paste soup
チョコレートケーキ	chokorēto kēki	chocolate cake
チョコレートサンデー	chokorēto sandē	chocolate sundae
なしの赤ぶどう酒煮	nashi no akabudōshu ni	pears baked in red wine
なしのクリーム煮	nashi no kurīmu ni	pears cooked with cream
バナナ揚げ	banana age	banana fritters
バナナフランベ	banana furanbe	banana flambé
ピーチメルバ	pīchi meruba	peach Melba
プティング	pudingu	pudding
フルーツサラダ	furūtsu sarada	fruit cocktail

Good with an afternoon cup of tea or coffee ...

スフレ	sufure	soufflé
ストロベリーサンデー	sutoroberī sandē	strawberry sundae
ぜんざい	zenzai	sweet redbean soup
みつ豆 (mitsu-mame)		jelly cubes with pieces of fruit served in syrup. Sometimes the syrup is served separately.
まんじゅう (manjū)		a bun stuffed with sweet bean-paste
和菓子 (wagashi)		confectionery of wheat or rice flour, mashed red beans, yams, arrowroot, egg and sugar
ようかん (yōkan)		bean-paste jelly served in long rectangles and sliced—very sweet!

Drinks 飲物

If you are eating in a Japanese restaurant you may not be able to get the same drinks as you have at home. However, the Japanese distil their own whisky, brew their own beer, and ferment a type of wine called *sake*.

What drinks do you have?	どんな飲物がありますか。	donna nomimono ga arimasu ka
I don't drink alcohol.	アルコールは飲みません。	arukōru wa nomi masen
Do you have non-alcoholic drinks?	アルコールの入らない飲物はありますか。	arukōru no hairanai nomimono wa arimasu ka

Beer ビール

Japanese-brewed beers are similar to English and German lager beers. *Nama biru* (unpasteurised beer) is also popular, either draught (on tap) or bottled.

I'd like a beer, please.	ビールを下さい。	bīru o kudasai
bottled beer	びん入り	bin iri
draught beer	ジョッキで	jokki de
light beer	ライトビール	raito bīru
dark beer	黒ビール	kuro bīru
foreign beer	外国産のビール	gaikokusan no bīru

Sake 酒

Locally distilled whisky is fast taking over as the favourite strong drink of the middle class, but *sake* remains the national alcohol par excellence. It's a colourless wine fermented from rice and usually served warm, but not hot, from porcelain carafes (*tokkuri*) in thimble-size cups (*ochoku*).

| May I have a carafe of sake, please? | お酒を一本頂けますか。 | o-sake o i-ppon itadake masu ka |

乾杯
(kanpai)
CHEERS!

NONALCOHOLIC DRINKS, see page 60

外食

Wine ワイン

Wine isn't an authentic Japanese drink, and until recently Japanese wine didn't exist. There are now a few wine-producing vineyards in the centre of the country, but most wines served in restaurants are still imported from abroad.

I'd like some wine.	ワインを頂きたいのですが。	wain o itadakitai no desu ga
Do you have ... wine?	…ワインはありますか。	... wain wa arimasu ka
American	アメリカの	amerika no
French	フランスの	furansu no
Italian	イタリアの	itaria no
Japanese	日本の	nihon no
May I have the wine list, please?	ワインリストを見せて頂けますか。	wain risuto o misete itadake masu ka
I'd like ... of white/ red wine.	白ワイン／赤ワインを…下さい。	shiro/aka wain o ... kudasai
a bottle	一本	i-ppon
half a bottle	ハーフボトルで	hāfu botoru de
a glass	グラス一杯	i-ppai
I don't want anything too sweet.	甘すぎるのは要りません。	ama sugiru no wa iri masen
A bottle of champagne, please.	シャンペンを一本、お願いします。	shanpen o i-ppon o-negai shimasu
What's the name of this wine?	このワインの名前は何といいますか。	kono wain no namae wa nan to ii masu ka
Where does this wine come from?	このワインはどこのものですか。	kono wain wa doko no mono desu ka

red wine	赤ワイン	aka wain
white wine	白ワイン	shiro wain
rosé wine	ローゼ（ワイン）	rōze (wain)
dry	ドライ／辛口	dorai/kara kuchi
sweet	甘口	amakuchi
sparkling	泡の立つ/スパークリング	awa no tatsu/supāku ringu
chilled	冷えた	hieta
at room temperature	室温で	shitsuon de

Other alcoholic drinks その他のアルコール飲料

aperitif	アペリティフ	aperitifu
brandy	ブランデー	burandē
gin	ジン	jin
gin and tonic	ジントニック	jin tonikku
liqueur	リキュール	rikyūru
port	ポートワイン	pōtowain
rum	ラム	ramu
sherry	シェリー	sherī
vermouth	ベルモット	berumotto
vodka	ウオッカ	uokka
whisky	ウイスキー	uisukī
neat (straight)	ストレート	sutorēto
on the rocks	オンザロック	onzarokku
with water	水割り	mizuwari
with soda water	ハイボール	haibōru

a glass	一杯	i-ppai
a bottle	一本	i-ppon
single	シングル	shinguru
double	ダブル	daburu

Japan produces its own whisky, although Scotch is imported
from Scotland. One of the best Japanese brands is *Suntory.*
Other brands are *Nikka* and *Ocean.*

I'd like to try Suntory Old, please.	サントリーオールドを味わってみたいのですが。	santorī ōrudo o ajiwatte mitai no desu ga

Another popular drink is *shōchū,* a spirit distilled from
sweet potatoes. It's fashionable to drink it "on the rocks".

Nonalcoholic drinks アルコールの入らない飲み物

I'd like a/an/some ...	…を下さい。	... o kudasai
(hot) chocolate	(熱い) ココア	(atsui) kokoa
coffee	コーヒー	kōhī
black coffee	ブラックコーヒー	burakku kōhī
coffee with cream	クリーム入りコーヒー	kurīmu iri kōhī
coffee with milk	ミルク入りコーヒー	miruku iri kōhī
espresso coffee	エスプレッソコーヒー	esupuresso kōhī
decaffeinated coffee	カフェイン抜きコーヒー	kafein nuki kōhī
grapefruit juice	グレープフルーツジュース	gurēpu furūtsu jūsu

(squeezed) lemon juice	レモンスカッシュ	remon sukasshu
lemonade	レモネード	remonēdo
mllk	ミルク	miruku
milkshake	ミルクセーキ	miruku sēki
mineral water	ミネラルウォーター	mineraru wōtā
orange juice	オレンジジュース	orenji jūsu
tomato juice	トマトジュース	tomato jūsu
tonic water	トニックウォーター	tonikku wōtā

Tea 茶

The green powdered tea (green because unfermented), brought originally from China, is prepared in lukewarm water. *Sencha* is the most common domestic tea, while *bancha,* the kind served in *sushi* bars and small restaurants, is coarser and needs boiling water. The *hoji-cha* served by the street vendors is brown, also brewed in boiling water, with a nice smoky tang to it.

I'd like some ...	…を下さい。	... o kudasai
(Indian) tea	紅茶	kōcha
with milk/lemon	ミルク入り／レモン入り	miruku iri/remon iri
Japanese tea	日本茶	nihon cha
green	緑茶	ryoku cha
powdered	抹茶	matcha
roasted	ほうじ茶	hōji cha

| Do you have iced tea? | アイスティーはありますか。 | aisu tī wa arimasu ka |

The tea ceremony 茶の湯

Drinking tea in Japan is not just a matter of having a "cuppa", it's a blend of formalism and courtesy that typifies Japan and the Japanese. This slightly bitter green tea (*matcha*), which comes from China, was first used by Zen Buddhist monks to help them stay awake while meditating. It became part of a more elaborate ceremony in the 15th century when Shogun Yoshimasa Ashikaga retired from politics to follow more spiritual pastimes. He felt that the tea ceremony induced the peace of mind necessary to further spiritual development.

外食

The tea should not only refresh you physically, but also give you time to appreciate the beauty of the tea bowls and other objects used in the ceremony, as well as the surroundings. You may find tea (ceremony) rooms in museums and gardens, where you'll be able to try a little *matcha* for a small fee.

The bill (check)　勘定

A service charge is added to restaurant bills. It is not customary to tip, and the practice is discouraged by the authorities.

May I have the bill (check), please?	お勘定をお願いします。	o-kanjō o o-negai shimasu
We'd like to pay separately.	別々に払いたいのですが。	betsubetsu ni haraitai no desu ga
Is there a cover charge?	席料は入りますか。	sekiryō wa hairimasu ka
Is service included?	サービス料は含まれていますか。	sābisuryō wa fukumarete imasu ka
Is everything included?	全部含まれていますか。	zenbu fukumarete imasu ka
What is this amount for?	これは何の金額ですか。	kore wa nan no kingaku desu ka
I think there's a mistake in this bill.	この勘定に間違いがあるようですが。	kono kanjō ni machigai ga aru yō desu ga
Do you accept traveller's cheques?	トラベラーチェックが使えますか。	toraberā chekku ga tsukaemasu ka
Can I pay with this credit card?	このクレジットカードで払えますか。	kono kurejitto kādo de haraemasu ka
That was a delicious meal.	おいしいお料理でした。	oishii o-ryōri deshita
We enjoyed it, thank you.	楽しかったです。ごちそうさまでした。	tanoshikatta desu, gochisō samadeshita

サービス料込み
SERVICE INCLUDED

Complaints 苦情

There is a plate/glass missing.	皿／コップがないんですが。	sara/koppu ga naindesu ga
I have no knife/fork/spoon.	ナイフ／フォーク／スプーンがありません。	naifu/fōku/supūn ga arimasen
That's not what I ordered.	それは注文したのと違います。	sore wa chūmonshita no to chigai masu
I asked for ...	…を注文しました。	... o chūmon shimashita
There must be some mistake.	きっと何か間違いがあったのでしょう。	kitto nanika machigai ga atta no deshō
May I change this?	換えて頂けますか。	kaete itadake masu ka
I asked for a small portion (for the child).	(子供用に)少量注文しました。	(kodomo yō ni) shōryō chūmon shimashita
The meat is ...	肉が…です。	niku ga ... desu
overdone	焼け過ぎ	yakesugi
underdone (too rare)	生焼け	nama yake
too tough	固い	katai
This is too ...	これは…過ぎます。	kore wa ... sugimasu
bitter/salty/sweet	苦／辛／甘	niga/kara/ama
I don't like this.	これはいりません。	kore wa irimasen
The food is cold.	料理が冷めています。	ryōri ga samete imasu
This isn't fresh.	これは新鮮ではありません。	kore wa shinsen de wa arimasen
What's taking so long?	どうしてそんなに長くかかるんですか。	dōshite sonnani nagaku kakarun desu ka
Have you forgotten our drinks?	飲み物がまだ来ていませんが。	nomimono ga mada kite imasen ga
The wine tastes of cork.	このワインはコルクの味がします。	kono wain wa koruku no aji ga shimasu
This isn't clean.	これはきれいではありません。	kore wa kirei de wa arimasen
Would you ask the head waiter to come over?	チーフにここに来るように言って頂けますか。	chīfu ni koko ni kuru yō ni itte itadakemasu ka

Snacks—Picnic スナック-ピクニック

Fast food chains selling all the familiar hamburger and fried chicken take-aways are as plentiful as in any Western country. Japan's homegrown version of fast food is the neat little *obento* lunch box of traditional rice, fish and vegetable goodies which you can buy at railway stations. You'll also get snacks in the *kissaten* coffee houses (see page 33) and at the *yatai* street stalls that set up shop in the evening and stay open until late at night.

I'll have one of these, please.	これを一つ頂けますか。	kore o hitotsu itadakemasu ka
It's to take away.	持ち帰ります。	mochikaerimasu
I'd like a/some ...	…を下さい。	... o kudasai

biscuits	ビスケット	bisuketto
(Japanese) box lunch	弁当	bentō
chips (french fries)	ポテトフライ	poteto furai
(bar of) chocolate	チョコレート	chokorēto
cookies	クッキー	kukkī
pancake	パンケーキ	pankēki
pastries	ペストリー	pesutorī
sandwich	サンドイッチ	sandoitchi
cheese	チーズ	chīzu
chicken	チキン	chikin
egg	卵	tamago
ham	ハム	hamu
vegetables	野菜	yasai
yoghourt	ヨーグルト	yōguruto

At street stalls you'll find ...

たこ焼き (tako-yaki)	wheat-flour dumpling containing bits of octopus *(tako)*, ginger and green onions or cabbage
大判焼き (ōban-yaki)	a kind of pancake stuffed with sweetened redbean paste
みたらしだんご (mitarashi dango)	skewered rice-flour dumpling grilled on charcoal, dipped in a sweet soy sauce
鯛焼 (taiyaki)	a kind of waffle in the shape of a fish, filled with sweet bean jam

Travelling around

While you're in Japan you'll probably want to travel around a bit. Use public transport. Japan's public transport system is one of the best in the world. Avoid driving as traffic conditions can be dangerous and most road signs are written in Japanese characters.

Note: Most of the phrases under "Plane" and "Train" can be used or adapted for travelling on all kinds of transport—underground (subway), bus, boat, etc.

Plane　飛行機

Three major air lines run regular connecting flights between the biggest Japanese cities.

Is there a flight to Sapporo?	札幌行きの便はありますか。	sapporo yuki no bin wa ari masu ka
Is it a direct flight?	直行便ですか。	chokkō bin desu ka
When's the next flight to Fukuoka?	次の福岡行きの便は何時ですか。	tsugi no fukuoka yuki no bin wa nan-ji desu ka
Is there a connection to Oita?	大分への乗り継ぎはありますか。	ōita e no noritsugi wa ari masu ka
I'd like a ticket to Nagasaki.	長崎までの切符を下さい。	nagasaki made no kippu o kudasai
single (one-way)	片道	katamichi
return (roundtrip)	往復	ōfuku
What time do we take off?	何時の出発ですか。	nanji no shuppatsu desu ka
What time do I have to check in?	何時にチェックインしなければなりませんか。	nanji ni chekku in shina-kereba narimasen ka
What's the flight number?	空港はどこですか。	nan-bin desu ka
What time do we arrive?	何便ですか。	nanji ni tsuki masu ka
Where is the airport?	何時に着きますか。	kūkō wa doko desu ka

Is there a/an ... to the airport?	空港行きの…はあります か。	kūkō yuki no ... wa ari masu ka
airport bus	空港バス	kūkō basu
bus	バス	basu
train	電車	densha
underground (subway) line	地下鉄	chikatetsu
I'd like to ... my reservation on flight no 123.	123便の予約を…したい のですが。	123 bin no yoyaku o ... shitai no desu ga
cancel	キャンセル	kyanseru
change	変更	henkō
confirm	確認	kakunin
Where can I get an airport bus to (the) ...?	…行きの空港バスはどこ で乗れますか。	... yuki no kūkō basu wa doko de nore masu ka
... airport	…空港	... kūkō
... hotel	…ホテル	... hoteru
town centre	市内	shinai

到着
ARRIVAL

出発
DEPARTURE

Train 列車

If you're worried about train tickets, times of departure, etc., go to a *kōtsūkōsha* (Japan Travel Bureau, JTB) office, where they speak English, or ask at your hotel.

The railway network covers the whole country; it is reputed to be clean, safe and punctual. First-class carriages are called *gurīn sha* ("green cars"), marked with a green four-leaf sign. To take a green-car coach, you'll have to buy a special ticket in addition to a regular ticket. Second-class coaches are often crowded.

All station names and important signs are printed in English.

Tourists can obtain special rail passes which allow unlimited travel on the Japanese railway system, as well as on buses and ferries throughout Japan. These passes must be obtained *outside* Japan, from offices of Japan Air Lines, from travel agents or from Japan Travel Bureau offices.

Types of trains 列車の種類

新幹線 (shinkansen)	super express or "bullet train". It has one westbound (*Tokaido-Sanyo*) and two north-bound lines (*Tohoku* and *Joetsu shinkansen*). Each offers two kinds of service: a faster one which stops only at major stations, and a slower one stopping at every station.

The rest of the Japanese railway network has three major categories of train:

特急 (tokkyū)	limited express for long-distance travel; supplementary fare required.
急行 (kyūkō)	ordinary express for medium-distance travel; supplementary fare required.
普通 (futsū)	local train stopping at all stations.

To the railway station 鉄道の駅へ行くには

Which station does the train to ... leave from?	…行きの電車はどの駅から出ますか。	... yuki no densha wa dono eki kara demasu ka
Where's the (railway) station?	(鉄道の) 駅はどこですか。	(tetsudō no) eki wa doko desu ka
Taxi!	タクシー！	takushī
Take me to the (railway) station.	(鉄道の) 駅まで連れていって下さい。	(tetsudō no) eki made tsurete itte kudasai
What's the fare?	料金はいくらですか。	ryōkin wa ikura desu ka

入口	ENTRANCE
出口	EXIT
ホームへ	TO THE PLATFORMS
案内	INFORMATION

TAXI, see page 21

Where is ...?   …はどこですか。

Where is/are the ...?	…はどこですか。	... wa doko desu ka
bar	バー	bā
booking office	予約窓口	yoyaku madoguchi
change machine	両替機	ryōgae ki
currency exchange office	両替所	ryōgaejo
information office	案内所	annaijo
left-luggage office (baggage check)	手荷物一時預かり所	tenimotsu ichiji azukarijo
lost property (lost and found) office	遺失物取扱所	ishitsubutsu toriatsu-kaijo
luggage lockers	手荷物ロッカー	tenimotsu rokkā
newsstand	新聞売場	shinbun uriba
platform 7	7番線ホーム	7 bansen hōmu
reservations office	予約窓口	yoyaku madoguchi
restaurant	食堂	shokudō
snack bar	スナックバー	sunakku bā
ticket machine	切符販売機	kippu hanbaiki
ticket office	切符売場	kippu uriba
toilets	洗面所	senmenjo
waiting room	待合室	machiaishitsu

Inquiries   案内

Is there a timetable in English?	英語の時刻表はありますか。	eigo no jikokuhyō wa arimasu ka
I'd like a timetable (in English), please.	(英語の) 時刻表を下さい。	(eigo no) jikokuhyō o kudasai
When is the ... train to Osaka?	大阪行きの…列車は何時ですか。	ōsaka yuki no ... ressha wa nanji desu ka
first/last/next	始発/最終/次の	shihatsu/saishū/tsugi no
What's the fare?	料金はいくらですか。	ryōkin wa ikura desu ka
What time does the train to Kobe leave?	神戸行きの列車は何時に出ますか。	kōbe yuki no ressha wa nanji ni demasu ka
Is it a through train?	直通列車ですか。	chokutsū ressha desu ka
Is there a connection to ...?	…への連絡はありますか。	... e no renraku wa arimasu ka

NUMBERS, see page 146

周遊旅行

Do I have to change trains?	列車を乗り換えなければなりませんか。	ressha o norikae nakereba narimasen ka
Is there enough time to change?	乗り換える時間は十分ありますか。	norikaeru jikan wa jūbun arimasu ka
How long do I have to wait?	どのくらい待たなければなりませんか。	donokurai matanakereba narimasen ka
What time does the train arrive in Nara?	その列車は奈良に何時に着きますか。	sono ressha wa nara ni nanji ni tsukimasu ka
Is there a ... on the train?	その列車に…はありますか。	sono ressha ni ... wa arimasu ka
buffet car	ビュッフェ	byuffe
dining-car	食堂車	shokudō sha
sleeping-car	寝台車	shindai sha
Does the train stop in Kofu?	その列車は甲府に止まりますか。	sono ressha wa kōfu ni tomarimasu ka
What platform does the train to Osaka leave from?	大阪行きの列車は何番ホームから出ますか。	ōsaka yuki no ressha wa nanban hōmu kara demasu ka
What platform does the train from Kyoto arrive at?	京都からの列車は何番ホームに着きますか。	kyōto kara no ressha wa nanban hōmu ni tsuki masu ka
Where do I board the train to Kamakura?	鎌倉行きの列車にはどこから乗るんでしょうか。	kamakura yuki no ressha wa doko kara norum deshō ka

---

直通列車です。	It's a through train.
…で乗り換えて下さい。	You have to change at ...
…で普通列車に乗り換えて下さい。	Change at ... and get a local train.
7番線ホームは…です。	Platform 7 is ...
あそこ／上の階 左側／右側	over there/upstairs on the left/on the right
あなたの列車は8番線ホームから出ます。	Your train will leave from platform 8.
…分遅れる見込みです。	There'll be a delay of ... minutes.

Tickets 切符

Ticket windows are usually classified according to destination, except for reserved seats (Shinkansen and other long distance trains), for which tickets are sold at "green windows" (みどりの窓口 – *midorino madoguchi*). For tickets to nearby destinations a vending machine is often provided.

Where can I buy a ticket to ...?	…行きの切符はどこで買えますか。	... yuki no kippu wa doko de kaemasu ka
Which ticket machine do I use to buy a ticket to ...?	…行きの切符を買うにはどの販売機を使ったらいいですか。	... yuki no kippu o kau ni wa dono hanbaiki o tsukattara iidesu ka
How much is the fare to Kofu?	甲府までの料金はいくらですか。	kōfu made no ryōkin wa ikura desu ka
A ticket to ..., please.	…行きの切符を一枚下さい。	... yuki no kippu o ichi-mai kudasai
single (one-way)	片道	katamichi
return (roundtrip)	往復	ōfuku
first class (green-coach seat)	グリーン車	gurīn sha
reserved seat	指定席	shitei seki
ordinary(-coach) seat	普通車	futsū sha
half price	半額	hangaku

Reservation 予約

I want to reserve a ...	…を予約したいのですが。	... o yoyaku shitai no desu ga
seat	席	seki
by the window	窓側の	mado gawa
smoking/ nonsmoking	喫煙／禁煙	kitsuen/kin-en
berth	寝台	shindai
upper	上段の	jōdan no
middle	中段の	chūdan no
lower	下段の	gedan no
berth in the sleeping car	寝台車の寝台	shindaisha no shindai

喫煙者 SMOKER	禁煙者 NONSMOKER

All aboard 列車

Is this the right plat-form for the train to Osaka?	大阪行きの列車は確かにこのホームから出ますか。	ōsaka yuki no ressha wa tashikani kono hōmu kara demasu ka
Is this the train to Yokohama?	これは横浜行きの列車ですか。	kore wa yokohama yuki no ressha desu ka
Where is platform 3?	3番ホームはどこですか。	3 ban hōmu wa doko desu ka
Excuse me. May I get by?	すみません。通らせて頂けますか。	sumimasen. toorasete itadakemasu ka
Is this seat taken?	この席はふさがっていますか。	kono seki wa fusagatte imasu ka
What station is this?	ここはどこの駅ですか。	koko wa doko no eki desu ka
How many train stops to ...?	…はいくつめの駅ですか。	... wa ikutsume no eki desu ka
Would you let me know before we get to Kyoto?	京都に着く前に教えていただけますか。	kyōto ni tsuku mae ni oshiete itadakemasu ka
How long does the train stop here?	列車はここにどの位停車しますか。	ressha wa koko ni dono kurai teisha shimasu ka
When do we get to Okayama?	岡山にはいつ着きますか。	okayama ni wa itsu tsuki masu ka

Sleeping 寝台車

Are there any free compartments in the sleeping-car?	寝台車に空いた寝台がありますか。	shindai sha ni aita shindai ga arimasu ka
Where's the sleeping-car?	寝台車はどこですか。	shindai sha wa doko desu ka
Where's my berth?	私の寝台はどこですか。	watashi no shindai wa doko desu ka
I'd like a lower berth.	下の段の寝台がいいのですが。	shita no dan no shindai ga iinodesu ga
Would you make up our berths?	寝台を用意して下さいますか。	shindai o yōi shite kudasaimasu ka
Would you wake me at 7 o'clock?	7時に起こして下さいますか。	7 ji ni okoshite kudasaimasu ka

Eating 食事

Many trains have dining cars or buffet cars where you can get snacks and drinks. On the train and at railway stations all over Japan you can buy *ekiben* (*eki* = station, *ben* = lunch), also called *obento*. These very popular lunch boxes contain traditional food, usually some speciality of the region: rice, raw or cooked fish and vegetables prepared in many different ways, and even the boxes come in different shapes and sizes.

Is there a dining car?	食堂車はありますか。	shokudō sha wa arimasu ka
I'd like a/some ...	…を下さい。	... o kudasai
beer	ビール	bīru
box lunch	お弁当	o-bentō
sandwich	サンドイッチ	sandoitchi
(Japanese) tea	（日本）茶	(nihon) cha

Baggage and porters 手荷物とポーター

Porter!	ポーター／赤帽さん！	pōtā/akabō san
Can you help me with my luggage?	荷物を運ぶのを手伝って下さいますか。	nimotsu o hakobu no o tetsudatte kudasaimasu ka
Where are the luggage trolleys (carts)?	荷物用カートはどこですか。	nimotsu yō kāto wa doko desu ka
Where are the luggage lockers?	荷物用ロッカーはどこですか。	nimotsu yō rokkā wa doko desu ka
Where's the left-luggage office (baggage check)?	手荷物一時預かり所はどこですか。	tenimotsu ichiji azukari jo wa doko desu ka
I'd like to leave my luggage, please.	荷物を頂けたいのですが。	nimotsu o azuketai no desu ga
I'd like to register (check) my luggage.	この荷物をチッキにしたいのですが。	kono nimotsu o chikki ni shitai no desu ga

---

小荷物取扱所
REGISTERING (CHECKING) BAGGAGE

周遊旅行

Underground (subway) 地下鉄

Tokyo, Osaka, Nagoya and other big cities have very efficient underground (subway) services. A map showing the various lines and stations is displayed outside every *chikatetsu* station.

You buy your ticket from a vending machine or from a ticket window and show it at the gate, where it will be punched. When you reach your destination you will have to hand it in. The station platform signs are in large Japanese and Roman letters. The smaller letters at the bottom of the sign indicate the previous and following stations. It is best to avoid the rush hours, 7 to 9 a.m. and 5 to 7 p.m.

Where's the underground (subway) station?	地下鉄はどこですか。	chikatetsu no eki wa doko desu ka
Does this train go to ...?	これは…へ行きますか。	kore wa ... e ikimasu ka
Where do I change for ...?	…へはどこで乗り換えるのでしょうか。	... e wa doko de norikaeru no deshō ka
Where is the ticket machine?	切符販売機はどこですか。	kippu hanbaiki wa doko desu ka
Which line should I take for ...?	…へ行くにはどの線に乗ればいいんですか。	... e iku ni wa dono sen ni nore ba iin desu ka
How many train stops to ...?	…はいくつめの駅ですか。	... wa ikutsume no eki desu ka
Is the next station ...?	次の駅は…ですか。	tsugi no eki wa ... desu ka
How late do the trains run?	電車はどのくらい遅くまで走っていますか。	densha wa dono kurai osoku made hashitte imasu ka
What time is the last train to ...?	…行きの最終電車は何時ですか。	... yuki no saishū ressha wa nanji desu ka
Where is the exit?	出口はどこですか。	deguchi wa doko desu ka
Which exit do I take for ...?	…へ行くにはどの出口がいいですか。	... e iku ni wa dono deguchi ga iidesu ka
How do I get to the street level?	地上に出るにはどう行ったらいいのですか。	chijō ni deru ni wa dō ittara īno desu ka

Bus — Tram (streetcar)　バス-市電

A complicated network of buses connects most areas of the large cities. In Kyoto and Nagoya this is a very useful and economical means of transport, but in Tokyo it is easier to take the subway.

The buses are usually one-man operated; the driver will tell you the fare, which you should put in a box by his seat. In some cities you pay when you get off the bus. Carry several ¥100 coins with you as the driver may not have change. You can buy a booklet of tickets *(kaisūken)* for multiple journeys.

Which bus goes to the town centre?	中心街に行くバスはどれですか。	chūshingai ni iku basu wa dore desu ka
Which bus/tram do I take to ...?	…へはどのバス／市電に乗るんでしょうか。	... e wa dono basu/shiden ni norun deshō ka
Where can I get a bus to ...?	…行きのバスにはどこで乗れますか。	... yuki no basu ni wa doko de noremasu ka
Where's the bus stop?	バス停はどこですか。	basu tei wa doko desu ka
When does the ... bus go?	…バスはいつですか。	... basu wa itsu desu ka
first/last/next	始発／最終／次の	shihatsu/saishū/tsugino
A ticket to ..., please.	…行きの切符を一枚下さい。	... yuki no kippu o ichi mai kudasai
I'd like a booklet of tickets.	回数券を下さい。	kaisūken o kudasai
How much is the fare to ...?	…までいくらですか。	... made ikura desu ka
Do I have to change buses?	バスを乗り換えなければなりませんか。	basu o norikae nakereba narimasen ka
How many bus stops are there to ...?	…はいくつめの停留所ですか	... wa ikutsume no teiryū jo desu ka
Will you tell me when to get off?	降りる時が来たら教えて下さいますか。	oriru toki ga kitara oshiete kudasaimasu ka
I want to get off at ...	…で降りたいのですが。	... de oritai no desu ga
When's the next coach (long-distance bus) to ...?	次の…行きの直通バスはいつですか。	tsugi no ... yuki no chokutsū basu wa itsu desu ka

How long does the journey (trip) take?	時間はどのくらいかかりますか。	jikan wa dono kurai kakari masu ka
Does it stop in ...?	…に止まりますか。	... ni tomari masu ka
Where does this bus go?	このバスはどこへ行きますか。	kono basu wa doko e iki masu ka

バス停留所　　　BUS STOP

Boat service　ボート・船

To discover the considerable charms of the Inland Sea, leave the plane, train, bus or taxi behind and take the ferryboat or hydrofoil, or try the longer cruises between Honshu and Shikoku island.

Where is there a boat information office?	ボート案内所はどこですか。	bōto annaijo wa doko desu ka
I'd like to take a boat trip/cruise.	ボート／遊覧船に乗りたいのですが。	bōto/yūransen ni nori tai no desu ga
When does the next ... leave?	次の…はいつ出ますか。	tsugi no ... wa itsu demasu ka
boat	ボート	bōto
ferry	フェリー	ferī
hydrofoil	水中翼船	suichūyokusen
ship	船	fune
Where's the embarkation point?	乗船場はどこですか。	jōsenjō wa doko desu ka
How long does the crossing take?	渡るのにどれ位かかりますか。	wataru noni dorekurai kakari masu ka
At which ports do we stop?	どの港に止まりますか。	dono minato ni tomari masu ka
cabin	船室	senshitsu
single/double	シングル／ダブル	singuru/daburu
deck	デッキ	dekki
harbour	港	minato
life belt/boat	救命ベルト／ボート	kyūmei beruto/bōto
pier	埠頭	futō
Can we take a tour of the harbour?	湾内遊覧は出来ますか。	wannai yūran wa dekimasu ka

Car 車

We've kept this section short because driving in Japan presents several sizable problems. Traffic keeps to the left, which will not unduly worry British drivers; however, most Westerners will be discouraged by the traffic conditions. The streets are extremely congested and it is forbidden to park or even to stop in some of them. Very few streets have names, and most traffic signs are written in Japanese characters. Roads are poorly surfaced and bumpy.

Where is there a filling station?	ガソリンスタンドはどこですか。	gasorin sutando wa doko desu ka
Full tank, please.	満タンにして下さい。	mantan ni shite kudasai
... litres of petrol (gasoline), please.	ガソリン…リットル入れて下さい。	gasorin ... rittoru irete kudasai
super (premium)	スーパー	sūpā
regular	レギュラー	regyurā
unleaded	無鉛	muen
diesel	ディーゼル	dīzeru
Please check the ...	…を調べて下さい。	... o shirabete kudasai
battery	バッテリー	batterī
brake fluid	ブレーキオイル	burēki oiru
oil	オイル	oiru
tyre pressure	タイヤの空気圧	taiya no kūkiatsu
water	水	mizu
Please check the spare tyre, too.	スペアタイヤも調べて下さい。	supea taiya mo shirabete kudasai
Can you mend this puncture (fix this flat)?	パンクを修理して頂けますか。	panku o shūri shite itadakemasu ka
Would you change the ..., please.	…を取り換えて下さい。	... o torikaete kudasai
bulb	電球	denkyū
fan belt	ファンベルト	fan beruto
spark(ing) plugs	点火プラグ	tenka puragu
tyre	タイヤ	taiya
wipers	ワイパー	waipā
Would you clean the windscreen (windshield)?	フロントガラスをふいて下さいますか。	furonto garasu o fuite kudasaimasu ka

CAR HIRE, see page 20

Asking the way 道を尋ねる

Excuse me ...	すみません…	sumimasen
Where is ...?	…はどこですか。	... wa doko desu ka
Can you tell me the way to ...?	…へ行く道を教えて頂けますか。	... e iku michi o oshiete itadakemasu ka
Is this the road to ...?	これは…へ行く道ですか。	kore wa ... e iku michi desu ka
How do I get to ...?	…へはどう行くんですか。	... e wa dō ikun desu ka
Can you show me on the map where I am?	この地図で私がどこにいるか示して下さい。	kono chizu de watashi ga doko ni iru ka shimeshite kudasai
How can I find this place/address?	この場所／住所にはどう行けばいいのでしょうか。	kono basho/jūsho ni wa dō ikeba iideshō ka
Is it far from here?	ここから遠いですか。	koko kara tōi desu ka
How long does it take by car/on foot?	車で／歩いてどの位かかりますか。	kuruma de/aruite dono kurai kakari masu ka
Can I drive to the centre of town?	中心街へ車で行けますか。	machi no chūshin e kuruma de ikemasu ka
What's the name of this place?	ここは何と言う所ですか。	koko wa nan to yū tokoro desu ka
Is there a road with little traffic?	車の通りの少ない道はありますか。	kuruma no tōri no sukunai michi wa arimasu ka
Is there a motorway (expressway)?	高速道路はありますか。	kōsoku dōro wa arimasu ka

NORTH
北
(kita)

WEST
西
(nishi)

EAST
東
(higashi)

SOUTH
南
(minami)

道が違います。	You're on the wrong road.
まっすぐ行きなさい。	Go straight ahead.
あそこの…です。	It's down there ...
左側／右側 反対側／…の裏 …のとなり／次	on the left/right opposite/behind ... next to/after ...
最初の／二番目の交差点 に行きなさい。	Go to the first/second crossroads (intersection).
…左／右に曲りなさい。	Turn left/right ...
信号で 角で	at the traffic lights at the corner
一方通行です。	It's a one-way street.
…へ戻らなければいけません。	You have to go back to ...
案内しますから、私につ いて来て下さい。	I'll show you. Follow me, please.

Parking 駐車

You may find parking a problem as there is little street parking space available in Tokyo and other large cities, nor is all-night parking allowed. The best solution is to use a car park, if your hotel has no facilities.

| Where can I park? | どこに駐車出来ますか。 | doko ni chūsha dekimasu ka |
| How's it | | |

Where can I park?	どこに駐車出来ますか。	doko ni chūsha dekimasu ka
Is there a car park nearby?	近くに駐車場がありますか。	chikaku ni chūshajō ga arimasu ka
May I park here?	ここに駐車してもいいですか。	koko ni chūsha shitemo ii desu ka
How long can I park here?	ここにどれくらい駐車出来ますか。	koko ni dorekurai chūsha dekimasu ka
What's the charge per hour?	一時間いくらですか。	ichi-jikan ikura desu ka
Do you have some change for the parking meter?	パーキングメーターに入れたいのでくずしていただけますか。	pākingu mētā ni iretai no de kuzushite itadake masu ka

Breakdown—Road assistance 故障-道路サービス

Where's the nearest garage?	最寄りの修理工場はどこですか。	moyori no shūrikōjō wa doko desu ka
Excuse me. My car has broken down.	すみません。車が故障してしまいました。	sumimasen. kuruma ga koshō shite shimai mashi ta
May I use your phone?	電話を使ってもよろしいですか。	denwa o tsukatte mo yoroshii desu ka
I've had a breakdown at ...	…で車が故障しました。	... de kuruma ga koshō shimashita
Can you send a mechanic?	修理工をよこして下さい。	shūriko o yokoshite kudasai
My car won't start.	エンジンがかかりません。	enjin ga kakari masen
The battery is dead.	バッテリーが上ってしまいました。	batterī ga agatte shimai mashita
I've run out of petrol. (gasoline).	ガス欠になりました。	gasuketsu ni nari mashita
I have a flat tyre.	タイアがパンクしました。	taiya ga panku shimashita
The engine is overheating.	エンジンがオーバーヒートしています。	enjin ga ōbāhīto shiteimasu
There is something wrong with the ...	…の調子が悪いのです。	... no chōshi ga warui desu
brakes	ブレーキ	burēki
carburettor	キャブレター	kyaburetā
exhaust pipe	マフラー	mafurā
radiator	ラジエーター	rajiētā
wheel	車輪	sharin
Can you send a breakdown van (tow truck)?	けん引車をよこして下さい。	ken-insha o yokoshite kudasai
How long will you be?	どのくらい時間がかかりますか。	dono kurai jikan ga kakari masu ka

Accident—Police 事故-警察

| Please call the police. | 警察を呼んで下さい。 | keisatsu o yonde kudasai |
| There's been an accident. It's about 2 km. from ... | 事故がありました。…から2キロ程の所です。 | jiko ga arimashita. ... kara 2 kiro hodo no tokoro desu |

| Call a doctor/an ambulance quickly. | 医者／救急車を早く呼んで下さい。 | isha/kyūkyūsha o hayaku yonde kudasai |
| There are people injured. | 怪我人がいます。 | keganin ga imasu |

Road signs 道路標識

One of the drawbacks of driving in Japan is that, although some of the road signs are visual, the remainder are written in Japanese characters.

一方通行	One-way traffic
追越し禁止	No overtaking (passing)
危険	Danger
重量制限	Weight limit
車両通行止め	No vehicles
徐行	Slow
スピード落せ	Reduce speed
道路工事中	Roadworks in progress
止まれ	Stop
歩行者専用	Pedestrians only
まわり道	Diversion (detour)
路肩弱し	Soft shoulder
路面凹凸あり	Bad road surface

Bicycle hire (rental) 貸自転車

Bicycles can be hired in tourist resorts. Ask at the tourist office for the address of a rental firm.

| I'd like to hire (rent) a bicycle. | 自転車を借りたいのですが。 | jitensha o karitai no desu ga |

Other means of transport その他の交通手段

cable car	ケーブルカー	kēburukā
helicopter	ヘリコプター	herikoputā
moped	モーター付自転車	mōtā tsuki jitensha
motorbike	モーターバイク	mōtā baiku
scooter	スクーター	sukūtā

Or perhaps you prefer:

| hitchhiking | ヒッチハイク | hitchi haiku |
| walking | 歩く | aruku |

Sightseeing

The JNTO (Japan Tourist Organisation) operates Tourist Information Centres (TIC), where you can obtain maps, information, tour itineraries and advice on transport. Some provide English-speaking guides.

Note: On visiting temples don't be surprised when you are asked to remove your shoes. This custom applies to any establishment where the floors are covered with *tatami* matting.

Where's the tourist information centre?	観光案内所はどこですか。	kankō annaijo wa doko desu ka
What's the "travel phone" number?	トラベルフォンの番号は何番ですか。	toraberufon no bangō wa nan-ban desu ka
What are the main points of interest?	何が特に面白いですか。	nani ga toku ni omoshiroi desu ka
We're here for ...	ここには…います。	koko ni wa ... imasu
a few hours/a day/ a week	二三時間／一日／一週間	ni-san jikan/ichi-nichi/ isshūkan
Can you recommend a/an ...?	…はありますか。	... wa arimasu ka
excursion	小旅行	shō ryokō
sightseeing tour	観光ツアー	kankō tsuā
Where's the point of departure?	出発点はどこですか。	shuppatsu ten wa doko desu ka
Will the bus pick us up at the hotel?	そのバスはホテルに迎えに来てくれますか。	sono basu wa hoteru ni mukae ni kitekuremasu ka
How much does the tour cost?	そのツアーはいくらかかりますか。	sono tsuā wa ikura kakari masu ka
What time does the tour start?	そのツアーは何時に出ますか。	sono tsuā wa nanji ni demasu ka
Is lunch included?	昼食は含まれていますか。	chūshoku wa fukumare- teimasu ka
Do we have free time in ...?	…で自由時間がありますか。	... de jiyū jikan ga arimasu ka

TRAVEL PHONE, see inside back-cover

観光

What time do we get back?	何時に戻って来られますか。	nanji ni modotte korare masu ka
Is there an English-speaking guide?	英語を話すガイドがいますか。	eigo o hanasu gaido ga imasu ka
I'd like to hire a private guide ...	個人のガイドを…頼みたいのですが。	kojin no gaido o ... tanomitai no desu ga
for half a day	半日	han-nichi
for a full day	一日	ichi-nichi

Where ...? どこ？

Where is/are the ...?	…はどこですか。	... wa doko desu ka
abbey	修道院	shūdōin
aquarium	水族館	suizokukan
art gallery	画廊	garō
botanical garden	植物園	shokubutsuen
business district	ビジネス街	bijinesu gai
castle	城	shiro
cathedral	大聖堂	daiseidō
cave	洞窟	dōkutsu
cemetery	墓地	bochi
church	町の中心	kyōkai
city centre	教会	machi no chūshin
convent	修道院	shūdōin
court house	裁判所	saibansho
downtown area	繁華街	hankagai
embankment	堤防	teibō
exhibition	展覧会	tenrankai
factory	工場	kōjō
fair	博覧会	hakurankai
flea market	のみの市	nomi no ichi
fortress	城砦	jōsai
fountain	噴水	funsui
gardens	庭園	teien
gate	門	mon
harbour	港	minato
kabuki theatre	歌舞伎座	kabukiza
library	図書館	toshokan
market	市場	ichiba
monastery	僧院	sōin
monument	記念碑	kinenhi
museum	博物館／美術館	hakubutsukan/bijutsukan
observatory	天文台	tenmondai
open-air museum	野外美術館	yagai bijutsukan

palace	宮殿	kyūden
park	公園	kōen
parliament building	国会議事堂	kokkai gijidō
ruins	遺跡	iseki
shopping area	ショッピング街	shoppingu gai
shrine	神社	jinja
square	広場	hiroba
(Olympic) stadium	(オリンピック) 競技場	(orinpikku) kyōgijō
statue	像	zō
stock exchange	証券取引所	shōken torihikijo
temple	寺	tera
(national) theatre	(国立) 劇場	(kokuritsu) gekijō
tomb	墓	haka
tower	塔	tō
town hall	市役所	shiyakusho
university	大学	daigaku
zoo	動物園	dōbutsuen

入場無料	ADMISSION FREE
カメラ持込禁止	NO CAMERAS ALLOWED

Admission 入場

Is ... open on Sundays?	…は日曜日に開いてますか。	... wa nichiyōbi ni aite imasu ka
When does it open?	いつ開きますか。	itsu akimasu ka
When does it close?	いつ閉りますか。	itsu shimarimasu ka
How much is the entrance fee?	入場料はいくらですか。	nyūjōryō wa ikura desu ka
Is there any reduction for (the) ...?	…割引はありますか。	... waribiki wa arimasu ka
children	子供	kodomo
disabled	身体障害者	shintai shōgaisha
groups	団体	dantai
students	学生	gakusei
Do you have a guidebook (in English)?	(英語の)案内書はありますか。	(eigo no) annaisho wa arimasu ka
Can I buy a catalogue?	カタログを買えますか。	katarogu o kaemasu ka
Is it all right to take pictures?	写真をとっても構いませんか。	shashin o totte mo kamai masen ka

観光

What are your special interests?　何に特に興味がありますか。

I'd like to see (a/the) ...	…が見たいのですが。	... ga mitai no desu ga

Buddhist temple	寺	tera
historical site	史跡	shiseki
Imperial Palace	皇居	kōkyo
Japanese garden	日本庭園	nihon teien
rock garden	石庭	sekitei
National Museum	国立美術館	kokuritsu bijutsukan
pagoda	塔	tō
Shinto shrine	神社	jinja
teahouse	茶室	chashitsu
Zen temple	禅寺	zendera

What do you suggest we should see?	何を見たらいいでしょうか。	nani o mitara ii deshō ka

We're interested in ...	…に興味を持っています。	... ni kyōmi o motte imasu

antiques	骨董品	kottōhin
archaeology	考古学	kōkogaku
architecture	建築	kenchiku
modern	近代	kindai
religious	宗教	shūkyō
traditional	伝統	dentō
art	芸術	geijutsu
calligraphy	書道	shodō
ceramics	陶磁器	tōjiki
coins	古銭／硬貨	kosen/kōka
drawings	デッサン	dessan
flower arranging	いけ花	ikebana
folk arts	民芸品	mingeihin
furniture	家具	kagu
handicrafts	手工芸品	shukōgeihin
history	歴史	rekishi
lacquerware	漆器	shikki
ornithology	鳥類学	chōruigaku
painting	絵画	kaiga
papercrafts	紙工芸	shikōgeihin
pottery	陶器	tōki
ukiyoe prints	浮世絵	ukiyoe
religion	宗教	shūkyō
sculpture	彫刻	chōkoku
textiles	織物	orimono
woodcraft	木彫	kibori

Who — What — When?　誰-何-いつ？

What's that building?	あの建物は何ですか。	ano tatemono wa nan desu ka
When was it built?	いつ建てられましたか。	itsu tateraremashita ka
Is it original?	原形のままですか。	genkei no mama desu ka
Who was the ...?	…は誰ですか。	... wa dare desu ka
architect	建築家	kenchikuka
artist	芸術家	geijutsuka
painter	画家	gaka
sculptor	彫刻家	chōkokuka
When did he live?	いつの時代の人ですか。	itsu no jidai no hito desu ka
Who painted that picture?	あの絵は誰が描いたのですか。	ano e wa dare ga kaita no desu ka
It's ...	…ですね。	... desu ne
beautiful	美しい	utsukushii
interesting	面白い	omoshiroi
magnificent	立派	rippa
strange	奇妙	kimyō
terrifying	恐ろしい	osoroshii

Religious services　礼拝

Although Shinto and Buddhism are the major religions, there are over 900,000 Christians in Japan, with churches in nearly every town. Few services are conducted in English.

Is there a ... near here?	この近くに…はありますか。	kono chikaku ni ... wa ari masu ka
Catholic church	カトリック教会	katorikku kyōkai
Protestant church	プロテスタント教会	purotesutanto kyōkai
mosque	回教寺院	kaikyō jiin
synagogue	ユダヤ教会	yudaya kyōkai
Is it open to visitors?	訪問者に公開されていますか。	hōmonsha ni kōkai sarete imasu ka
What time is mass/ the service?	礼拝は何時からですか。	reihai wa nanji kara desu ka
I'd like to visit the church.	その教会に行きたいのですが。	sono kyōkai ni iki tai no desu ga

観光

In the countryside 郊外で

Is there a scenic route to ...?	…に行く景色の良いコースはありますか。	... ni iku keshiki no yoi kōsu wa arimasu ka
How far is it to ...?	…まেどの位ありますか。	... made dono kurai arimasu ka
Can we walk?	歩いて行けますか。	aruite ikemasu ka
How high is that mountain?	あの山の高さはどれ位ありますか。	ano yama no takasa wa dore kurai arimasu ka
What ... is this?	これは何という…ですか。	kore wa nan to yū ... desu ka
animal/bird	動物／鳥	dōbutsu/tori
flower/tree	花／木	hana/ki

bridge	橋	hashi
cedar	西洋すぎ	seiyō sugi
cherry tree	桜	sakura
farm	農場	nōjō
field	野原	nohara
forest	森	mori
garden	庭	niwa
hill	丘	oka
hot spring	温泉	onsen
house	家	ie
island	島	shima
lake	湖	mizuumi
meadow	牧場	bokujō
mountain	山	yama
(foot)path	小道	komichi
peak	峰	mine
pine	松	matsu
pond	池	ike
river	川	kawa
road	道	michi
rock	岩	iwa
sea	海	umi
stone	石	ishi
valley	谷	tani
village	村	mura
wall	壁／へい	kabe/hei
waterfall	滝	taki
watermill	水車	suisha
wood	林	hayashi

Relaxing

You'll find all the usual kinds of entertainment, such as concerts, plays, films, cabarets, sports, etc. But there are also typically Japanese spectacles like the famous *kabuki, noh* and *bunraku* theatres, and sports displays like *sumo* wrestling or *kendo* (see page 91). At your hotel or in tourist information centres you'll find publications like the "Visitor's guide", or consult the English-language newspapers.

Theatre—Concert—Cinema 劇場-コンサート-映画

Can you recommend a/an ...?	何かよい…はありません か。	nani ka yoi ... wa arimasen ka
concert	コンサート	konsāto
film	映画	eiga
opera	オペラ	opera
play	芝居	shibai
What's playing at the National Theatre?	国立劇場では何をやって いますか。	kokuritsu gekijō de wa nani o yatte imasu ka
What sort of play is it?	どんな芝居ですか。	donna shibai desu ka
Who's it by?	誰の作品ですか。	dare no sakuhin desu ka
Do you think I'll understand it?	私にわかるでしょうか。	watashi ni wakaru deshō ka
I'd like to go to a concert.	コンサートに行きたいの ですが。	konsāto ni ikitai no desu ga
Where's the concert hall?	コンサートホールはどこ ですか。	konsāto hōru wa doko desu ka
Which orchestra is playing?	どこのオーケストラが演 奏していますか。	doko no ōkesutora ga ensōshite imasu ka
What are they playing?	何を演奏していますか。	nani o ensō shite imasu ka
Who's the conductor/ soloist?	指揮者／独奏者は誰です か。	shikisha/dokusōsha wa dare desu ka
Is there a ballet I can see?	バレーは上演されていま すか。	barē wa jōen sarete imasu ka
Who is dancing the lead role?	主演は誰ですか。	shuen wa dare desu ka

What's on at the cinema tonight?	今夜どんな映画をやっていますか。	kon-ya donna eiga o yatte imasu ka
Who's in it?	誰が出ていますか。	dare ga dete imasu ka
Who's the director?	監督は誰ですか。	kantoku wa dare desu ka

The traditional Japanese theatre　日本の伝統芸能

There are three major forms of traditional theatre which are unique to Japan. They are *Noh, Kabuki* and *Bunraku.*

Noh, the oldest of Japanese stage arts dating back to the 13th century, is performed in slow motion by an all-male cast wearing colourful, stiff 15th-century brocade costumes and wooden masks. The stage has no scenery except a backdrop of painted pine trees and is open to the audience on three sides. *Noh* is not necessarily to everyone's taste.

Kabuki, originated in the 16th century, is just the opposite of *Noh.* The stage is vast, costumes and settings gorgeous, the action fast and continuous. All the players are men, and the female characters are played by actors who have been specially trained since early childhood. Shows, comprising several pieces, last up to four hours, but you can buy tickets for just a part of the programme.

Bunraku is a form of puppet theatre found only in Japan, using the same dramatic themes, stories and conventions as *noh* and *kabuki.* It isn't always easy for foreigners to appreciate. Each doll, 3 to 4½ feet high, is manipulated by a master puppeteer and two black-clad assistants. The dolls move on a waist-high platform on stage.

I'd like to see ...	…を見たいのですが。	... o mitai no desu ga
bunraku	文楽	bunraku
kabuki	歌舞伎	kabuki
noh	能	nō
Where are they playing?	どこでやっていますか。	doko de yatte imasu ka
How long will the performance last?	その公演は何時間かかりますか。	sono kōen wa nanjikan kakarimasu ka

Tickets 切符

Where can I buy tickets?	切符はどこで買えますか。	kippu wa doko de kae masu ka
What time does it begin?	何時に始まりますか。	nanji ni hajimarimasu ka
What time does it end?	何時に終りますか。	nanji ni owarimasu ka
Are there any seats for tonight?	今夜の席はまだあります か。	kon-ya no seki wa mada arimasu ka
I'd like to reserve 2 seats ...	…2席予約したいのです が。	... 2 seki yoyaku shitai no desu ga
for the show on ... evening	…の晩のショーを	... no ban no shō o
for the matinée on ...	…の昼の部を	... no hiru no bu o
How much are the tickets?	切符はいくらになります か。	kippu wa ikura ni nari masu ka
I'd like a seat ...	…席を下さい。	... seki o kudasai
in the stalls (orchestra)	オーケストラボックス	ōkesutora bokkusu
in the circle (mezzanine)	二階の	nikai no
not too far forward	余り前の方でない	amari mae no hō denai
not too far back	余り後の方でない	amari ushiro no hō denai
somewhere in the middle	真中あたりの	mannaka atari no
Do you have a pro-gramme (in English)?	(英語の)プログラムはあ りますか。	(eigo no) puroguramu wa arimasu ka
Where's the cloak-room?	クロークはどこですか。	kurōku wa doko desu ka

Nightclubs—Discos ナイトクラブ-ディスコ

It's best to ask a Japanese friend or at your hotel, which nightclub or discotheque they'd recommend—nightlife can be very expensive.

Where's the nightclub section of the city?	この町のナイトクラブ街 はどこですか。	kono machi no naito kurabu gai wa doko desu ka

DAYS OF THE WEEK, see page 150

Can you recommend a good ...?	よい…を教えて下さい。	yoi ... o oshiete kudasai
bar	バー	bā
discotheque	ディスコ	disuko
jazz club	ジャズクラブ	jazu kurabu
nightclub	ナイトクラブ	naito kurabu

Is there a floor show?	フロアショーはあります か。	furoa shō wa arimasu ka
What kind of band is playing?	どんなバンドが入ってい ますか。	donna bando ga haitte imasu ka
Where can we go dancing?	どこでダンスが出来ます か。	doko de dansu ga deki masu ka

Geisha 芸者

Geisha are highly accomplished hostess-entertainers trained since early childhood to sing, dance, play the *shamisen* (a Japanese string instrument) and pour *sake* (Japanese rice wine) for guests. Most of them start their career as *geisha* servants when they are quite young (at the age of seven or eight). The apprenticeship won't be over until they reach the age of twenty or so.

Geisha are mostly engaged by rich Japanese businessmen to entertain and relax their guests. A *geisha's* main function is to break the ice. As a non-Japanese, you are unlikely to see a genuine *geisha* actually performing.

What you are most likely to come across are very distant cousins of the geisha, the *hosutessu* in the *kara oke* bars. These small bars can be found in entertainment districts all over Japan. People like to come here after work to unwind for a while. It's the *hosutessu's* job to keep the whisky glass or sake cup topped up, and the conversation going.

Here you will be surrounded by the sound of non-stop taped popular music—both Japanese and Western—and periodically one of the clientele will climb up onto the small spotlighted stage and sing his or her favourite number.

Sports スポーツ

Practically all sports played in the West are also popular in Japan: golf, tennis, football (soccer), rugby, basketball, etc. Baseball is at least as popular in Japan as in the United States.

Many cities have martial arts halls in which you can watch *kendo* (fencing with bamboo staves), and the now internationally practised sports of *judo, aikido* and *karate*.

But Japan's real national sport is *sumo* (fat-power wrestling). This ancient, highly ritualized sport goes back 15 centuries and more to Shinto religious ceremonies, when contests were held at the harvest festivals. *Sumo* wrestlers weigh anything from 200 to 350 pounds. Seasonal 15-day tournaments are held alternatively in Tokyo, Nagoya, Osaka and Fukuoka.

I'd like to see a *sumo* match.	相撲の試合が見たいのですが。	sumō no shiai ga mitai no desu ga
Is there a tournament now?	今競技がありますか。	ima kyōgi ga arimasu ka
Can you get me a ticket?	切符を手配して下さいますか。	kippu o tehaishite kudasai masu ka
Is there a/an ... demonstration?	…の実演がありますか。	... no jitsuen ga arimasu ka
aikido	合気道	aikidō
judo	柔道	jūdō
karate	空手	karate
kendo	剣道	kendō

baseball	野球	yakyū
basketball	バスケットボール	basuketto bōru
boxing	ボクシング	bokushingu
football (soccer)	サッカー	sakkā
horse racing	競馬	keiba
rugby	ラグビー	ragubī
skiing	スキー	sukī
swimming	水泳	suiei
tennis	テニス	tenisu
volleyball	バレーボール	barēbōru

What's the admission charge?	入場料はいくらですか。	nyūjōryō wa ikura desu ka
Where can I play golf/tennis?	どこでゴルフ／テニスが出来ますか。	doko de gorufu/tenisu ga dekimasu ka
Is there a public golf course/tennis court?	パブリックのゴルフコース／テニスコートがありますか。	paburikku no gorufu kōsu/tenisu kōto ga arimasu ka
Can I hire (rent) ...?	…を借りられますか。	... o kariraremasu ka
clubs	クラブ	kurabu
equipment	用具	yōgu
rackets	ラケット	raketto
What's the charge per ...?	…の料金はいくらですか。	... no ryōkin wa ikura desu ka
hour/day/round	一時間／一日／一ラウンド	ichi-jikan/ichi-nichi/ichi-raundo
I'd like to go swimming.	泳ぎに行きたいのですが。	oyogi ni ikitai no desu ga
Is there a swimming pool here?	ここにプールがありますか。	koko ni pūru ga arimasu ko
Is it open-air or indoor?	屋外ですか屋内ですか。	okugai desu ka okunai desu ka
Is it heated?	温水ですか。	onsui desu ka
What's the temperature of the water?	水温は何度ですか。	suion wa nando desu ka
Is there a good beach nearby?	近くにいい海水浴場がありますか。	chikaku ni ii kaisuiyokujō ga arimasu ka

Winter sports ウインタースポーツ

Japan is a mountainous country, so there are numerous ski-resorts.

I'd like to ski.	スキーがしたいのですが。	sukī ga shitai no desu ga
What are the skiing conditions like at ...?	…のスキーコンディションはどうですか。	... no sukī kondishon wa dō desu ka
Can I hire ...?	…を借りられますか。	... o kariraremasu ka
ski boots	スキー靴	sukī gutsu
skiing equipment	スキー用具	sukī yōgu
skis	スキー	sukī

Making friends

Japanese society is very formal, and people prefer to be introduced through others rather than initiate a conversation with a stranger. This does not mean, though, that you won't speak to any Japanese, as they are happy to practise their languages if they can be of help to a tourist.

Rather than shaking hands the Japanese bow to each other in greeting—this isn't expected of foreign visitors.

Introductions 紹介

Would you introduce me to Mr./Mrs./Ms. ...?*	…さんを私に紹介して頂けますか。	... san o watashi ni shō-kaishite itadake masu ka
My name is ...	私は…と申します。	watashi wa ... to mōshi-masu
How do you do? (Pleased to meet you.)	はじめまして。	hajimemashite
What's your name?	あなたのお名前は何ですか。	anata no o-namae wa nan desu ka
This is ...	こちらは…です。	kochira wa ... desu
Mr./Mrs./Ms. ...*	…さん	... san
my wife/husband	家内／主人	kanai/shujin
my son/daughter	私のむすこ／むすめ	watashi no musuko/musume
a friend/colleague	友達／同僚	tomodachi/dōryō
How are you?	お元気ですか。	o-genki desu ka
Fine, thanks. And you?	元気です、お蔭様で。あなたは？	genki desu. okagesama de. anata wa

Follow up 打ちとけるために

Do you live here?	ここにお住いですか。	koko ni o-sumai desu ka
I'm here on holiday/on a business trip.	ここには休暇で来ています／仕事で来ています。	koko ni wa kyūka de kiteimasu/shigoto de kiteimasu
Where do you come from?	どちらからいらっしゃいましたか。	dochira kara irasshai mashita ka

* When addressing a Japanese you should use their family name followed by *san*. (*San* should never be used when referring to oneself.)

I'm from ...	私は…からです。	watashi wa ... kara desu
What nationality are you?	国籍はどちらですか。	kokuseki wa dochira desu ka
I'm ...	私は…です。	watashi wa ... desu
American	アメリカ人	amerika jin
Australian	オーストラリア人	ōsutoraria jin
British	英国人	eikoku jin
Canadian	カナダ人	kanada jin
English	イギリス人	igirisu jin
Irish	アイルライド人	airurando jin
Scottish	スコットランド人	sukottorando jin
How long have you been here?	ここにもうどの位いらっしゃいますか。	koko ni mō donokurai irasshaimasu ka
Is this your first visit to Japan?	日本には初めていらっしゃったのですか。	nihon ni wa hajimete irasshatta no desu ka
I've been here several times.	ここにはもう何回か来ています。	koko ni wa mō nankai ka kiteimasu
Where are you staying?	どちらに御滞在ですか。	dochira ni go-taizai desu ka
Are you enjoying your stay?	ここがお気に入りましたか。	koko ga o-kiniirimashita ka
Yes, I like it very much.	はい、非常に気に入っています。	hai hijō ni kiniitte imasu
I like the ...	…が好きです。	... ga suki desu
city	町	machi
country	この国	kono kuni
food	ここの食べ物	koko no tabemono
landscape	景色	keshiki
people	ここの人々	koko no hitobito
Do you travel a lot?	よく旅行なさいますか。	yoku ryokō nasaimasu ka
Where have you been travelling?	今までどこを旅行なさいましたか。	imamade doko o ryokō nasaimashita ka
Are you on your own?	おひとりですか。	o-hitori desu ka
I'm with my ...	…と一緒です。	... to issho desu
husband/wife	主人／家内	shujin/kanai
family/children	家族／子供	kazoku/kodomo
brother/sister	兄弟／姉妹	kyōdai/shimai
father/mother	父／母	chichi/haha
boyfriend/girlfriend	ボーイフレンド／ガールフレンド	bōifurendo/gārufurendo

COUNTRIES, see page 145

友達を作る

Are you married/single?	結婚していらっしゃいますか／独身ですか。	kekkon shite irasshaimasu ka/dokushin desu ka
What do you do?	どんなお仕事をしていらっしゃいますか。	donna o-shigoto o shitei-rasshaimasu ka
I'm a ...	私は…です。	watashi wa ... desu
businessman	ビジネスマン	bijinesuman
journalist	ジャーナリスト	jānarisuto
secretary	秘書	hisho
student	学生	gakusei
teacher	教師	kyōshi
I work in a factory/an office/a shop.	私は工場／オフィス／店で働いています。	watashi wa kōjō/ofuisu/mise de hataraite imasu

Invitations 招待

May I invite you for dinner?	夕食にご招待させて頂けますか。	yūshoku ni go-shōtai sasete itadakemasu ka
We're giving a small party tomorrow. I hope you can come.	明日ささやかなパーティーをしようと思っています。いらして頂けるとうれしいのですが。	asu sasayakana pātī o shiyōto omotte imasu. irashite itadakeruto ureshii no desu ga
That's very kind of you.	御親切にどうもありがとうございます。	go-shinsetsu ni dōmo arigatō gozaimasu
What time shall we come?	何時にお伺いすればいいでしょうか。	nanji ni o-ukagaisureba iideshō ka

Talking about the weather 天気について話す

What a lovely day!	すばらしい天気ですね。	subarashii tenki desu ne
It's nice/awful weather.	いい／ひどい天気ですね。	ii/hidoi tenki desu ne
It's windy today.	今日は風が強いです。	kyō wa kaze ga tsuyoi desu
Is it usually as humid as this?	いつもこんなに湿気がありますか。	itsumo konnani shikke ga arimasu ka
What is the weather forecast?	天気予報はどうですか。	tenki yohō wa dō desu ka
Is it going to ... tomorrow?	明日は…でしょうか。	asu wa ... deshō ka
clear up/be sunny rain/snow	お天気になる／晴れる 雨が降る／雪が降る	o-tenki ni naru/hareru ame ga furu/yuki ga furu

Dating デート

Are you waiting for someone?	誰かをお待ちですか。	dareka o o-machi desu ka
Do you mind if I sit here?	ここに座ってもかまいませんか。	koko ni suwatte mo kamaimasen ka
Shall we have a cup of coffee?	コーヒーでも御一緒にいかがですか。	kōhī demo go-issho ni ikaga desu ka
Do you mind if I smoke?	たばこを吸ってもよろしいですか。	tabako o suttemo yoroshii desu ka
Do you have a light, please?	火をお待ちですか。	hi o o-mochi desu ka
Would you like to go out tonight?	今夜私と一緒に出掛けませんか。	konban watashi to issho ni dekakemasen ka
Would you like to go dancing?	ダンスをしに行きませんか。	dansu o shini ikimasen ka
Shall we go to the cinema?	一緒に映画に行きましょうか。	issho ni eiga ni ikimashō ka
Shall we go for a walk?	一緒に散歩に行きましょうか。	issho ni sanpo ni ikimashō ka
Where shall we meet?	どこでお会いしましょうか。	doko de o-aishimashō ka
I'll call for you at 8.	8時にお迎えに参ります	8 ji ni o-mukae ni mairi masu
May I take you home?	お宅までお送りしましょうか。	o-taku made o-okuri shimashō ka
Can I see you again?	又お会い出来ますか。	mata o-ai dekimasu ka

... and you might answer:

I'd love to, thank you.	ありがとう、よろこんで。	arigotō, yorokonde
Thank you, but I'm busy.	ありがとう、でも約束がありますから。	arigatō, demo yakusoku ga arimasu kara
No, I'm not interested, thank you.	いいえ結構です、興味がありません。	iie kekkō desu kyōmi ga arimasen
Thank you for the evening.	今晩はどうもありがとうございました。	konban wa dōmo arigatō gozaimashita
I've enjoyed myself.	大変楽しかったです。	taihen tanoshikatta desu

Shopping Guide

This shopping guide is designed to help you find what you want with ease, accuracy and speed. It features:

1. A list of all major shops, stores and services (p. 98).
2. Some general expressions required when shopping to allow you to be specific and selective (p. 100).
3. Full details of the shops and services most likely to concern you. Here you'll find advice, alphabetical lists of items, and conversion charts listed under the headings below.

		page
Bookshop/ Newsstand/ Stationer's	books, magazines, newspapers, stationery	104
Chemist's (drugstore)	medicine, first-aid, cosmetics, toilet articles	106
Clothes shop	clothes and accessories, fabrics, shoes	110
Department store	list of departments	117
Electrical appliances/ Leisure	household appliances, hi-fi equipment	118
Grocery/ Supermarket	some general expressions, weights, measures and packaging	120
Jeweller's/ Watchmaker's	jewellery, watches, watch repairs	121
Optician's	glasses, lenses, binoculars	123
Photography	cameras, films, developing, accessories	124
Tobacconist's— Kiosk	smoker's supplies, sweets, cookies ...	126
Miscellaneous	souvenirs, records, cassettes, toys	127

ショッピングガイド

Shops, stores and services 小売店、デパートそしてサービス

Shops in Japan usually open between 9 and 11 a.m. and stay open until 8 p.m., except department stores which close at 6 or 6.30 p.m. All shops close one day per week; many are open on Saturdays and Sundays. If you need something urgently, go to a major railway station where you'll usually find a shopping centre open until around 8 p.m.

There are many "cut-price" shops where you can save from 5–40%, and if you are willing to fill in lengthy forms you can buy goods that are exempt from tax where you see a "tax-free" sign (you will need to produce your passport).

The Japanese are not a haggling nation and are in fact embarrassed, even offended, by any attempt to argue over prices. Exceptions exist, but overall posted prices are fair and non-negotiable.

You will find detailed information about sales in the English-language newspapers.

Where's (the nearest) ...?	(最寄りの)…はどこですか。	(moyori no) ... wa doko desu ka
antique shop	骨董屋	kottōya
art gallery	画廊	garō
baker's	パン屋	pan-ya
bookshop	本屋	hon-ya
butcher's	肉屋	nikuya
camera shop	カメラ屋	kameraya
cake shop	ケーキ屋	kēkiya
candy store	菓子屋	kashiya
ceramics shop	陶器屋	tōkiya
chemist's	薬屋	kusuriya
clothes shop (men's/women's)	洋装店 (紳士用／婦人用)	yōsōten (shinshi yō/fujin yō)
computer equipment store	コンピューター機器店	konpūta kikiten
delicatessen	デリカテッセン	derikatessen
department store	デパート	depāto
discount shop	安売りの店	yasuuri no mise
dressmaker's	洋服屋	yōfukuya
drugstore	薬屋	kusuriya
electrical shop	電気店	denkiten
fish market	魚市場	uoichiba

ショッピングガイド

fishmonger's	魚屋	sakanaya
flea market	のみの市	nomi no ichi
florist's	花屋	hanaya
furrier's	毛皮屋	kegawaya
greengrocer's	八百屋	yaoya
grocery	食料品店	shokuryōhinten
handicrafts shop	手工芸品店	shukōgeihinten
hardware store	金物屋	kanamonoya
health food shop	健康食品店	kenkō shokuhinten
ironmonger's	金物屋	kanamonoya
jeweller's	宝石店	hōsekiten
kimono shop	呉服屋	gofukuya
kiosk	キヨスク	kiyosuku
launderette	コインランドリー	koinrandorī
library	図書館	toshokan
liquor store	酒屋	sakaya
market	市場	ichiba
newsstand	新聞売場	shinbun uriba
off-licence	酒屋	sakaya
optician	眼鏡屋	meganeya
pastry shop	ケーキ屋	kēkiya
pharmacy	薬屋	kusuriya
photographer	写真屋（カメラマン）	shashinya (kamera man)
photo store	写真屋	shashinya
record shop	レコード店	rekōdoten
shoe shop	靴屋	kutsuya
shopping centre	ショッピングセンター	shoppingu sentā
souvenir shop	みやげ物屋	miyagemonoya
sporting goods shop	スポーツ用品店	supōtsuyōhinten
stationer's	文房具店	bunbōguten
supermarket	スーパーマーケット	sūpāmāketto
sweet shop	菓子屋	kashiya
tailor's	洋服屋	yōfukuya
textile shop	生地屋	kijiya
tobacconist's	たばこ屋	tabakoya
toy shop	おもちゃ屋	omochaya
travel agency	旅行代理店	ryokō dairiten
vegetable store	八百屋	yaoya
video shop	ビデオ用品店	bideo yōhinten
watchmaker's	時計屋	tokeiya
wine merchant's	酒屋	sakaya
woodblock print shop	木版画店	mokuhangaten

入口	ENTRANCE
出口	EXIT
非常口	EMERGENCY EXIT

General expressions 般的な表現

Where? どこですか。

Where's there a good ...?	良い…はどこですか。	yoi ... wa doko desu ka
Where can I find a ...?	…はどこにありますか。	... wa doko ni arimasu
Where do they sell ...?	…はどこで売ってますか。	... wa doko de uttemasu
Where's the main shopping area?	主要なショッピング街はどの辺にありますか。	shuyō na shoppingu gai wa donohen ni arimasu ka
Is there a department store there?	そこにデパートはありますか。	soko ni depāto wa arimasu ka
Is it far from here?	ここから遠いですか。	koko kara tōi desu ka
How do I get there?	そこにはどうやって行けますか。	sokoni wa dōyatte ikemasu ka

大売出し（セール） SALE	在庫一掃セール CLEARANCE

Service サービス

Can you help me?	お願いします。	o-negai shimasu
I'm just looking.	見るだけです。	mirudake desu
Do you sell ...?	…はありますか。	... wa arimasu ka
I'd like ...	…が欲しいのですが。	... ga hoshii no desu ga
Can you show me some ...?	…を見せて下さい。	... o misete kuda sai
Do you have any ...?	…はありますか。	... wa arimasu ka
I'd like to buy ...	…を買いたいのですが。	... o kaitai no desu ga

That one あれ

Can you show me ...?	…を見せて下さい。	... o misete kudasai
this/that	これ／あれ	kore/are
the one in the window/in the display case	ショーウインドーに出ている／ショーケースの中にあるもの	shōuindō ni deteiru/ shōkēsu no naka ni aru mono

DEPARTMENT STORE, see page 117

I want a ... one.	…のが欲しいのですが。	... no ga hoshiino desu ga
big	大きい	ōkii
cheap	安い	yasui
dark	色の濃い	iro no koi
good	良い	yoi
heavy	重い	omoi
large	大きい	ōkii
light (weight)	軽い	karui
light (colour)	色の薄い	iro no usui
oval	だ円形の	daenkei no
rectangular	長方形	chōhōkei
round	丸い	marui
small	小さい	chīsai
square	四角い	shikakui

I don't want anything too expensive.	余り高いのは入りません。	amari takai no wa irimasen
I'd prefer something of better quality.	もっと質の良いのが欲しいのですが。	motto shitsu no yoi no ga hoshii no desu ga
Can you show me some others?	他のを見せて下さい。	hoka no o misete kudasai
Don't you have anything ...?	何か…のはありませんか。	nanika ... no wa arimasen ka
cheaper/better	もっと安い／もっと良い	motto yasui/motto yoi
larger/smaller	もっと大きな／もっと小さな	motti ōki na/motto chiisa na

How much? おいくらですか。

How much is this?	これはいくらですか。	kore wa ikura desu ka
I don't understand.	分かりません。	wakarimasen
Please write it down.	書いて下さい。	kaite kudasai
I don't want to spend more than ... yen.	…円以上は使いたくないのですが。	... yen ijō wa tsukaitaku nai do desu ga

Decision 決める

It's not quite what I want.	私が欲しいのと少し違います。	watashi ga hoshii noto sukoshi chigaimasu
No, I don't like it.	これは好みに合いません。	kore wa konomi ni aimasen
I'll take it.	これを頂きます。	kore o itadakimasu

COLOURS, see page 114

Ordering 注文

| Can you order it for me? | それを注文して頂けますか。 | sore a chūmon shite itadakemasu ka |
| How long will it take? | どの位かかりますか。 | dono kurai kakarimasu ka |

Delivery 配達

I'll take it with me.	持って帰ります。	motte kaerimasu
Deliver it to the ... hotel, please.	…ホテルに届けて下さい。	... hoteru ni todokete kudasai
Send it to this address, please.	この住所に送って下さい。	kono jūsho ni okutte kudasai
Could you send it overseas for me?	外国に送って頂けますか。	gaikoku ni okutte itadake masu ka
Will I have any difficulty with the customs?	税関で問題になるような事はありませんか。	zeikan de mondai ni naru yō na koto wa arimasen ka

Paying 支払い

How much is it?	いくらですか。	ikura desu ka
Can I pay by ...?	…で払えますか。	... de haraemasu ka
credit card	クレジットカード	kurejitto kādo
traveller's cheque	トラベラーチェック	toraberā chekku
Do you accept dollars/pounds?	ドル／ポンドでもよろしいですか。	doru/pondo demo yoroshii desu ka
Can I buy this tax-free?	これは免税で買えますか。	kore wa menzei de kae masu ka
I think there's a mistake in the bill.	勘定に間違いがあるように思いますが。	kanjō ni machigai ga aruyō ni omoimasu ga
Can I have a receipt, please?	領収書を下さい。	ryōshūsho o kudasai

Anything else? 他に何か？

| No, thanks, that's all. | いいえ、結構です。 | iie kekkō desu. sore de zenbu desu |

Yes, I'd like ...	ええ、…が欲しいのですが。	ee ... ga hoshii no desu ga
Show me ..., please.	…を見せて下さい。	... o misete kudasai
May I have a bag, please?	袋をいただけますか。	fukuro o itadakemasu ka
Could you wrap it up for me, please?	それを包んで頂けますか。	sore o tsutsunde itadake masu ka

Dissatisfied 不満

Can you exchange this, please?	これを交換して下さい。	kore o kōkan shitekudasai
I'd like to return this.	これを返したいのですが。	kore o kaeshitai no desu ga
I'd like a refund.	払い戻ししたいのですが。	harai modoshi shitai no desu ga
Here's the receipt.	これが領収書です。	kore ga ryōshūsho desu

いらっしゃいませ。	Welcome.
何をお求めていらっしゃいますか。	What are you looking for?
…をお求めていらっしゃいますか。	What ... would you like?
どういう色／どういう形 どんな質／どの位	colour/shape quality/quantity
あいにく全然ございません。	I'm sorry, we haven't any.
注文いたしましょうか。	Shall we order it for you?
お持ち帰りになりますか。 それともお届けしましょうか。	Will you take it with you or shall we send it?
これは…円です。	That's ... yen, please.
…はお断わりしております。	We don't accept ...
クレジットカード トラベラーチェック 銀行小切手	credit cards traveller's cheques personal cheques
品切れでございます。	We're out of stock.
他に何か？	Anything else?
お支払いはあちらでございます。	The cash desk is over there.

Bookshop—Newsstand—Stationer's 本屋-新聞売場-文房具

Foreign books, magazines and newspapers can be found in large bookshops and hotels. Several newspapers are published in English; they are on sale in hotels and in newspaper kiosks.

The Kanda district in Tokyo is devoted almost entirely to second-hand books—the biggest neighbourhood of its kind in the world, selling books in most European languages as well as Japanese.

Where's the nearest ...?	最寄りの…はどこですか。	moyori no ... wa doko desu ka
bookshop	本屋	hon-ya
newsstand	新聞売場	shinbun uriba
stationer's	文房具店	bunbōguten
Where can I buy an English-language newspaper?	英語の新聞はどこで買えますか。	eigo no shinbun wa doko de kaemasu ka
Do you have books in ...?	…の本はありますか。	... no hon wa arimasu ka
English	英語	eigo
French	フランス語	furansugo
German	ドイツ語	doitsugo
Have you any of ...'s books in English?	…の英語の本はありますか。	... no eigo no hon wa arimasu ka
The title/author is ...	タイトル／著者は…です。	taitoru/chosha wa ... desu
Is there an English translation of ...?	…の英語訳はありますか。	... no eigo yaku wa arimasu ka
Do you have second-hand books?	古本はありますか。	furu hon wa arimasu ka
I'd like a ...	…が欲しいのですが。	... ga hoshii no desu ga
book	本	hon
(Japanese) novel	（日本語の）小説	(nihongo no) shōsetsu
short stories	短編小説	tanpen shōsetsu
for learning Japanese	日本語学習用の本	nihongo gakushū yō no hon
dictionary	辞書	jisho
English–Japanese	英和	eiwa
pocket	ポケット	poketto

guidebook	ガイドブック	gaido bukku
magazine	雑誌	zasshi
map	地図	chizu
map of the town	市街地図	shigai chizu
road map	道路地図	dōro chizu
newspaper	新聞	shinbun
American/English	アメリカの/イギリスの	amerika no/igirisu no
paperback	文庫本	bunko bon
travel guide	旅行案内書	ryokō annaisho

At the stationer's:

| I'd like a/an/some ... | …が欲しいのですが。 | ... ga hoshii no desu ga |

ball-point pen	ボールペン	bōru pen
cellophane tape	セロテープ	serotēpu
crayons	クレヨン	kureyon
drawing paper	画用紙	gayōshi
envelopes	封筒	fūtō
eraser	消しゴム	keshi gomu
felt-tip pen	フェルトペン	fueruto pen
fine/medium/broad tip	細字/中字/太字	hosoji/chūji/futoji
fountain pen	万年筆	mannenhitsu
glue	糊	nori
ink	インク	inku
India ink	墨	sumi
(adhesive) labels	札（糊付)	fuda (noritsuki)
mechanical pencil	シャープペンシル	shāpu penshiru
notebook	ノート	nōto
origami paper	折り紙	origami
paintbox	絵具	enogu
paintbrush	絵筆	efude
paper	紙	kami
paperclips	紙挟み	kamibasami
paper napkins	紙ナプキン	kami napukin
paste	糊	nori
pen	ペン	pen
pencil	鉛筆	enpitsu
pencil sharpener	鉛筆削り	enpitsu kezuri
playing cards	トランプ	toranpu
(picture) postcard	(絵)葉書	(e) hagaki
propelling pencil	シャープペンシル	shāpu penshiru
refill (for a pen)	カートリッジ	kātorijji
rubber	消しゴム	keshi gomu
string	紐	himo
writing paper	便箋	binsen
wrapping paper	包装紙	hōsōshi

Chemist's (drugstore) 薬局（ドラッグストアー）

Japanese chemists normally stock a range of goods as wide as those at home. All cities have excellent stores and some offer round-the-clock service.

薬局 *(yakkyoku)* is the Japanese name for pharmacies; 漢方薬局 *(kampoyakkyoku)* sell traditional Chinese herbal remedies.

This section is divided into two parts:

1. Pharmaceutical—medicine, first-aid, etc.
2. Toiletry—toilet articles, cosmetics

General 一般的な質問

Where's there a chemist's (drugstore)?	薬局（ドラッグストアー）はどこですか。	yakkyoku (doraggu-sutoā) wa doko desu ka
Is it open all night?	一晩中開いていますか。	hitobanjū aite imasu ka
What time does it open/close?	何時に開きますか／締りますか。	nan-ji ni akimasu ka/shimarimasu ka
Do they sell ...?	…を売っていますか。	... o utte imasu ka
American products	アメリカ製品	amerika seihin
European products	ヨーロッパ製品	yōroppa seihin
herbal remedies	漢方薬	kanpōyaku
homoeopathic remedies	同種療法薬	dōshuryōhōyaku

1—Pharmaceutical 薬品

I'd like something for ...	…にきく薬が欲しいのですが。	... ni kiku kusuri ga hoshii no desu ga
a cold/a cough	風邪／咳	kaze/seki
constipation	便秘	benpi
diarrhoea	下痢	geri
hay fever	枯草熱／花粉症	karekusa netsu/kafunshō
a headache	頭痛	zutsū
insect bites	虫刺され	mushi sasare

DOCTOR, see page 136

sunburn	日焼け	hiyake
toothache	歯痛	haita
travel sickness	乗り物酔い	norimono yoi
an upset stomach	胃のもたれ	i no motare

| Can you make up this prescription for me? | この処方箋の薬を作って頂けますか。 | kono shohōsen no kusuri o tsukutte itadake masu ka |

| Can I get it without a prescription? | 処方箋なしで買えますか。 | kore wa shohōsen nashide kaemasu ka |

| Shall I wait? | 待っていましょうか。 | matte imashō ka |

| 毒
POISON | 飲用しないで下さい
DO NOT SWALLOW |

| Can I have a/an/some ... | …を下さい。 | ... o kudasai |

analgesic	鎮痛剤	chintsūzai
antiseptic cream	消毒クリーム	shōdoku kurīmu
aspirin	アスピリン	asupirin
bandage	繃帯	hōtai
elastic bandage	伸縮性のある繃帯	shinshukusei no aru hōtai
Band-Aids	絆創膏	bansōkō
contraceptives	避妊具	hiningu
contraceptive pills	避妊薬	hinin yaku
corn plasters	魚目膏薬	uomomekōyaku
cotton wool (absorbent cotton)	脱脂綿	dasshimen
cough drops	咳止め薬	sekidome
disinfectant	消毒薬	shōdokuyaku
ear drops	耳薬	mimigusuri
Elastoplast	絆創膏	bansōkō
eye drops	目薬	megusuri
gauze	ガーゼ	gāze
herbal tea	ハーブティー	hābutī
insect repellent/spray	防虫剤／防虫スプレー	bōchūzai/bōchū supurē
iodine	ヨードチンキ	yōdochinki
laxative	下痢	gezai
mouthwash	うがい薬	ugaigusuri
nose drops	鼻薬	hanagusuri
painkiller	鎮痛剤	chintsūzai
sanitary towels (napkins)	生理用ナプキン	seiriyō napukin
sleeping pills	睡眠薬	suimin yaku

suppositories	座薬	zayaku
... tablets	…錠剤	... jōzai
tampons	タンポン	tanpon
thermometer	体温計	taionkei
throat lozenges	喉薬	nodogusuri
tranquillizers	鎮静剤	chinseizai
vitamin pills	ビタミン剤	bitaminzai

2—Toiletry 化粧品類

I'd like a/an/some ...	…が欲しいのですが。	... ga hoshii no desu ga
after-shave lotion	アフターシェーブローション	afutā shēbu rōshon
astringent	アストリンゼント	asutorinzento
bath salts	バスソルト	basu soruto
blusher	ほおべに	ho-o beni
bubble bath	入浴剤	nyūyokuzai
body lotion	ボディーローション	bodē rōshon
cream	クリーム	kurīmu
for dry/normal/	ドライ／ノーマル／	dorai/nōmaru/
greasy skin	油性肌用	abura shō hada yō
cleansing cream	クレンジングクリーム	kurenjingu kurīmu
foundation cream	ファンデーションクリーム	fandēshon kurīmu
moisturizing cream	モイスチャーライジングクリーム	moisuchāraijingu kurīmu
night cream	ナイトクリーム	naito kurīmu
deodorant	デオドラント	deodoranto
emery board	つめやすり	tsumeyasuri
eyebrow pencil	アイペンシル	aipenshiru
eye liner	アイライナー	airainā
eye shadow	アイシャドー	aishadō
face powder	おしろい	oshiroi
foot cream	足のクリーム	ashi no kurīmu
hand cream	ハンドクリーム	hando kurīmu
lipsalve	リップクリーム	rippu kurīmu
lipstick	口紅	kuchibeni
make-up remover pads	化粧落とし用パッド	keshōotoshi yō paddo
nail brush	つめブラシ	tsume burashi
nail clippers	つめ切り	tsumekiri
nail file	つめやすり	tsumeyasuri
nail polish	マニキュア	manikyua
nail polish remover	マニキュアリムーバー	manikyua rimūbā
nail scissors	つめ切りばさみ	tsumekiribasami
perfume	香水	kōsui
powder	おしろい	oshiroi

razor	かみそり	kamisori
razor blades	かみそりの刃	kamisori no ha
rouge	口紅	kuchibeni
safety pins	安全ピン	anzenpin
shampoo	シャンプー	shanpū
shaver	かみそり	kamisori
shaving cream	ひげそり用クリーム	higesori yō kurīmu
soap	石けん	sekken
sponge	スポンジ	suponji
sun-tan cream	サンタンクリーム	santan kurīmu
sun-tan oil	サンタンオイル	santan oiru
talcum powder	タルカムパウダー	tarukamu paudā
tissues	ティッシュペーパー	tisshu pēpā
toilet bag	化粧袋	keshōbukuro
toilet paper	トイレットペーパー	toiretto pēpā
toilet water	オードトワレ	ōdotoware
toothbrush	歯ブラシ	haburashi
toothpaste	ねり歯みがき	nerihamigaki
towel	タオル	taoru
tweezers	毛抜き	kenuki

For your hair 髪の手入れのために

bobby pins	ピン止め	pin dome
colour shampoo	カラーシャンプー	karā shanpū
comb	くし	kushi
curlers	カーラー	kārā
dry shampoo	ドライシャンプー	dorai shanpū
hairbrush	ヘアーブラシ	heā burashi
hairgrips	ピン止め	pin dome
hair lotion	ヘアーローション	heā rōshon
hair slide	髪止め	kamidome
hairspray	ヘアースプレー	heā supurē
setting lotion	セットローション	setto rōshon
shampoo	シャンプー	shanpū
for dry/greasy (oily) hair	乾性／油性用	kansei/yusei yō

For the baby 乳児のために

baby food	ベビーフード	bebī fūdo
dummy (pacifier)	おしゃぶり	oshaburi
feeding bottle	哺乳びん	honyūbin
nappies (diapers)	おむつ	omutsu

HAIRDRESSER—BARBER, see page 31

Clothing 衣類

Shopping for clothes can be fun as there is a wide variety of styles available: from high fashion, with an element of the fantastic, to simple well-cut classics. Japanese designs can be bought from boutiques in large department stores.

Japanese silks are very expensive but of magnificent quality, especially in Kyoto and Kobe. If you can't afford a silk kimono, you might like to settle for the more modest, but still very elegant *yukata,* fine cotton kimono, traditionally in indigo-blue and white. Western-style pyjamas and dressing gowns are to be found in the same materials as the yukata.

If you want to buy something specific, prepare yourself in advance. Look at the list of clothing on the next page, and get some idea of the colour, size and material you'd like. They're all listed on the following pages.

General 一般的な表現

I'd like ...	…が欲しいのですが。	... ga hoshii no desu ga
for a (10-year-old) boy/girl	(10歳の)男の子／女の子に	(jussai no) otoko no ko/onna no ko ni
for my husband/wife	主人／家内	shujin/kanai ni
for a man/woman/ child	男性／女性／子供に	dansei/josei/kodomo ni
Something like this.	これに似たもの。	kore ni nita mono
I like the one in the window.	ウインドーに出ているのがいいです。	uindō ni deteiru no ga ii desu
Is it ...?	…ですか。	... desu ka
handmade	手作り	tezukuri
imported	輸入品	yunyū hin
made here	ここの特産	koko no tokusan
traditional Japanese	日本の伝統的なもの	nihon no dentōtekina mono
Can you show me how to wear it?	着方を教えて下さいますか。	kikata o oshiete kudasai masu ka

Clothes and accessories 衣料品

I'd like a/an(some) ...	…が欲しいのですが。	... ga hoshii no desu ga
anorak	アノラック	anorakku
bathing cap	水泳帽	suieibō
bathing suit	水着	mizugi
bathrobe	バスローブ	basu rōbu
blouse	ブラウス	burausu
braces	ズボン吊り	zubon tsuri
briefs	ブリーフ	brīfu
cap	帽子	bōshi
cardigan	カーデガン	kādegan
coat	上着	uwagi
dress	ドレス	doresu
dressing gown	バスローブ	basu rōbu
girdle	ガードル	gādoru
gloves	手袋	tebukuro
handbag	ハンドバッグ	handobaggu
handkerchief	ハンカチーフ	hankachīfu
hat	帽子	bōshi
jacket	ジャケット	jaketto
jeans	ジーパン	jīpan
kimono	着物	kimono
lingerie	下着	shitagi
nightdress	寝間着	nemaki
overalls	オーバーオール	ōbāōru
pair of ...	…一対	... ittsui
panties	パンティー	pantī
pants (Am.)	ズボン	zubon
panty hose	パンティーストッキング	pantī sutokkingu
pullover	プルオーバー	puru ōbā
roll-neck (turtleneck)	タートルネック	tātoru nekku
round-neck	丸首	maru kubi
V-neck	Vネック	bui nekku
with long/short sleeves	長/半そで	naga/han sode
without sleeves	そでなし	sode nashi
pyjamas	パジャマ	pajama
raincoat	レインコート	reinkōto
scarf	スカーフ	sukāfu
shirt	ワイシャツ	waishatsu
shorts	ショートパンツ	shōto pantsu
skirt	スカート	sukāto
slip	スリップ	surippu
socks	くつ下	kutsushita
stockings	ストッキング	sutokkingu
suit (man's)	背広	sebiro

SHOES, see page 116

suit (woman's)	スーツ	sūtsu
suspenders (Am.)	ズボン吊り	zubon tsuri
sweater	セーター	sētā
sweatshirt	トレーナー	torēnā
swimming trunks	海水パンツ	kaisui pantsu
swimsuit	水着	mizugi
T-shirt	Tシャツ	tīshatsu
tie	ネクタイ	nekutai
tights	パンティーストッキング	pantī sutokkingu
tracksuit	トレーナー	torēnā
trousers	ズボン	zubon
umbrella	傘	kasa
underpants	パンツ	pantsu
undershirt	シャツ	shatsu
vest (Am.)	チョッキ	chokki
vest (Br.)	シャツ	shatsu
waistcoat	チョッキ	chokki

belt	ベルト	beruto
buckle	バックル	bakkuru
button	ボタン	botan
collar	えり	eri
pocket	ポケット	poketto
press stud (snap fastener)	スナップ	sunappu
zip (zipper)	チャック	chakku

Note that the Japanese have shorter arms and legs than Westerners, and that Japanese underwear will probably not suit the Western figure.

Size サイズ

I take size 38.	サイズは38です。	saizu wa 38 desu
Could you measure me?	計って下さいますか。	hakatte kudasaimasu ka
I don't know the Japanese sizes.	日本のサイズは知りません。	nihon no saizu wa shiri masen

Sizes can vary somewhat from one manufacturer to another, so be sure to try on clothing and shoes before you buy.

NUMBERS, see page 146

Women

	Dresses/suits					
American	8	10	12	14	16	18
British	32	34	36	38	40	42
Japanese	9	11	13	15	17	19

	Stockings					Shoes			
American British }	8	8½	9½	9½	10	6 4½	7 5	8 6½	9 7
Japanese	20	21	22	23	24	23½	24½	25	25½

Men

	Suits/overcoats						Shirts			
American British }	36	38	40	42	44	46	15	16	17	18
Japanese	90	95	100	105	110	115	38	41	43	45

	Shoes									
American British }	5	6	7	8	8½	9	9½	10	11
Japanese	23	24	25	26	26½	27	27½	28	29

A good fit? 体に合いますか。

Can I try it on?	これを試していいですか。	kore o tameshite ii desu ka
Where's the fitting room?	試着室はどこですか。	shichaku shitsu wa doko desu ka
Is there a mirror?	鏡はありますか。	kagami wa arimasu ka
It fits very well.	大変よく合います。	taihen yoku aimasu
It doesn't fit.	サイズが合いません。	saizu ga aimasen
It's too ...	…すぎます。	... sugi masu
short/long	短／長	mijika/naga
tight/loose	きつ／ゆる	kitsu/yuru

| Can you alter it? | 直せますか。 | naosemasu ka |
| How long will it take? | どれくらいかかりますか。 | dore kurai kakarimasu ka |

Colour 色

I'd like something in ...	…のものが欲しいのですが。	... no mono ga hoshii no desu ga
I'd like a darker/lighter shade.	もっと暗い／もっと明るい色のが欲しいのですが。	motto kurai/motto akarui iro no ga hoshii no desu ga
I want something to match this.	これに合うものが欲しいのですが。	kore ni au mono ga hoshii no desu ga
I don't like the colour.	色が気に入りません。	iro ga kini irimasen

beige	ベージュ	bēju
black	黒	kuro
blue	青	ao
brown	茶色	cha iro
golden	金色	kin iro
green	緑色	midori iro
grey	灰色	hai iro
mauve	ふじ色	fuji iro
orange	オレンジ	orenji
pink	ピンク	pinku
purple	紫色	murasaki iro
red	赤	aka
scarlet	緋色	hi iro
silver	銀色	gin iro
turquoise	トルコブルー	toruko burū
white	白	shiro
yellow	黄色	ki iro
light ...	明るい…	akarui
dark ...	暗い…	kurai

無地
(muji)

縞
(shima)

水玉模様
(mizutama-moyō)

格子縞
(kōshijima)

連続模様
(renzoku-moyō)

Fabric 織物

If you're in town for a few days, why not have the garments made, at little extra cost, from the wide range of materials available off the roll.

I'd like something in silk/cotton.	絹／木綿のものが欲しいのですが。	kinu/momen no mono ga hoshii no desu ga
I want something thinner.	もっと薄手のものが欲しいのですが。	motto usude no mono ga hoshii no desu ga
Do you have any better quality?	もっと品質のいいものはありませんか。	motto hinshitsu no ii mono wa arimasen ka
Do you have anything in ...?	…のものはありますか。	... no mono wa arimasu ka

camel-hair	キャメル	kyameru
chiffon	絹モスリン／シフォン	kinu mosurin/shifon
corduroy	コージュロイ	kōjuroi
cotton	木綿	momen
denim	デニム	denimu
flannel	フランネル	furanneru
lace	レース	rēsu
leather	革／レザー	kawa/rezā
linen	リンネル／麻	rinneru/asa
poplin	ポプリン	popurin
rubber	ゴム	gomu
satin	サテン	saten
silk	絹	kinu
suede	スエード	suēdo
towelling	タオル地	taoruji
velvet	ビロード	birōdo
velveteen	綿ビロード／べっちん	men birōdo/betchin
wool	羊毛／ウール	yōmō/ūru
worsted	ウーステッド	ūsuteddo

Is it ...?	…ですか。	... desu ka

pure cotton/wool	純綿／毛	jun men/mō
synthetic	合繊	gōsen
colourfast	脱色防止加工	dasshoku bōshikakō
crease (wrinkle) resistant	しわ防止加工	shiwa bōshikakō

Is it hand washable/ machine washable?	手で／機械で洗えますか。	te de/kikai de araemasu ka
Will it shrink?	縮みますか。	chijimimasu ka
How much is that per metre?	一メートルいくらですか。	ichi-mētoru ikura desu ka

1 centimetre (cm.)	= 0.39 in.	1 inch = 2.54 cm.
1 metre (m.)	= 39.37 in.	1 foot = 30.5 cm.
10 metres	= 32.81 ft.	1 yard = 0.91 m.

Shoes 靴

Japanese shoes do not fit the broader Western foot well, and large sizes are rather difficult to find. Size charts vary, so it's best to get your feet measured.

I'd like a pair of ...	…が欲しいのですが。	... ga hoshii no desu ga
(rain)boots	(レイン) ブーツ	(rein) būtsu
moccasins	モカシン	mokashin
plimsolls (sneakers)	スニーカー	sunīkā
sandals	サンダル	sandaru
shoes	靴	kutsu
flat	ヒールなし	hīru nashi
with a heel	ヒールのある	hīru no aru
slippers	スリッパ	surippa
Could you measure my feet?	足のサイズを計って下さいますか。	ashi no saizu o hakatte kudasaimasu ka
These are too ...	…すぎます。	... sugimasu
narrow/wide	きつ／ゆる	kitsu/yuru
large/small	大き／小さ	ōki/chīsa
Do you have a larger/smaller size?	もっと大きい／小さいのはありませんか。	motto ōkii/chīsai no wa arimasen ka
Do you have the same in black?	黒で同じものがありますか。	kuro de onaji mono ga ari masu ka
I need some shoe polish/shoelaces.	靴みがき／靴ひもを下さい。	kutsu migaki/kutsu himo o kuda sai

Shoe repairs 靴修理

Can you repair these shoes?	この靴を直して下さいますか。	kono kutsu o naoshite kudasaimasu ka
I'd like new soles/heels.	靴底／ヒールを取り替えて下さい。	kutsuzoko/hīru o torikaete kudasai
When will they be ready?	いつ出来上りますか。	itsu dekiagarimasu ka

SIZES, see page 113

Department store   デパート

There is hardly anything you can't find in a Japanese department store. Even if you don't want to buy anything, it's worth taking a look at the tasteful products of traditional arts and crafts, the mountains of electronic gadgets and precision instruments, the delightful textiles or the vast food section (usually in the basement).

Most department stores have an information desk near the entrance, with a list of items sold on each floor; a lady posted near the escalators can answer enquiries. Some of the staff will speak English.

Where's the ... department?	…コーナーはどこですか。	... kōnā wa doko desu ka
arts and crafts	工芸品	kōgeihin
china	陶磁器	tōjiki
clothing	衣類	irui
children's	子供用	kodomo yō
men's/women's	紳士用／婦人用	shinshi yō/fujin yō
computer equipment	コンピューター機器	konpūtā kiki
electronics	エレクトロニクス	erekutoronikusu
fabric	織物	orimono
food	食品	shoku hin
furniture	家具	kagu
housewares	家庭用品	kateiyōhin
jewellery	宝石	hōseki
photographic equipment	写真用品	shashin yōhin
records	レコード	rekōdo
shoe	靴	kutsu
stationary	文房具	bunbōgu
toys	おもちゃ	omocha
watch	時計	tokei
toiletry	化粧品／洗面用具	keshōhin/senmen yōgu
video equipment	ビデオ機器	bideo kiki
Is there a tax-free department?	免税コーナーはあります か。	menzei kōnā wa arimasu ka
Where is/are the ...?	…はどこですか。	... wa doko desu ka
cash desk	レジ	reji
escalator	エスカレーター	esukarētā
information desk	案内係	annai gakari
lift (elevator)	エレベーター	erebētā
staircase	階段	kaidan

ショッピングガイド

Electrical appliances—Hi-fi equipment　電気製品-ハイファイセット

Electric current in Japan is 100–110 volt, AC, but the cycles are different depending on the region. The country's eastern half, including Tokyo, has 50 cycles; the western half is on a 60-cycle basis. The dividing line is near Shizuoka. Sockets (outlets) are American style.

In Tokyo, the place to go for electronic goods—stereos, radios, calculators—is Akihabara, a whole neighbourhood devoted to multi-floor discount stores selling electronic equipment at interesting prices. The tax-free department, usually found on the top floor, has English-speaking sales staff but a smaller range of products.

Osaka's equivalent discount-shopping neighbourhood, Nipponbashi, specializes in the latest computer equipment.

I'd like a/an/some …	…が欲しいのですが。	… ga hoshii no desu ga
adaptor	アダプター	adaputā
amplifier	アンプ	anpu
antenna	アンテナ	antena
dish antenna	パラボラアンテナ	parabora antena
battery	電池	denchi
bulb	電球	denkyū
cassette player/	カセットプレーヤー／	kasetto purēyā/rekōdā
recorder	レコーダー	
clock-radio	時計付ラジオ	tokei tsuki rajio
compact disc player	コンパクトディスクプレーヤー	konpakuto disuku purēyā
(personal) computer	(パーソナル)コンピューター	(pāsonaru) konpūtā
lap computer	ポータブルコンピューター	pōtaburu konpūtā
pocket computer	ポケットコンピューター	poketto konpūtā
dictating machine	口述録音機	kōjutsu rokuonki
disk drive	ディスクドライブ	disuku doraibu
electric toothbrush	電気歯ブラシ	denki haburashi
electronic game	電子ゲーム	denshi gēmu
extension lead (cord)	継ぎ足しレコード	tsugitashi kōdo
hair dryer	ヘヤードライヤー	heyā doraiyā
headphones	ヘッドホーン	heddohōn
(travelling) iron	(旅行用)アイロン	(ryokōyō) airon
lamp	ランプ	ranpu
laser disc	レーザーディスク	rēzā disuku
micro cassette	マイクロカセットレコーダー	maikuro kasetto rekōdā
recorder	ダー	

RECORDS—CASSETTES, see page 128

personal cassette player	パーソナルカセットプレーヤー	pāsonaru kasetto purēya
plug	プラグ	puragu
pocket calculator	ポケット計算機	poketto keisanki
pocket copier	ポケットコピー	poketto kopī
portable ...	ポータブル…	pōtaburu ...
printer	プリンター	purintā
radio	ラジオ	rajio
car radio	カーラジオ	kā rajio
radio cassette recorder	ラジオカセットレコーダー	rajio kasetto rekōdā
record player	レコードプレーヤー	rekōdo purēya
shaver	カミソリ	kamisori
speakers	スピーカー	supīkā
stereo system	ステレオ装置	sutereo sōchi
tape recorder	テープレコーダー	tēpu rekōdā
television	テレビ	terebi
colour TV	カラーテレビ	karā terebi
miniature TV	超小型テレビ	chōkogata terebi
flat-screen TV	フラットスクリーンテレビ	furatto sukurīn terebi
wrist TV	腕時計テレビ	udedokei terebi
transformer	トランス	toransu
tuner	チューナー	chūnā
video recorder	ビデオレコーダー	bideo rekōdā
word processor	ワープロ	wāpuro

What's the voltage?	何ボルトですか。	nan boruto desu ka
Do you have one for ...?	…に合うものがありますか。	... ni au mono ga arimasu ka
American voltage	アメリカの電圧	amerika no den-atsu
European voltage	ヨーロッパの電圧	yōroppa no den-atsu

110/220/240 volt	110／220／240ボルト	hyaku-jū/nihyaku-nijū/nihyaku-yonjū boruto
50/60 Hz.	50／60ヘルツ	go-jū/roku-jū herutsu

Can you show me how it works?	動かし方を教えて下さい。	ugokashi kata o oshiete kudasai
Do you have a battery for this?	これの電池はありますか。	kore no denchi wa arimasu ka
This is broken.	これはこわれています。	kore wa kowarete imasu
Can you repair it?	修理して頂けますか。	shūri shite itadakemasu ka
When will it be ready?	いつ出来ますか。	itsu dekimasu ka

Grocery — Supermarket 食料品-スーパーマーケット

I'd like some bread.	パンを下さい。	pan o kudasai
What sort of cheese do you have?	どんな種類のチーズがありますか。	don-na shurui no chīzu ga arimasu ka
I'll have one of those.	あそこのを一つ下さい。	asokono o hitotsu kudasai
that one	あれ	are
the one on the shelf	棚の上の	tana no ue no
May I help myself?	自分でしてもいいですか。	jibun de shite mo ii desu ka
I'd like ...	…下さい。	... kudasai
a kilo of apples	リンゴを一キロ	ringo o ichi kiro
half a kilo of tomatoes	トマトを半キロ	tomato o han kiro
100 grams of butter	バターを100グラム	batā o 100 guramu
a litre of milk	牛乳を一リットル	gyūnyū o ichi rittoru
half a dozen eggs	卵を半ダース	tamago o han dāsu
4 slices of ham	ハムを4切れ	hamu o 4 kire
a packet of tea	紅茶を一パック	kōcha o hito pakku
a jar of jam	ジャムを一瓶	jamu o hito bin
a tin (can) of peaches	ももを一缶	momo o hito kan
a tube of mustard	チューブ入りからしを一本	chūbu-iri karashi o ippon
a box of chocolates	チョコレートを一箱	choko rēto o hito hako
a bottle of soy sauce	しょうゆを一瓶	shōyu o hito bin

---

1 kilogram or kilo (kg.) = 1000 grams (g.)

100 g. = 3.5 oz.	½ kg. = 1.1 lb.	1 oz. = 28.35 g.
200 g. = 7.0 oz.	1 kg. = 2.2 lb.	1 lb. = 453.60 g.

---

1 litre (l.) = 0.88 imp. qt. or 1.06 U.S. qt.

1 imp. qt. = 1.14 l.	1 U.S. qt. = 0.95 l.
1 imp. gal. = 4.55 l.	1 U.S. gal. = 3.8 l.

These items may come in handy:

a bottle-opener	栓抜き	sennuki
a corkscrew	コルク抜き	korukunuki
matches	マッチ	matchi
paper napkins	紙ナプキン	kami napukin
scissors	罐切り	hasami
a tin (can) opener	はさみ	kankiri

FOOD, see also page 64

Jeweller's—Watchmaker's 宝石店-時計屋

Japan is a producer of world-famous cultured pearls and offers a far greater variety than anywhere else in the world. The price depends on regularity, size and lustre.

Whether you're buying a present for yourself or for somebody else, you will find that Japanese shopkeepers take great pride in wrapping the purchase attractively.

I'd like a small present for a ...	…へのちょっとした贈物が欲しいのですが。	… e no chottoshita okurimono ga hoshii no desu ga
man/woman/child	男性／女性／子供	dansei/josei/kodomo
I'd like something in gold/silver.	金製品／銀製品が欲しいのですが。	kinsēhin/ginsēhin ga hoshii no desu ga
How many carats is it?	それは何カラットですか。	sore wa nan karatto desu ka
Is this real silver?	これは本当の銀ですか。	kore wa hontō no gin desu ka
I'd like a piece of jewellery with pearls.	真珠の入っている宝石が欲しいのですが。	shinju no haitteiru hōseki ga hoshii no desu ga
Can you repair this watch?	この時計を修理して預けますか。	kono tokei o shūri shite itadakemasu ka
I need a new battery.	電池を下さい。	denchi o kudasai
I'd like a/an/some ...	…が欲しいのですが。	… ga hoshii no desu ga
alarm clock	目覚し時計	mezamashi dokei
bangle	ブレスレット	buresuretto
bracelet	ブレスレット	buresuretto
brooch	ブローチ	burōchi
chain	鎖	kusari
cigarette lighter	ライター	raitā
clip	クリップ	kurippu
clock	置時計	oki dokei
cross	十字架	jūjika
cuff links	カフスボタン	kafusu botan
cutlery	食卓用ナイフ類	shokutaku yo naifu rui
earrings	イヤリング	iyaringu
gem	宝石	hōseki
jewel box	宝石箱	hōseki-bako
necklace	ネックレス	nekkuresu
pendant	ペンダント	pendanto

pin	ピン	pin
ring	指輪	yubiwa
silverware	銀器	ginki
tie clip	ネクタイ止め	nekutai dome
tie pin	ネクタイピン	nekutai pin
watch	時計	tokei
automatic	自動巻	jidōmaki
digital	デジタル	dejitaru
with an (electronic) alarm	（電子）目覚し付	(denshi) mezamashi tsuki
with a calculator	計算機付	keisanki tsuki
with a calendar function	カレンダー付	karendā tsuki
waterproof	防水	bōsui
watchstrap	時計バンド	tokei bando

| What's it made of? | それは何製ですか。 | sore wa nani sei desu ka |
| What kind of stone is this? | これはどんな種類の石ですか。 | kore wa donna shurui no ishi desu ka |

amber	琥珀	kohaku
amethyst	アメジスト	amejisuto
brass	しんちゅう	shinchū
copper	銅	dō
coral	珊瑚	sango
(cut) crystal	（カット）水晶	(katto) suishō
diamond	ダイアモンド	daiamondo
emerald	エメラルド	emerarudo
enamel	エナメル	enameru
glass	ガラス	garasu
gold	金	kin
gold plate	金メッキ	kin mekki
ivory	象牙	zōge
jade	翡翠	hisui
onyx	オニックス	onikkusu
pearl	真珠	shinju
cultured pearl	養殖真珠	yōshoku shinju
pewter	ピューター	pyūtā
platinum	プラチナ	purachina
ruby	ルビー	rubī
sapphire	サファイア	safaia
silver	銀	gin
silver plate	銀メッキ	gin mekki
stainless steel	ステンレス	sutenresu
topaz	トパーズ	topāzu
turquoise	トルコ石	toruko ishi

Optician 眼鏡屋

I've broken my glasses.	眼鏡をこわしてしまいました。	megane o kowashite shimai mashita
Can you repair them for me?	直して頂けますか。	naoshite itadake masu ka
When will they be ready?	いつ出来上りますか。	itsu dekiagari masu ka
Can you change the lenses?	レンズを取り替えて頂けますか。	renzu o torikaete itadake masu ka
I want tinted lenses.	色の入ったレンズが欲しいのですが。	iro no haitta renzu ga hoshii no desu ga
The frame is broken.	フレームがこわれました。	furēmu ga koware mashita
I'd like a spectacle case.	眼鏡ケースが欲しいのですが。	megane kēsu ga hoshii no desu ga
I'd like to have my eyesight checked.	視力検査をして頂きたいのですが。	shiryoku kensa o shite itadakitai no desu ga
I'm short-sighted/long-sighted.	私は近視／遠視です。	watashi wa kinshi/enshi desu
I want some contact lenses.	コンタクトレンズが欲しいのですが。	kontakuto renzu ga hoshii no desu ga
I've lost one of my contact lenses.	コンタクトレンズの片方をなくしてしまいました。	kontakuto renzu no katahō o naku shite shimai mashita
Could you give me another one?	もう一つ別のを頂けますか。	mō-hitotsu betsu no o itadake masu ka
I have hard/soft lenses.	ハード／ソフトレンズです。	hādo/sofuto renzu desu
Do you have any contact-lens fluid?	コンタクトレンズ用液はありますか。	kontakuto renzu yōeki wa ari masu ka
I'd like to buy a pair of sunglasses.	サングラスを買いたいのですが。	sangurasu o kaitai no desu ga
May I look in a mirror?	鏡を見せて下さいますか。	kagami o misete kudasai masu ka
I'd like to buy a pair of binoculars.	双眼鏡を買いたいのですが。	sōgankyō o kaitai no desu ga

Photography 写真

I'd like to buy a/an ... camera.	…カメラが欲しいのですが。	... kamera ga hoshii no desu ga
automatic	オートマチックの	ōtomachikku no
inexpensive	安い	yasui
medium price	手頃な値段の	tegoro na nedan no
Polaroid	ポラロイド	poraroido
simple	扱いの簡単な	atsukai no kantan na
sophisticated	性能のいい	seinō no ii
Show me some cine (movie) cameras, please.	撮影機を見せて下さい。	satsueiki o misete kudasai
I'd like to have some passport photos taken.	パスポート用の写真を撮って頂きたいのですが。	pasupōto yō no shashin o totte itadakitai no desu ga

Film フィルム

I'd like a film for this camera.	このカメラ用のフィルムが欲しいのですが。	kono kamera yō no firumuga hoshii no desu ga
black and white film	白黒フィルム	shiro kuro firumu
colour film	カラーフィルム	karā firumu
disc film	ディスクフィルム	disuku firumu
colour slide film	スライド用フィルム	suraido yō firumu
cartridge	カートリッジ	kātorijji
cassette	カセット	kasetto
roll film	巻きフィルム	makifirumu
24/36 exposures	24/36枚どり	nijū-yon/sanjū-roku maidori
single 8	シングル8	singuru eito
super 8	スーパー8	sūpā eito
this size	このサイズ	kono saizu
this ASA/DIN number	このフィルム感度	kono firumu kando
artificial light type	タングステンタイプ	tangusuten taipu
daylight type	デイライトタイプ	deiraito taipu
fast (high-speed)	ハイスピード	haisupīdo
fine grain	微粒子	biryūshi

Processing 現像

How long will it take to develop this film?	このフィルムを現像するのに何日ぐらいかかりますか。	kono firumu o genzō suru no ni nan-nichi gurai kakarimasu ka
How much will it cost?	いくらぐらいかかりますか。	ikura gurai kakari masu ka
I want ... prints of each negative.	このネガを…枚づつプリントして欲しいのですが。	kono nega o ... mai zutsu purinto shite hoshii no desu ga
with a mat finish	マット仕上げで	matto shiage de
with a glossy finish	光沢仕上げで	kōtaku shiage de
Will you enlarge this, please?	これを引伸して頂けますか。	kore o hikinobashite itadakemasu ka
When will it be ready?	いつ出来上りますか。	itsu dekiagarimasu ka

Accessories and repairs 備品と修理

I'd like a/an/some ...	…が欲しいのですが。	... ga hoshii no desu ga
battery	電池	denchi
cable release	シャッターレリーズ	shattā rerīzu
camera case	カメラケース	kamera kēsu
(electronic) flash	(電子) フラッシュ	(denshi) furasshu
filter	フィルター	firutā
for black and white	白黒用	shirokuro yō
for colour	カラー用	karā yō
lens	レンズ	renzu
telephoto lens	望遠レンズ	bōen renzu
wide-angle lens	広角レンズ	kōkaku renzu
zoom lens	ズームレンズ	zūmu renzu
lens cap	レンズキャップ	renzu kyappu
tripod	三脚	sankyaku
Can you repair this camera?	このカメラを修理して頂けますか。	kono kamera o shūrishite itadakemasu ka
The film is jammed.	フィルムが動きません。	firumu ga ugokimasen
There's something wrong with the ...	…に何か悪い点があるうです。	... ni nanika warui ten, ga aruyō desu
exposure counter	露出計	roshutsukei
film winder	フィルムワインダー	firumu waindā
flash attachment	フラッシュの固定部	furasshu no koteibu
light meter	ライトメーター	raito mētā
rangefinder	レンジファインダー	renji faindā
shutter	シャッター	shattā

NUMBERS, see page 146

ショッピングガイド

Tobacconist's—Kiosk たばこ屋-キヨスク

Cigarettes can be purchased at tobacconists', newsstands, coffee shops and from vending machines. Packets bear English names such as *Hi-lite, Cherry* or *Seven Stars*. Imported brands are also available.

A packet of cigarettes, please.	たばこを一箱下さい。	tabako o hito hako kudasai
cigarette holder	パイプ	paipu
cigarettes	たばこ	tabako
mild/strong	マイルド／ストロング	mairudo/sutorongu
menthol	はっか／メンソール	hakka/mensōru
cigars	葉巻	hamaki
lighter	ライター	raitā
lighter fluid/gas	ライター用オイル／ガス	raitā yō oiru/gasu
matches	マッチ	matchi
pipe	パイプ	paipu
pipe cleaners	パイプクリーナー	paipu kurīnā
pipe tobacco	パイプたばこ	paipu tabako
pipe tool	パイプ用器具	paipu yō kigu
wick	芯	shin
Do you have American/English cigarettes?	アメリカの／イギリスのたばこはありますか。	amerika no/igirisu no tabako wa arimasu ka
I'd like a carton.	ワンカートン下さい。	wan kāton kudasai

filter-tipped	フィルター付き	firutā tsuki
without filter	フィルターなし	firutā nashi

At the kiosk you might ask for:

biscuits	ビスケット	bisuketto
candy	キャンディー	kyandī
chewing gum	チューインガム	chūin gamu
chocolate	チョコレート	chokorēto
cookies	クッキー	kukkī
sweets	キャンディー	kyandī

Miscellaneous その他

Souvenirs おみやげ

It need hardly be said in this section that Japanese electronic and optical products enjoy a world-wide reputation. But Japan also offers a wide choice of other items: superbly finished cloisonné and lacquerware, colourful woodblock prints, decorative straw-ware and beautiful, hand-decorated paper are some of the glories of Japanese craftsmanship.

Can you show me a/some ...?	…を見せて頂けますか。	... o misete itadake masu ka
bamboo products	竹製品	takeseihin
brocades	錦織	nishiki ori
ceramics	陶磁器	tōjiki
(Japanese) chess sets	将棋	shōgi
chopsticks	箸	hashi
clocks	置時計	oki dokei
cloisonné	七宝焼	shippō yaki
cutlery	食卓用ナイフ類	shokutaku yō naifu rui
damask	ダマスク織	damasuku ori
dolls	人形	ningyō
fans	扇子	sensu
fishing tackle	釣道具	tsuri dōgu
folkcrafts	民芸品	mingeihin
hanging-picture scrolls	掛物	kake mono
kimono	着物	kimono
kites	凧	tako
lacquerware	漆器	shikki
lanterns	ちょうちん	chōchin
masks	面	men
music boxes	オルゴール	orugōru
origami paper	折り紙	origami
painted screens	屏風	byōbu
paper products	紙製品	kamiseihin
(cultured) pearls	(養殖) 真珠	(yōshoku) shinju
porcelain	磁器	jiki
pottery	陶器	tōki
sake cups	酒盃	shuhai
silks	絹	kinu
swords	刃剣類	tōken rui
tea bowls/cups	茶碗	chawan
tea pots	きゅうす	kyūsu
watches	時計	tokei
woodblock prints	木版画	mokuhanga

Records—Cassettes レコード-カセット

I'd like a ...	…が欲しいのですが。	... ga hoshii no desu ga

cassette	カセット	kasetto
compact disc	コンパクトディスク	konpakuto disuku
laser disc	レーザーディスク	rēza disuku
record	レコード	rekōdo
video cassette	ビデオカセット	bideo kasetto

Do you have any records by ...?	…のレコードはありますか。	... no rekōdo wa arimasu ka
Can I listen to this record?	このレコードを聴いてみたいんですが。	kono rekōdo o kīte mitain desu ga

L.P. (33 rpm)	L. P.（33回転）盤	eru-pī (sanjū-san kaiten) ban
E.P. (45 rpm)	E. P.（45回転）盤	ī-pī (yonjū-go kaiten) ban
single	シングル盤	shinguru ban

chamber music	室内楽	sitsunai gaku
classical music	クラッシック音楽	kurasshiku ongaku
folk music	民謡	min-yō
instrumental music	器楽	kigaku
jazz	ジャズ	jazu
light music	軽音楽	kei ongaku
modern music	現代音楽	gendai ongaku
orchestral music	管弦楽	kangen gaku
pop music	ポップミュージック	poppu mūjikku
traditional Japanese music	日本の伝統音楽	nihon no dentō ongaku

Toys おもちゃ

I'd like a toy/game ...	…おもちゃ／ゲームをいただきたいのですが。	... omocha/gēmu o itadakitai no desu ga

for a boy	男の子に	otoko no ko ni
for a 5-year-old girl	5歳の女の子に	5 sai no onna no ko ni

ball	ボール	bōru
building blocks (bricks)	つみ木	tsumiki
card game	カードゲーム	kādo gēmu
chess set	チェスセット	chesu setto
doll	人形	ningyō
electronic game	電子ゲーム	denshi gēmu
roller skates	ローラースケート	rōrā sukēto

Your money: banks—currency

Bank—Currency exchange office 銀行-両替所

Banks are open from 9 a.m. to 3 p.m. Monday to Friday, from 9 a.m. to noon on Saturdays; they are closed on Sundays and second Saturdays of the month. All banks are closed on Sundays, except Tokyo Airport's bank which is open 24 hours a day, the year round.

Most banks have a special foreign exchange section where foreign cash and traveller's cheques may be exchanged for yen. You must present your passport.

Money and traveller's cheques can be exchanged only at authorized currency exchange offices, such as leading Western-style hotels, banks and top shops catering for foreign visitors.

International credit cards and traveller's cheques are accepted by hotels, *ryokans* and stores.

Currency 通貨

The monetary system is based on the *yen* (円), abbreviated ¥.

Banknotes: ¥ 500, 1,000, 3,000, 5,000 and 10,000.
Coins: ¥ 1, 5, 10, 50, 100 and 500.

General 一般表現

Where is there a ...?	…はどこですか。	... wa doko desu ka
bank	銀行	ginkō
currency exchange office	両替所	ryōgaejo
When does it open/ close?	いつ開きますか／締りますか。	itsu aki masuka/shimari masu ka
Where can I change ...?	…はどこで両替出来ますか。	... wa doko de ryōgae deki masu ka
money	お金	o-kane
dollars	ドル	doru
pounds	ポンド	pondo

At the bank 銀行で

I'd like to change some ...	…を替えたいのですが。	... o kaetai no desu ga
U.S. dollars	U. S.ドル	yūesu doru
Canadian dollars	カナダドル	kanada doru
pounds	ポンド	pondo
I'd like to cash a traveller's cheque.	トラベラーチェックを現金に替えたいのですが。	toraberā chekku o genkin ni kaetai no desu ga
What's the exchange rate?	交換レートはいくらですか。	kōkan rēto wa ikura desu ka
How much commission do you charge?	手数料はいくらですか。	tesūryō wa ikura desu ka
Can you cash a personal cheque?	銀行小切手を現金に替えられますか。	ginkō kogitte o genkin ni kaerare masu ka
Can you telex my bank in London?	ロンドンの私の銀行にテレックスを打って頂けますか。	rondon no watashi no ginkō ni terekkusu o utte itadakemasu ka
I have a/an ...	…を持っています。	... o motte imasu
credit card	クレジットカード	kurejitto kādo
introduction from ...	…の紹介状	... no shōkaijō
letter of credit	信用状	shin-yōjō
I'm expecting some money from New York.	ニューヨークからのお金を待っているんですが。	nyūyōku kara no o-kane o matte irun desu ga
Has it arrived?	着いていますか。	tsuite imasu ka
Give me ..., please.	…を下さい。	... o kudasai
large/small notes (bills)	高額／小額紙幣	kōgaku/shōgaku shihei
some small change	小銭	kozeni

Deposit—Withdrawal 預金-引出

I'd like to ...	…たいのですが。	... tai no desu ga
open an account	口座を開き	kōza o hiraki
withdraw ... yen	…円を引出し	... en o hikidashi
deposit this in my account	これを私の口座に入れ	kore o watashi no kōza ni ire
Where should I sign?	どこにサインするんでしょうか。	doko ni sain surun deshō ka

NUMBERS, see page 146

Business terms ビジネス

My name is ...	私は…と申します。	watashi wa ... to mōshi masu
Here's my card.	これが私の名刺です。	kore ga watashi no meishi desu
I have an appointment with ...	…とお会いする約束をしているんですが。	... to o-aisuru yakusoku o shiteirun desu ga
Can you give me an estimate of the cost?	コストの見積りを頂けますか。	kosuto no mitsumori o itadakemasu ka
What's the rate of inflation?	インフレ上昇率はどれだけですか。	infure jōshōritsu wa doredake desu ka
Can you provide me with a/an ...?	…をつけて頂けますか。	... o tsukete itadake-masu ka

interpreter	通訳	tsūyaku
secretary	秘書	hisho
translator	翻訳者	hon-yakusha

amount	額	gaku
balance	残高	zandaka
(to) borrow	借りる	kariru
capital	資本	shihon
cheque (check)	小切手	kogitte
contract	契約	keiyaku
discount	割引	waribiki
expenses	支出	shishutsu
export	輸出	yushutsu
import	輸入	yunyū
interest	利子	rishi
investment	投資	tōshi
invoice	請求書	seikyūsho
(to) lend	貸す	kasu
loan	ローン	rōn
loss	損害	songai
mortgage	担保	tanpo
payment	支払	shiharai
percentage	率	ritsu
price	価格	kakaku
profit	利益	rieki
purchase	購入	kōnyū
sale	販売	hanbai
share	株	kabu
transfer (of funds)	送金	sōkin
value	価値	kachi

At the post office

Post offices are indicated by a red and white double-capped 〒 sign. They are open from 9 a.m. to 5 p.m. from Monday to Friday, from 9 a.m. to noon on Saturdays, and are closed on Sundays. Main post offices in large cities are open from 8 a.m. to 8 p.m. on weekdays, from 8 a.m. to noon on Sundays.

Stamps are on sale in post offices, in hotels and from some tobacconists' and chemists'. Letter boxes (mailboxes) are red.

Where's the post office?	郵便局はどこですか。	yūbin kyoku wa doko desu ka
What time does it open/close?	何時に開き／締りますか。	nan-ji ni aki/shimarimasu ka
A ...-yen stamp, please.	…円切手を一枚下さい。	... en kitte o ichimai kudasai
A stamp for this letter/postcard, please.	この手紙／葉書用の切手を下さい。	kono tegami/hagaki yō no kitte o kudasai
What's the postage for a letter/postcard to ...?	…向の手紙／葉書はいくらですか。	... muke no tegami/hagaki wa ikura desu ka
Australia	オーストラリア	ōsutoraria
Great Britain	イギリス	igirisu
Canada	カナダ	kanada
Europe	ヨーロッパ	yōroppa
U.S.A.	アメリカ	amerika
Where's the letter box (mailbox)?	郵便箱はどこですか。	yūbinbako wa doko desu ka
I want to send this by ...	これを…で送りたいのですが。	kore o ... de okuritai no desu ga
airmail	航空便	kōkūbin
express (special delivery)	速達	sokutatsu
registered mail	書留	kakitome

NUMBERS, see page 146

I'd like to send this parcel.	この小包を送りたいので すが。	kono kozutsumi o okuritai no desu ga
How much will it cost ...?	いくらになりますか。	... ikura ni narimasu ka
by air	航空便で	kōkūbin de
by sea	船便で	funabin de

切手	STAMPS
小包	PARCELS
(外国) 為替	(INTERNATIONAL) MONEY ORDERS

Where's the poste restante (general delivery)?	局留め郵便の窓口はどこ ですか。	kyokudome yūbin no madoguchi wa doko desu ka
Is there any post (mail) for me?	私宛の郵便はありますか。	watashi ate no yūbin wa arimasu ka
My name is ...	私の名前は…です。	watashi no namae wa ... desu

Telegrams 電報

Overseas telegrams can be sent from main post offices or from the KDD office (see next page); you can also ask for help at the hotel desk. Rates differ according to the type of telegram—ordinary, urgent or letter. For prices, ask at the post office.

I'd like to send a telegram/telex.	電報／テレックスを打ち たいのですが。	denpō/terekkusu o uchitai no des
May I have a form, please?	用紙を頂けますか。	yōshi o ita
How much is it (per word)?	(一語につき)いくらです か。	(ichi de
ordinary telegram	普通電報	
urgent telegram	至急電報	
letter telegram	書信電報	
How long will it take?	どのくらいかかりま	
How much will this telex cost?	このテレックスは になりますか。	

PS, see page 146

COUNTRIES, see page 145

Telephone 電話

Public telephones are differentiated by colour and shape; all can be used for local, inter-city or long-distance calls. The yellow and blue phones can be used for reverse-charge (collect) calls, but not the red ones. International calls can be made from the light green public telephones by dialing 0051 for the international operator. Kokusai Denshin Denwa (KDD) is a private company which offers special services such as personal (person-to-person) calls, reverse-charge (collect) calls, credit calls, etc.

Where's there a ...?	…はどこにありますか。	... wa doko ni arimasu ka
telephone	電話	denwa
telephone booth	公衆電話	kōshū denwa
KDD office	KDD	kēdīdī
May I use your phone?	電話を使ってもいいですか。	denwa o tsukatte mo yoroshii desu ka
I want to call ...	…に電話したいんですが。	... ni denwa shitain desu ga
Great Britain	イギリス	igirisu
Canada	カナダ	kanada
the U.S.A.	アメリカ	amerika
How do I get the (international) operator?	(国際通話の)交換手を呼び出すにはどうしたらいいですか。	(kokusai tsūwa no) kōkanshu o yobidasu ni wa dōshitara iidesu ka
Can you help me get this number?	この番号にかけて頂けますか。	kono bangō ni kakete itadake masu ka
What is the number for the KDD?	KDDは何番ですか。	kēdīdī wa nan-ban desu ka
I want to place a ...	…をお願いします。	... o o-negai shimasu
credit call	クレジットコール	kurejitto kōru
international call	国際通話	kokusai tsūwa
personal (person-to-person) call	指名通話	shimei tsūwa
reversed charge (collect) call	コレクトコール	korekuto kōru
...phone	テレホンカードをいただけますか。	terehon kādo o itadake masu ka
	ダイヤル直通でかけられますか。	daiyaru chokutsū de kakeraremasu ka

Speaking 電話口で

Hello. This is ... speaking.	もしもし…です。	moshi moshi ... desu
I'd like to speak to ...	…とお話ししたいんですが。	... to o-hanashi shitain desu ga
Extension ..., please.	内線…お願いします。	naisen ... o-negai shimasu
Speak louder, please.	もっと大きい声で話して下さい。	motto ōkii koe de hanashite kudasai
More slowly, please.	もっとゆっくり話して下さい。	motto yukkuri hanashite kudasai
Could you repeat that, please?	もう一度言って頂けますか。	mō ichido itte itadakemasu ka

Bad luck 不運

Would you try again later?	後でもう一度かけて頂けますか。	ato de mōichido kakete itadakemasu ka
Operator, you gave me the wrong number.	交換手さん、番号が間違っていました。	kōkanshu-san bangō ga machigatte imashita
We were cut off.	切れてしまいました。	kirete shimai mashita

Not there いません

When will he/she be back?	いつお戻りになりますか。	itsu o-modori ni narimasu ka
Will you tell him/her I called?	電話があったと伝えて下さいますか。	denwa ga atta to tsutaete kudasaimasu ka
My name is ...	私は…です。	watashi wa ... desu
Would you ask him/her to call me?	私に電話するようお願いして頂けますか。	watashi ni denwa suru yō o-negai shite itadake masu ka
Would you take a message, please?	伝言を控えて頂けますか。	dengon o hikaete masu ka

Charges 料金

| What was the cost of the call? | 通話料はいくらになりましたか。 | |
| I want to pay for the call. | 電話代を払いたいので | が。 |

TRAVEL PHONE, see inside back-cove

Doctor

For minor ailments, your hotel can contact an English-speaking doctor. In case of serious illness or accident, you can ask to be taken to a hospital with English-speaking staff. There are two in Tokyo, and at least one in any other large city.

General 一般的な表現

Can you get me a doctor?	医者を呼んで下さいますか。	isha o yonde kudasai masu ka
Is there a doctor here?	ここに医者はいますか。	koko ni isha wa imasu ka
I need a doctor, quickly.	すぐ医者を呼んで下さい。	sugu isha o yonde kudasai
Where can I find a doctor who speaks English?	英語を話す医者にはどこでみてもらえますか。	eigo o hanasu isha ni wa doko de mite moraemasu ka
Where's the surgery (doctor's office)?	診察室はどこですか。	shinsatsu shitsu wa doko desu ka
What are the surgery (office) hours?	診察時間はいつですか。	shinsatsu jikan wa itsu desu ka
Could the doctor come to see me here?	ここに往診に来てもらえますか。	koko ni ōshin ni kitemorae masu ka
What time can the doctor come?	医者には何時に来てもらえますか。	isha ni wa nanji ni kite morae masu ka
Can you recommend a/an ...?	…を紹介して頂けますか。	... o shōkaishite itadake masu ka
general practitioner	一般医	ippan-i
children's doctor	小児科	shōnika
eye specialist	眼科	ganka
gynaecologist	婦人科	fujinka
Can I have an appointment ...?	…見て頂けますか。	... mite itadakemasu ka
tomorrow	明日	asu
as soon as possible	出来るだけ早く	dekirudake hayaku

Parts of the body　体の部分

appendix	盲腸	mōchō
arm	腕	ude
back	背中	senaka
bladder	膀胱	bōkō
bone	骨	hone
bowel	腸	chō
breast	乳房	chibusa
chest	胸	mune
ear	耳	mimi
eye	目	me
face	顔	kao
finger	指	yubi
foot	足	ashi
genitals	生殖器	seishokuki
gland	腺	sen
hand	手	te
head	頭	atama
heart	心臓	shinzō
heel	踵	kakato
hip	尻	shiri
jaw	顎	ago
joint	関節	kansetsu
kidney	腎臓	jinzō
knee	膝	hiza
leg	脚	ashi
lip	唇	kuchibiru
liver	肝臓	kanzō
lung	肺	hai
mouth	口	kuchi
muscle	筋肉	kinniku
neck	首	kubi
nerve	神経	shinkei
nervous system	神経系統	shinkei keitō
nose	鼻	hana
rib	肋骨	rokkotsu
shoulder	肩	kata
skin	皮膚	hifu
spine	背骨	sebone
stomach	胃	i
tendon	腱	k...
thigh	腿	...o yubi
throat	喉	...ta
thumb	親指	...entōsen
toe	足の指	kekkan
tongue	舌	
tonsils	扁桃腺	
vein	血管	

Accident — Injury 事故-けが

There has been an accident.	事故が起きました。	jiko ga okimashita
My child has had a fall.	子供が落ちました。	kodomo ga ochimashita
He/She has hurt his/her head.	彼／彼女は頭にけがをしました。	kare/kanojo wa atama ni kega o shimashi ta
He's/She's un-conscious.	意識不明です。	ishiki fumei desu
He's/She's bleeding.	出血しています。	shukketsu shiteimasu
He's/She's (seriously) injured.	(ひどい)けがをしています。	(hidoi) kega o shiteimasu
His/Her arm is broken.	腕を折りました。	ude o orimashita
His/Her ankle is swollen.	足首が腫れています。	ashikubi ga hareteimasu
I've been stung.	何かに刺されました。	nanika ni sasaremashita
I've got something in my eye.	目に何か入りました。	me ni nanika hairi mashita
I've got a/an ...	私は…。	watashi wa
blister	水腫が出来ました	suishu ga dekimashita
boil	できものが出来ました	dekimono ga dekimashita
bruise	打撲傷をおいました	dabokushō o oimashita
burn	火傷をおいました	yakedo o oimashita
cut	切り傷をしました	kirikizu o shimashita
graze	かすり傷をしました	kasurikizu o shimashita
insect bite	虫に刺されました	mushi ni sasaremashita
lump	瘤が出来ました	kobu ga dekimashita
rash	発疹があります。	hasshin ga arimasu
sting	刺し傷があります	sashikizu ga arimasu
swelling	腫物が出来ました	hare mono ga dekimashita
wound	傷をおいました	kizu o oirnashita
Could you have a look at it?	それを見て頂けますか。	sure o mite itadakemasu ka
I can't move it.	…を動かせません。	... o ugokasemasen
It hurts.	痛みます。	itamimasu

どこが痛みますか。	Where does it hurt?
どんな痛みですか。	What kind of pain is it?
鈍い／鋭い／ズキズキと 絶え間なく／時々	dull/sharp/throbbing constant/on and off
…います。	It's ...
折れて／挫いて 脱臼して／裂けて	broken/sprained dislocated/torn
レントゲンが必要です。	I want you to have an X-ray.
ギプスをはめましょう。	It needs to be put in plaster.
化膿しています。	It's infected.
破傷風の予防注射をして ありますか。	Have you been vaccinated against tetanus?
化膿止め／痛み止めをあ げましょう。	I'll give you an antiseptic/ a painkiller.

Illness 病気

I'm not feeling well.	気分がすぐれません。	kibun ga suguremasen
I'm ill.	具合が悪いのです。	guai ga warui no desu
I feel ...	私は…がします。	watashi wa ... ga shi-masu
dizzy	めまい	memai
nauseous	吐気	hakike
shivery	寒気	samuke
I've got a fever.	熱があります。	netsu ga arimasu
My temperature is 38 degrees.	38度の熱があります。	38 do no netsu ga arimasu
I've been vomiting.	戻しました。	modoshimashita
I'm constipated.	便秘しています。	benpi shiteimas
I've got diarrhoea.	下痢しています。	geri shiteimasu
My ... hurt(s).	…が痛みます。	... ga itaimma

医者

I've got (a/an) ...	私は…。	watashi wa
asthma	喘息です。	zensoku desu
backache	背中が痛みます。	senaka ga itamimasu
cold	風邪をひきました。	kaze o hikimashita
cough	咳が出ます。	seki ga demasu
cramps	けいれんします。	keiren shimasu
earache	耳が痛みます。	mimi ga itamimasu
hay fever	花粉症です。	kafunshō desu
headache	頭痛がします。	zutsū ga shimasu
indigestion	消化不良を起こしました。	shōkafuryō o okoshi mashita
nosebleed	鼻血が出ました。	hanaji ga demashita
palpitations	動悸がします。	dōki ga shimasu
rheumatism	リューマチです。	ryūmachi desu
sore throat	のどが痛みます。	nodo ga itamimasu
stiff neck	首が廻りません。	kubi ga mawarimasen
stomach ache	胃が痛みます。	i ga itamimasu
sunstroke	日射病です。	nisshabyō desu
I have difficulties breathing.	呼吸が困難です。	kokyū ga konnan desu
I have a pain in my chest.	胸部に痛みがあります。	kyōbu ni itami ga arimasu
I had a heart attack ... years ago.	…年前心臓発作を起こしました。	... nen mae shinzō hossa o okoshimashita
My blood pressure is too high/too low.	私は血圧が高すぎ／低すぎます。	watashi wa ketsuatsu ga takasugi/hikusugi masu
I'm allergic to ...	…にアレルギーです。	... ni arerugī desu
I'm diabetic.	私は糖尿病です。	watashi wa tōnyōbyō desu

Women's section　婦人科

I have period pains.	生理痛があります。	seiritsū ga arimasu
I have a vaginal infection.	腟炎にかかっています。	chitsuen ni kakatte imasu
I'm on the pill.	避妊薬を使っています。	hinin yaku o tsukatte imasu
I haven't had my period for 2 months.	2ヶ月間生理がありません。	2 kagetsu kan seiri ga arimasen
I'm (3 months) pregnant.	妊娠（3ヶ月）です。	ninshin (3 kagetsu) desu

こんな状態がどの位続いていますか。	How long have you been feeling like this?
こうなったのは初めてですか。	Is this the first time you've had this?
体温／血圧を計りましょう。	I'll take your temperature/ blood pressure.
袖をまくって下さい。	Roll up your sleeve, please.
服を脱いで下さい。	Please undress.
ここに横になって下さい。	Please lie down over here.
口を開けて下さい。	Open your mouth.
深呼吸をして下さい。	Breathe deeply.
咳をして下さい。	Cough, please.
どこが痛みますか。	Where do you feel the pain?
あなたは…	You've got (a/an) ...
盲腸炎です。	appendicitis
膀胱カタルです。	cystitis
胃炎です。	gastritis
インフルエンザです。	flu
…の炎症です。	inflammation of ...
食中毒です。	food poisoning
黄疸です。	jaundice
性病です。	venereal disease
肺炎です。	pneumonia
はしかです。	measles
注射をしましょう。	I'll give you an injection.
血液の／便の／尿の検査をしましょう。	I want a specimen of your blood/stools/urine.
…日間安静にしている必要があります。	You must stay in bed for ... days.
専門医に見てもらって下さい。	I want you to see a specialist.
検診のため病院へ行って下さい。	I want you to go to the hospital for a general check-up.

Prescription—Treatment 处方-治疗

This is my usual medicine.	これがいつも飲んでいる薬です。	kore ga itsumo nondeiru kusuri desu
Can you give me a prescription for this?	これの処方箋を頂けますか。	kore no shohōsen o itadakemasu ka
Can you prescribe a/an/some ...?	…を処方して頂けますか。	... o shohōshite itadakemasu ka
antidepressant	アンチデプレサント	anchidepuresanto
sleeping pills	睡眠薬	suimin yaku
tranquillizer	鎮静剤	chinseizai
I'm allergic to antibiotics/penicillin.	抗生物質／ペニシリンに対してアレルギーです。	kōsei busshitsu/penishirin ni taishite arerugī desu
I don't want anything too strong.	強すぎるのは要りません。	tsuyosugiru no wa irimasen
How many times a day should I take it?	一日何回飲むんでしょうか。	ichi-nichi nankai nomundeshō ka
Must I swallow them whole?	かまずに丸ごと飲み込まなければいけませんか。	kamazu ni maru goto nomiko ma nakereba ikemasen ka

---

どんな治療を受けていますか。	What treatment are you having?
どんな薬を使っていますか。	What medicine are you taking?
注射ですか経口ですか。	By injection or orally?
この薬を…さじ飲んで下さい。	Take ... teaspoons of this medicine.
…一錠をコップ一杯の水で飲んで下さい。	Take one pill with a glass of water ...
毎…時間	every ... hours
一日…回	... times a day
毎食前／毎食後	before/after each meal
朝／夜	in the morning/at night
痛みのある時	in case of pain
…日間	for ... days

医者

CHEMIST'S, see page 106

Fee 料金

How much do I owe you?	おいくらですか。	o-ikura desu ka
May I have a receipt for my health insurance?	健康保険用に領収書を頂けますか。	kenkōhoken yō ni ryōshūsho o itadake masu ka
Can I have a medical certificate?	診断証明書を頂けますか。	shindan shōmeisho o itadake masu ka
Would you fill in this health insurance form, please?	この健康保険の用紙に書き込んで頂きたいのですが。	kono kenkōhoken no yōshi ni kakikonde itadaki tai no desu ga

Hospital 病院

What are the visiting hours?	面会時間はいつですか。	menkai jikan wa itsu desu ka
When can I get up?	いつ起き上がれますか。	itsu okiagaremasu ka
When will the doctor come?	医師の往診はいつでしょうか。	ishi no ōshin wa itsu deshō ka
I'm in pain.	痛みます。	itamimasu
I can't eat/sleep.	食べること／眠ることが出来ません。	taberu koto/nemeru koto ga dekimasen
Can I have a pain-killer/some sleeping pills?	鎮痛剤／睡眠薬を頂けますか。	chintsūzai/suimin yaku o itadakemasu ka
Where is the bell?	呼び鈴はどこですか。	yobirin wa doko desu ka

nurse	看護婦	kangofu
patient	患者	kanja
surgeon	外科医	gekai
anaesthetic	麻酔	masui
blood transfusion	輸血	yuketsu
injection	注射	chūsha
operation	手術	shujutsu
bed	ベッド	beddo
bedpan	差し込み便器	sashikomi benki
thermometer	体温計	taion kei

Dentist 歯医者

Can you recommend a good dentist?	良い歯医者を紹介して頂けますか。	yoi haisha o shōkai shite itadakemasu ka
Can I make an (urgent) appointment to see Dr ...?	(至急)…先生に見て頂きたいのですが。	(shikyū) ... sensei ni mite itadakitai no desu ga
Couldn't you make it earlier than that?	もっと早く出来ませんでしょうか。	motto hayaku dekimasen deshō ka
I have a broken tooth.	歯が折れてしまいました。	ha ga orete shimai-mashita
I have a toothache.	歯が痛みます。	haga itamimasu
I have an abscess.	腫物が出来ています。	hare mono ga dekitei-masu
This tooth hurts.	この歯が痛みます。	kono ha ga itamimasu
at the top	上の	ue no
at the bottom	下の	shita no
in the front	前の	mae no
at the back	奥の	oku no
Can you fix it temporarily?	応急処置をして頂きますか。	ōkyūshochi o shite itadakemasu ka
I don't want it extracted.	抜かないで下さい。	nuka naide kudasai
Could you give me an anaesthetic?	麻酔をして頂けますか。	masui o shite itadake masu ka
I've lost a filling.	詰め物をなくしました。	tsumemono o nakushi-mashita
The gum ...	歯茎が…	haguki ga
is very sore	とても痛みます。	totemo itamimasu
is bleeding	出血しています。	shukketsu shiteimasu
I've broken this denture.	入歯をこわしてしまいました。	ireba o kowashite shimai-mashita
Can you repair this denture?	この入歯を直して頂けますか。	kono ireba o naoshite itadakemasu ka
When will it be ready?	いつ出来上りますか。	itsu dekiagarimasu ka

Reference section

Where do you come from? どこからいらっしゃいましたか。

Africa	アフリカ	afurika
Asia	アジア	ajia
Australia	オーストラリア	ōsutoraria
Europe	ヨーロッパ	yōroppa
North America	北米	hoku bei
South America	南米	nan bei

Austria	オーストリア	ōsutoria
Belgium	ベルギー	berugī
Burma	ビルマ	biruma
Canada	カナダ	kanada
China	中国	chūgoku
Denmark	デンマーク	denmāku
England	イングランド	ingurando
Finland	フィンランド	finrando
France	フランス	furansu
Germany	ドイツ	doitsu
Great Britain	イギリス	igirisu
Greece	ギリシャ	girisha
Holland	オランダ	oranda
India	インド	indo
Indonesia	インドネシア	indoneshia
Ireland	アイルランド	airurando
Israel	イスラエル	isuraeru
Italy	イタリー	itarī
Japan	日本	nippon/nihon
Korea	韓国	kankoku
Malaysia	マレーシア	marēshia
New Zealand	ニュージーランド	nyūjīrando
Norway	ノルウエー	noruē
Philippines	フィリッピン	firippin
Portugal	ポルトガル	porutogaru
Scotland	スコットランド	sukottorando
South Africa	南アフリカ	minami afurika
Soviet Union	ソ連	soren
Spain	スペイン	supein
Sweden	スウェーデン	suēden
Switzerland	スイス	suisu
Taiwan	台湾	taiwan
Thailand	タイ国	taikoku
United States	アメリカ（合衆国）	amerika (gasshū koku)
Wales	ウェールズ	uēruzu

Numbers 数

In Japanese, some cardinal numbers are pronounced in two or three different ways, depending on what is being counted, though they're written the same way. We do give some alternative pronunciation in parentheses, but given that the counting system is too complex to explain in two pages, you may use *ichi, ni, san,* etc. and still be understood, even if the form is not always grammatically correct.

The Japanese are also familiar with Western numerals.

0	ゼロ	zero (rei)
1	一	ichi (hitotsu)
2	二	ni (futatsu)
3	三	san (mittsu)
4	四	shi (yon, yo, yottsu)
5	五	go (itsutsu)
6	六	roku (muttsu)
7	七	shichi (nana, nanatsu)
8	八	hachi (yattsu)
9	九	kyū (ku, kokonotsu)
10	十	jū (tō)
11	十一	jū-ichi
12	十二	jū-ni
13	十三	jū-san
14	十四	jū-shi
15	十五	jū-go
16	十六	jū-roku
17	十七	jū-shichi
18	十八	jū-hachi
19	十九	jū-kyū (jūku)
20	二十	ni-jū
21	二十一	ni-jū-ichi
22	二十二	ni-jū-ni
23	二十三	ni-jū-san
24	二十四	ni-jū-shi
25	二十五	ni-jū-go
26	二十六	ni-jū-roku
27	二十七	ni-jū-shichi
28	二十八	ni-jū-hachi
29	二十九	ni-jū-kyū (ni-jū-ku)

30	三十	san-jū
31	三十一	san-jū-ichi
32	三十二	san-jū-ni
33	三十三	san-jū-san
40	四十	yon-jū
41	四十一	yon-jū-ichi
42	四十二	yon-jū-ni
43	四十三	yon-jū-san
50	五十	go-jū
51	五十一	go-jū-ichi
52	五十二	go-jū-ni
53	五十三	go-jū-san
60	六十	roku-jū
61	六十一	roku-jū-ichi
62	六十二	roku-jū-ni
63	六十三	roku-jū-san
70	七十	nana-jū
71	七十一	nana-jū-ichi
72	七十二	nana-jū-ni
73	七十三	nana-jū-san
80	八十	hachi-jū
81	八十一	hachi-jū-ichi
82	八十二	hachi-jū-ni
83	八十三	hachi-jū-san
90	九十	kyū-jū
91	九十一	kyū-jū-ichi
92	九十二	kyū-jū-ni
93	九十三	kyū-jū-san
100	百	hyaku
101	百一	hyaku-ichi
102	百二	hyaku-ni
103	百三	hyaku-san
110	百十	hyaku-jū
120	百二十	hyaku-ni-jū
130	百三十	hyaku-san-jū
140	百四十	hyaku-yon-jū
150	百五十	hyaku-go-jū
160	百六十	hyaku-roku-jū
170	百七十	hyaku-nana-jū
180	百八十	hyaku-hachi-jū
190	百九十	hyaku-kyū-jū

200	二百	ni-hyaku
300	三百	san-byaku
400	四百	yon-hyaku
500	五百	go-hyaku
600	六百	ro-ppyaku
700	七百	nana-hyaku
800	八百	ha-ppyaku
900	九百	kyū-hyaku
1000	千	sen
1100	千百	sen-hyaku
1200	千二百	sen-ni-hyaku
1300	千三百	sen-san-byaku
2000	二千	ni-sen
3000	三千	san-zen
5000	五千	go-sen
10,000	一万	ichi-man
50,000	五万	go-man
100,000	十万	jū-man
1,000,000	百万	hyaku-man
1,000,000,000	十億	jū-oku
first	一番	ichiban
second	二番	niban
third	三番	sanban
fourth	四番	yonban (yoban)
fifth	五番	goban
sixth	六番	rokuban
seventh	七番	shichiban (nanaban)
eighth	八番	hachiban
ninth	九番	kyūban (kuban)
tenth	十番	jūban
once	一度	ichido
twice	二度	nido
three times	三度	sando
a half	半分	hanbun
half a ...	…の半分	... no hanbun
half of ...	…の半分	... no hanbun
half (adj.)	半分	hanbun
a quarter	四分の一	yonbun no ichi
one third	三分の一	sanbun no ichi
a pair of	一組の	hitokumi no
a dozen	一ダース	ichi-dāsu
one per cent	1パーセント	ichi pāsento
3.4%	3・4パーセント	san ten yon pāsento

1981	千九百八十一	sen kyū-hyaku hachi-jū ichi
1992	千九百九十二	sen kyū-hyaku kyū-jū ni
2003	二千三	ni-sen san

Year and age 年と年齢

year	年	toshi
leap year	閏年	urūdoshi
decade	十年	jū-nen
century	世紀	seiki
this year	今年	kotoshi
last year	昨年、去年	saku-nen, kyo-nen
next year	来年	rai-nen
2 years ago	二年前	ni-nen mae
in one year	一年後	ich-nen go
the 16th century	十六世紀	jū-roku-seiki
in the 20th century	二十世紀に	ni-ju-seiki
How old are you?	おいくつですか。	o-ikutsu desu ka
I'm 30 years old.	三十歳です。	san-jū sai desu
He/She was born in 1960.	彼／彼女は1960年生まれです。	kare/kanojo wa 1960 nen umare desu

Seasons 季節

spring	春	haru
summer	夏	natsu
autumn	秋	aki
winter	冬	fuyu
in spring	春に	haru ni
during the summer	夏の間	natsu no aida
in autumn	秋に	aki ni
during the winter	冬の間	fuyu no aida

Months 十二ヶ月

The Japanese calendar corresponds mostly to our Gregorian calendar. However, a new era is proclaimed with the ascension of each emperor to the imperial Japanese throne so that years are counted according to the number of years in the reign of the emperor. Thus, with the enthronement of Hirohito in 1926, the Showa era was proclaimed. The year 1987, for instance, would be the 62nd year of Showa.

参用欄

In Japanese, months are literally called first month, second month, third month, etc., which correspond to our January, February, March. Although the Japanese calendar is the nation's official one, days and dates are sure to be written in Western style as well.

January	一月	ichigatsu
February	二月	nigatsu
March	三月	sangatsu
April	四月	shigatsu
May	五月	gogatsu
June	六月	rokugatsu
July	七月	shichigatsu
August	八月	hachigatsu
September	九月	kugatsu
October	十月	jūgatsu
November	十一月	jū-ichigatsu
December	十二月	jū-nigatsu
this month	今月	kongetsu
last month	先月	sengetsu
next month	来月	raigetsu
the beginning of May	五月上旬	gogatsu jōjun
the middle of June	六月中旬	rokugatsu chūjun
the end of July	七月下旬	shichigatsu gejun
during August	八月中	hachigatsu chū
in September	九月に	kugatsu ni
since October	十月から	jūgatsu kara
July 1	7月1日	shichigatsu tsuitachi
March 10	3月10日	sangatsu tōka

Days 日

Which day is it today?	今日は何曜日ですか。	kyō wa nan-yōbi desu ka
Sunday	日曜日	nichiyōbi
Monday	月曜日	getsuyōbi
Tuesday	火曜日	kayōbi
Wednesday	水曜日	suiyōbi
Thursday	木曜日	mokuyōbi
Friday	金曜日	kin-yōbi
Saturday	土曜日	doyōbi

morning	朝	asa
afternoon	午後	gogo
evening	晩	ban
night	夜	yoru
noon	正午	shōgo
midnight	午前零時	gozen reiji
yesterday	昨日	sakujitsu/kinō
today	今日	kyō
tomorrow	明日	asu
the day before	前の日	mae no hi
the next day	次の日	tsugi no hi
last week	先週	senshū
next week	来週	raishū
birthday	誕生日	tanjōbi
day	日	hi
day off	仕事休みの日	shigoto yasumi no hi
holiday	休日	kyūjitsu
holidays/vacation	休暇	kyūka
week	週	shū
weekend	週末	shū matsu
working day	平日	heijitsu

What time is it? 何時ですか。

What time is it?	何時ですか。	nan-ji desu ka
Excuse me. Can you tell me the time?	すみません。時間を教えて頂けますか。	sumimasen. jikan o oshiete itadakemasu ka
(It's) one o'clock.	1時（です）。	ichi-ji (desu)
(It's) two o'clock.	2時（です）。	ni-ji (desu)
(It's) three o'clock.	3時（です）。	san-ji (desu)
five past ...	…5分過ぎ	... go-fun sugi
ten past ...	…10分過ぎ	... ju-ppun sugi
a quarter past ...	…15分過ぎ	... jū-go-fun sugi
twenty past ...	…20分過ぎ	... niju-ppun sugi
twenty-five past ...	…25分過ぎ	... nijūgo-fun sugi
half past ...	…半	... han
twenty-five to ...	…25分前	... nijū go-fun mae
twenty to ...	…20分前	... niju-ppun mae
a quarter to ...	…15分前	... jūgo-fun mae
ten to ...	…10分前	... ju-ppun mae
five to ...	…5分前	... go-fun mae

NUMBERS, see page 146

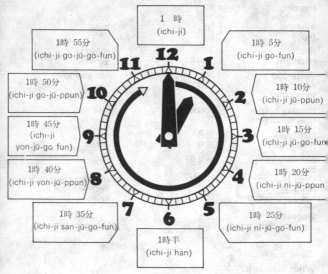

In ordinary conversation, time is expressed as shown above. However, airline and train timetables use a 24-hour clock which means that after noon hours are counted from 13 to 24.

The train leaves at ...	電車は…に出ます。	densha wa ... ni demasu
13.04 (1.04 p.m.)	13時 4 分	jū-san-ji yon-pun
0.40 (0.40 a.m.)	零時40分	rē-ji yon-ju-ppun
in 5 minutes	5分て	go-fun de
in a quarter of an hour	15分て	jū-go-fun de
half an hour ago	30分前	sanju-ppun mae
about 2 hours	約2時間	yaku ni-jikan
more than 10 minutes	10分以上	ju-ppun ijō
less than 30 seconds	30秒以下	sanjū-byō-ika
The clock is fast/slow.	その時計は進んで／遅れています。	sono tokei wa susunde/okurete imasu

参照欄

Public holidays　祝祭日

January 1	元日	New Year's Day
January 15	成人の日	Coming-of-Age Day
February 11	建国記念日	National Foundation Day
March 21	春分の日	Vernal Equinox Day
April 29	天皇誕生日	Emperor's Birthday
May 3	憲法記念日	Constitution Day
May 5	こどもの日	Children's Day
September 15	敬老の日	Respect for the Aged Day
September 23	秋分の日	Autumnal Equinox Day
October 10	体育の日	Health-Sports Day
November 3	文化の日	Culture Day
November 23	勤労感謝の日	Labour Thanksgiving Day

Note: Japanese shops and stores are mostly open on public holidays. When a holiday falls on a Sunday, the following Monday is counted as a holiday.

Greetings and wishes　挨拶と祝辞

Merry Christmas!	メリークリスマス。	merī kurisumasu
Happy New Year!	明けましておめでとうございます。	akemashite omedetō gozai masu
Happy Easter!	楽しい復活祭を。	tanoshii fukkatsusai o
Happy birthday!	お誕生日おめでとうございます。	o-tanjōbi omedetō gozai masu
Best wishes!/ Congratulations!	おめでとうございます。	omedetō gozai masu
Good luck!	御幸運をお祈りします。	go-kōun o o-inori shimasu
All the best!	すばらしい幸運をお祈りします。	subarashii kōun o o-inori shimasu
Have a good trip!	よい御旅行を。	yoi go-ryokō o
Have a good holiday!	よい休日を。	yoi kyūjitsu o
Best regards from ...	…からよろしくとのことです。	... kara yoroshiku tono koto desu
My regards to ...	…によろしくお伝え下さい。	... ni yoroshiku o-tsutae kudasai

Signs and notices 標示

空き	Vacancy
湯	Hot (water)
ベルを押して下さい	Please ring
注意	Caution
男子用	Gentlemen
出口	Exit
エレベーター	Lift (elevator)
閉店	Closed
非常口	Emergency exit
婦人用	Ladies
引く	Pull
触れるべからず	Don't touch
案内所	Information
犬に注意	Beware of the dog
入口	Entrance
会計係	Cash desk
貸します	For hire/For rent/To let
警告	Warning
危険	Danger
禁煙	No smoking
…禁止	… forbidden
故障中	Out of order
入場禁止	No entrance
入場お断わり	No admittance
起さないで下さい。	Do not disturb
押す	Push
ペンキ塗りたて	Wet paint
私有地	Private property
使用中	Occupied
立入禁止	Keep out
止まれ	Stop
釣禁止	No fishing
水	Cold (water)
売り切れ	Sold out
売ります	For sale
予約済	Reserved

Emergency　緊急事態

Call the police	警察を呼んで下さい。	keisatsu o yonde kudasai
Consulate	領事館	ryōjikan
Danger	危険	kiken
Embassy	大使館	taishikan
Fire	火事	kaji
Gas	ガス	gasu
Get a doctor	医者を呼んで下さい。	isha o yonde kudasai
Call an ambulance	救急車を呼んで下さい。	kyūkyūsha o yonde kudasai
Help	助けて。	tasukete
Get help quickly	早く助けを呼んで下さい。	hayaku tasuke o yonde kudasai
I'm ill	病気です。	byōki desu
I'm lost	道に迷いました。	michi ni mayoi mashita
Leave me alone	一人にしておいて下さい。	hitori ni shite oite kudasai
Look out	気をつけて。	ki o tsukete
Poison	毒	doku
Police	警察	keisatsu
Stop that man/ woman	あの男／女をつかまえて下さい。	ano otoko/on-na o tsuka maete kudasai
Stop thief	泥棒をつかまえて下さい。	dorobō o tsuka maete kudasai

Emergency telephone numbers　緊急時の電話番号

Dial **110**	for the police
Dial **119**	to report a fire or call an ambulance

Lost property　遺失物

Where's the ...?	…はどこですか。	... wa doko desu ka
lost property (lost and found) office	遺失物取り扱い所	ishitsubutsu toriatsukaijo
police station	交番	kōban
I want to report a theft.	盗難届を出したいのですが。	tōnan todoke o dashitai nodesu ga
My ... has been stolen.	…が盗まれました。	... ga nusumaremashita
I've lost my ...	…をなくしました。	... o nakushimashita
handbag	ハンドバッグ	handobaggu
passport	パスポート	pasupōto
wallet	札入れ	satsuire

DOCTOR, see page 136

参照項

Conversion tables

Kilometres into miles

1 kilometre (km.) = 0.62 miles

km.	10	20	30	40	50	60	70	80	90	100	110	120	130
miles	6	12	19	25	31	37	44	50	56	62	68	75	81

Miles into kilometres

1 mile = 1.609 kilometres (km.)

miles	10	20	30	40	50	60	70	80	90	100
km.	16	32	48	64	80	97	113	129	145	161

Fluid measures

1 litre (l.) = 0.88 imp. quarts = 1.06 U.S. quarts

1 imp. quart = 1.14 l.	1 U.S. quart = 0.95 l.
1 imp. gallon = 4.55 l.	1 U.S. gallon = 3.8 l.

litres	5	10	15	20	25	30	35	40	45	50
imp. gal.	1.1	2.2	3.3	4.4	5.5	6.6	7.7	8.8	9.9	11.0
U.S. gal.	1.3	2.6	3.9	5.2	6.5	7.8	9.1	10.4	11.7	13.0

Weights and measures

1 kilogram or kilo (kg.) = 1000 grams (g.)

100 g. = 3.5 oz.	½ kg. = 1.1 lb.
200 g. = 7.0 oz.	1 kg. = 2.2 lb.

1 oz. = 28.35 g.
1 lb. = 453.60 g.

CLOTHING SIZES, see page 113 / YARDS AND INCHES, see page 116

参照欄

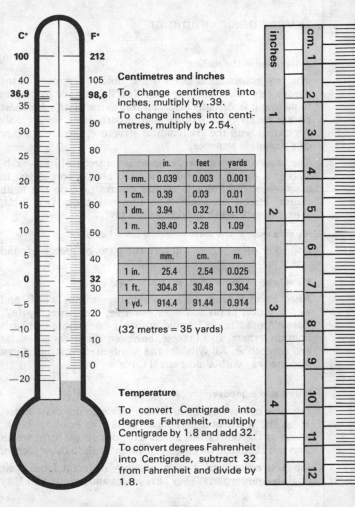

Centimetres and inches

To change centimetres into inches, multiply by .39.

To change inches into centimetres, multiply by 2.54.

	in.	feet	yards
1 mm.	0.039	0.003	0.001
1 cm.	0.39	0.03	0.01
1 dm.	3.94	0.32	0.10
1 m.	39.40	3.28	1.09

	mm.	cm.	m.
1 in.	25.4	2.54	0.025
1 ft.	304.8	30.48	0.304
1 yd.	914.4	91.44	0.914

(32 metres = 35 yards)

Temperature

To convert Centigrade into degrees Fahrenheit, multiply Centigrade by 1.8 and add 32.

To convert degrees Fahrenheit into Centigrade, subtract 32 from Fahrenheit and divide by 1.8.

A very basic grammar

A sentence in the making

The few grammatical notes below do not account for the psychology of Japanese speech. You'll just have to keep in mind that it is virtually inconceivable to translate a Japanese phrase by an exact English counterpart. Here we are only concerned with the grammatical structure, the architecture of a Japanese sentence.

The basic word order in Japanese is subject—object—verb. This is a rather rigid rule: the verb always comes last in a sentence. Subordinate clauses always precede the main clause. Here's an example to illustrate those two facts. Whereas an English speaker would say:

My wife wore a new dress when she came home,

a speaker of Japanese will turn the parts of speech around and say:

My wife home came when, she a new dress wore.

Also, English tends to stress syllables within words and words within phrases. In our example, the words "wife", "dress" and "home" would probably carry more emphasis than the others. In Japanese, however, the stress is regular and monotone. All syllables and words are pronounced in a staccato way with almost equal force.

Nouns and adjectives

Japanese nouns have no articles. Plurals do not exist either. Thus, the word **hon** may mean book, the book, a book, books or the books. All nouns have one single form which does not change according to the noun's role in the sentence.

Japanese adjectives, in turn, are very different from their English counterparts. They have tenses and moods as if they

文法

were verbs. The true Japanese adjective is an adjective with a sense of "to be" attached to it. An improvised rendition of "a new dress" in Japanese could be "a new-being dress". The past tense of these adjectives is formed by adding **katta** to their basic stem:

takai	expensive	**yasui**	cheap
takakatta	"was expensive"	**yasukatta**	"was cheap"

There are a certain number of adjectives which are formed differently: these are of Chinese origin. Bringing our Japanese phrase up to date, we say:

My wife home came when, she new-being dress wore.

Verbs

There is at least one field where (to a certain extent) Japanese is much simpler than English: verbs. The Japanese verb has only two tenses—present and past (where in most cases the ending is **ta**). A future tense does not exist but is understood from the context, just like the plurals of nouns. However, this simplicity is largely offset by the existence of numerous polite forms. These are basically the result of the sharply-defined social strata in Japan which gave birth to numerous graduations in polite speech. The way our speaker feels about the dress his wife wore, and above all the person he is speaking to, will define the grade of politeness of the verb form he'll choose. They can hardly be expressed in English. Here's an example:

taberu	to eat	**nomu**	to drink
tabemasu	to eat (polite)	**nomimasu**	to drink (polite)

Apart from politeness, a great number of other ways of feeling, moods and opinions are expressed through a complex web of verb forms. While you will be correct in using the verb forms given in this book, native Japanese speakers employ a great many others.

文法

And there is another difference. The verbs, apart from having only two tenses, have no special form to indicate person or number. On top of that, personal pronouns are usually omitted. They, too, are understood from the context, and the Japanese feel they are not necessary.

What's now left of our sentence? It has started taking the shape of a Japanese sentence—pared down to its essentials. But we're not ready yet.

Particles

Subject and direct object are not understood from the word order as in English. When a noun is used as a subject, either the particle **ga** or the particle **wa** is added after it to indicate this; a noun used as a direct object takes the postposition **o**. In fact, particles are to Japanese what word order and prepositions are to English. That is also true of questions. These are not formed by inversion of verb and subject and by intonation, as in many Western languages, but again a special particle **(ka)** is added and pronounced at the end of the phrase. It's roughly an equivalent of our question mark.

(My wife) *ga* **home came when, my wife** *wa* **new-being dress** *o* **wore.**

By now you must be curious how a real Japanese would say that. Here it is:

妻が家に帰って来た時、妻は新しいドレスを着ていました。

tsuma **ga** ie ni kaette kita toki, tsuma **wa** atarashii doresu **o** kite imashita.

That's Japanese for you. If you have a close look at it and compare the Japanese characters with the transliteration and our English "translation", you're sure to discover similarities illustrating the rules we've explained above.

Japanese characters

Traditionally, Japanese is written from top to bottom starting in the upper right-hand corner. But it's also written horizontally and from left to right (as in this book). Basically the Japanese script you will be looking at is a mixture of three different systems called *kanji, hiragana* and *katakana*.

Kanji

Kanji, adopted from the Chinese, are the basic ideograms, each character representing one word.

山 mountain	川 river	水 water	火 fire
太 陽 sun	月 moon	星 star	大 地 earth

Hiragana

Hiragana characters are used for words of Japanese origin and often also for particles (which designate subject or object) and endings or words spelled in *kanji. Hiragana* and *katakana* scripts represent individual syllables.

あ a	か ka	さ sa	た ta	な na	は ha	ま ma	や ya	ら ra	わ wa
い i	き ki	し shi	ち thi	に ni	ひ hi	み mi		り ri	
う u	く ku	す su	つ tsu	ぬ nu	ふ fu	む mu	ゆ yu	る ru	
え e	け ke	せ se	て te	ね ne	へ he	め me		れ re	
お o	こ ko	そ so	と to	の no	ほ ho	も mo	よ yo	ろ ro	を (w)o
			ん n						

GRAMMAR

Katakana

Katakana is often used for writing English and other foreign words and names – a kind of shorthand system.

ア a	カ ka	サ sa	タ ta	ナ na	ハ ha	マ ma	ヤ ya	ラ ra	ワ wa
イ i	キ ki	シ shi	チ chi	ニ ni	ヒ hi	ミ mi		リ ri	
ウ u	ク ku	ス su	ツ tsu	ヌ nu	フ fu	ム mu	ユ yu	ル ru	
エ e	ケ ke	セ se	テ te	ネ ne	ヘ he	メ me		レ re	
オ o	コ ko	ソ so	ト to	ノ no	ホ ho	モ mo	ヨ yo	ロ ro	ヲ (w)o
				ン n					

文法

Dictionary
and alphabetical index

English-Japanese

n noun

abalone *n* awabi あわび 47
abbey *n* shūdōin 修道院 82
above no maue ni の真上に 15
abscess *n* hare mono 腫物 144
absorbent cotton *n* dasshimen 脱脂綿 107
accept, to uke (ire) ru 受け (いれ) る 62,102
accessories *n* akusesari アクセサリー 111
accident *n* jiko 事故 79,138
accommodation *n* shukuhaku 宿泊 22
account *n* kōza 口座 130
adaptor *n* adaputā アダプター 27,118
address *n* jūsho 住所 21,77,102
adhesive nori tsuki 糊付き 105
admission *n* nyūjō 入場 92
Africa *n* afurika アフリカ 145
after no ato の後 15
afternoon *n* gogo 午後 32,151
after-shave lotion *n* afutā shēbu rōshon アフターシェーブローション 108
again mata また 96 ; mō ichido もう一度 135
age *n* nenrei 年齢 149
ago mae (ni) 前 (に) 149
air conditioner *n* reibō sōchi 冷房装置 29
air conditioning *n* reibō sōchi 冷房装置 24
airmail *n* kōkūbin 航空便 132
airplane *n* hikōki 飛行機 65
airport *n* kūkō 空港 21,65,66
airport bus *n* kūkō basu 空港バス 19,66
air terminal *n* eā tāminaru エアーターミナル 21
alarm clock *n* mezamashi dokei 目覚し時計 121
alcohol *n* arukōru アルコール 58
all zenbu (no) 全部 (の) 103

allergic arerugi (no) アレルギーの 140
almond *n* āmondo アーモンド 56
alone hitori (de) ひとり (で) 155
alter, to *(garment)* naosu 直す 114
amber *n* kohaku 琥珀 122
ambulance *n* kyūkyūsha 救急車 80,155
America *n* amerika アリカ 145
American amerika (no) アメリカ (の) 105,106,126 ; *(person)* amerikajin アメリカ人 94
American plan *n* san-shoku tsuki 三食付き 24
amethyst *n* amejisuto アメジスト 122
amount *n* (kin)gaku (金)額 62,131
amplifier *n* anpu アンプ 118
anaesthetic *n* masui(zai) 麻酔 (剤) 144
analgesic *n* chintsūzai 鎮痛剤 107
anchovy *n* anchobi アンチョビ 45,47
and to と 15
animal *n* dōbutsu 動物 86
anorak *n* anorakku アノラック 111
another betsu no 別の 123
antenna *n* antena アンテナ 118
antibiotic *n* kōsei busshitsu 抗生物質 142
antidepressant *n* anchi depuresanto アンチデプレサント 142
antique kottōhin 骨董品 84
antique shop *n* Kottōya 骨董屋 98
antiseptic kanō dome (no) 化膿止め (の) 139
antiseptic cream *n* shōdoku kurimu 消毒クリーム 107
anyone dareka 誰か 12,16
anything nani ka 何か 40
aperitif *n* aperitifu アペリティフ 60
appendicitis *n* mōchō(en) 盲腸(炎) 141
appendix *n* mōchō 盲腸 137
appetizer zensai 前菜, ōdoburu オードブル 45

apple *n* ringo りんご 56
appointment *n* yoyaku 予約 31 ; yakusoku 約束 131
apricot *n* anzu あんず 56
April *n* shigatsu 四月 150
aquarium *n* suizokukan 水族館 82
archaeology *n* kōkogaku 考古学 84
architect *n* kenchikuka 建築家 85
architecture *n* kenchiku 建築 84
arm *n* ude 腕 137
around *(time)* koro (ni) ころ（に）32 ; *(place)* chikaku (ni) 近く（に）38
arrival *n* tōchaku 到着 16,66
arrive, to tsuku 着く 65,69
art *n* geijutsu 芸術 84
art gallery *n* garō 画廊 82,98
artificial sweetener *n* jinkōkanmiryō 人口甘味料 42
artist *n* geijutsuka 芸術家 85
arts and crafts *n* kōgeihin 工芸品 117
ashtray *n* haizara 灰皿 27,41
Asia *n* ajia アジア 145
ask, to *(request)* negau 願う 135
ask for, to chūmon suru 注文する 63
asparagus *n* asuparagasu アスパラガス 45,54
aspirin *n* asupirin アスピリン 107
asthma *n* zensoku 喘息 140
astringent *n* asutorinzento アストリンゼント 108
at ni に 15
at least sukunakutomo 少くとも 25
at once suguni すぐに 32
aubergine *n* nasu なす 54
August *n* hachigatsu 八月 150
Australia *n* ōsutoraria オーストラリア 132,145
Australian ōsutoraria (no) オーストラリアの ; *(person)* ōsutoraria jin オーストラリア人 94
Austria *n* ōsutoria オーストリア 145
author *n* chosha 著者 104
automatic ōtomachikku (no) オートマチック（の）20,124 ; jidōmaki 自動巻き 122
autumn *n* aki 秋 149
avoid, to sakeru 避る 41
awful hidoi ひどい 95

B

baby *n* nyūji 乳児 24,109
baby food *n* bebī fūdo ベビーフード 109
babysitter *n* bebī shittā ベビーシッター 27
back, to be modoru 戻る 135
back *(body)* senaka 背中 137

backache *n* se no itami 背の痛み 140
bacon *n* bēkon ベーコン 51
bacon and eggs *n* bēkon eggu ベーコンエッグ 43
bad warui 悪い 14
bag *n* baggu バッグ 18 ; fukuro 袋 103
baggage *n* (te)nimotsu （手）荷物 18, 26,32,72
baggage cart *n* (te)nimotsu yō kāto （手）荷物用カート 18
baggage check *n* (te)nimotsu ichiji azukarijo （手）荷物一時預り所 68,72
baggage claim *n* (te)nimotsu uketori （手）荷物受取り所 18
baked tenpi de yaita 天火で焼いた 48, 51
baker's *n* pan-ya パン屋 98
balance *(account)* zandaka 残高 131
balcony *n* barukoni バルコニー 23
ball *n* bōru ボール 128
ballet *n* barē バレー 87
ballpoint pen *n* bōru pen ボールペン 105
bamboo *n* take 竹 127
banana *n* banana バナナ 56
band *(music)* n bando バンド 90
bandage *n* hōtai 包帯 107
Band-Aid *n* bansōkō 絆創膏 107
bangle *n* buresuretto ブレスレット 121
bank *(finance)* n ginkō 銀行 129
banknote *n* shihei 紙幣 130
bar *n* bā 33,90
barbecued bābekyūshita バーベキューした 51
barber's *n* tokoya 床屋 31
baseball *n* yakyū 野球 91
basketball *n* basuketto bōru バスケットボール 91
bath *n* basu バス 23 ; furo 風呂 28
bathing cap *n* suieibō 水泳帽 111
bathrobe *n* basu rōbu バスローブ 111
bathroom *n* furoba 風呂場 28
bath salts *n* basu soruto バスソルト 108
bath towel *n* basutaoru バスタオル 27
battery *n* denchi 電池 118,125 ; *(car)* batteri バッテリー 76,79
be, to desu です 14
beach *n* kaisuiyokujō 海水浴場 92
bean *n* sayaingen 莢いんげん 54
beard *n* ago hige あごひげ 31
beautiful utsukushii 美しい 14,85
beauty salon *n* biyō shitsu 美容室 31
bed *n* beddo ベッド 23,24,108
bedpan *n* sashikomi benki 差し込み便器 143

beef n gyūniku 牛肉 40,50
beefsteak n bifuteki ビフテキ 51
beer n bīru ビール 41,58
beer garden n biyagāden ビヤガーデン 33
before (no) mae （の）前 15
begin, to hajimaru 始まる 89
beginning (of month) n jōjun 上旬 150
behind ushiro 後ろ 15
beige bēju ベージュ 114
Belgium n berugii ベルギー 145
bell (electric) n yobirin 呼び鈴 143
bellboy n bōi ボーイ 26
below shita ni 下に 15
belt n beruto ベルト 112
berth n shindai 寝台 70
better yori yoi よりよい 14；motto yoi もっとよい 25
between, no aida の間 15
beware, to chūisuru 注意する 154
bicycle n jitensha 自転車 80
bicycle hire/rental n kashi jitensha 貸自転車 80
big ōkii 大きい 14,101
bill n kanjō 勘定 32,62,102；(banknote) shihei 紙幣 130
billion (Am.) n jū-oku 十億 147
binoculars n sōgankyō 双眼鏡 123
bird n tori 鳥 86
birthday n tanjōbi 誕生日 151,153
biscuit (Br.) n bisuketto ビスケット 64, 126
bitter nigai 苦い 63
black kuro 黒 114；(coffee) burakku ブラック 43
black and white (photography) shiro kuro 白黒 124,125
blackcurrant n kurosuguri 黒すぐり 56
bladder n bōkō 膀胱 137
blade n ha 刃 108
blanket n mōfu 毛布 27
bleach n burichi ブリーチ 31
bleed, to shukketsu suru 出血する 138, 144
blind (window) n buraindo ブラインド 30
blister n suishu 水腫 138
block, to tsumaru 詰る 29
blood n ketsueki 血液 141
blood pressure n ketsuatsu 血圧 140
blood transfusion n yuketsu 輸血 143
blouse n burausu ブラウス 111
blow-dry n burō ブロー 31
blue ao 青 114
blusher n ho-o beni ほおべに 108
boar (wild) n inoshishi いのしし 52

board, to noru 乗る 69
boat n bōto ボート 75
bobby pin n pin dome ピン止め 109
body n karada 体 137
body lotion n bodē rōshion ボデーローション 108
boil n dekimono でき物 138
boiled yudeta ゆでた 51
boiled egg n yude tamago ゆで卵 43
bone n hone 骨 137
book n hon 本 104
book, to yoyaku suru 予約する 39
booking office n yoyaku madoguchi 予約窓口 19,68
booklet (of tickets) n kaisūken 回数券 74
bookshop n hon-ya 本屋 98,104
boot n būtsu ブーツ 116
borrow, to kariru 借りる 131
botanical garden n shokubutsuen 植物園 82
bottle n hon, pon, bon 本 17,59,60
bottle-opener n sennuki 栓抜き 120
bottled (beer) bin iri びん入り 58
bottom n shita 下 144
bowel n chō 腸 137
box n hako 箱 120
boxing n bokushingu ボクシング 91
box lunch n bentō 弁当 64,72
boy n otoko no ko 男の子 110,128
boyfriend n bōifurendo ボーイフレンド 94
bracelet n buresuretto ブレスレット 121
braces (suspenders) n zubon tsuri ズボン吊り 111
braised torobi de nita とろ火で煮た 51
brake n burēki ブレーキ 79
brake fluid n burēki oiru ブレーキオイル 76
brandy n burandē ブランデー 60
bread n pan パン 41,43,120
break, to kowareru こわれる 30；kowasu こわす 123,144；o(re)ru 折(れ)る 138,144
break down, to koshō suru 故障する 79
breakdown n koshō 故障 79
breakdown van n ken-insha けん引車 79
breakfast n chōshoku 朝食 24,27,42
breast n chibusa 乳房 137
breathe, to kokyū o suru 呼吸をする 141
bridge n hashi 橋 86
briefs n burifu ブリーフ 111
bring, to mottekuru 持って来る 13
British (person) eikoku jin 英国人 94

辞書

brocade n nishiki ori 錦織 127
broiled yaita 焼いた 48,51
broken dakkyūshita 脱臼した 139
brooch n burōchi ブローチ 121
brother n kyōdai 兄弟 94
brown chairo 茶色 114
bruise n dabokushō 打撲傷 138
brush n burashi ブラシ 109
Brussels sprout n mekyabetsu 芽キャベ
ツ 54
bubble bath n nyūyoku zai 入浴剤 108
buckle n bakkuru バックル 112
Buddhist temple n tera 寺 84
buffet car n byuffe ビュッフェ 69
build, to tateru 建てる 85
building blocks/bricks n tsumiki 積み木
128
bulb n denkyū 電球 29,76,118
bunraku n bunraku 文楽 88
Burma n biruma ビルマ 145
burn n yakedo やけど 138
burn out, to (bulb) kireru 切れる 29
bus n basu バス 18,66,74
business n shigoto 仕事 16,93
business district n bijinesu gai ビジネス
街 82
businessman n bijinesuman ビジネスマ
ン 95
bus stop n basu tei バス停 74,75
busy isogashii 忙しい 96
butcher's n nikuya 肉屋 98
butter n batā バター 41,43
button n botan ボタン 30,112
buy, to kau 買う 13,70,89,100,104

C

cabbage n kyabetsu キャベツ 54
cabin (ship) n senshitsu 船室 75
cable (telegramme) n denpō 電報 133
cable car n kēburukā ケーブルカー 80
cable release n shattā rerīzu シャッタ
ーレリーズ 125
cake n kēki ケーキ 41,57
cake shop n kēkiya ケーキ屋 98
calculator n keisanki 計算機 119,122
calendar n karendā カレンダー 122
call, to (give name) iu 言う 11 ; (sum-
mon) yobu 呼ぶ 79 ; (phone) denwa
suru 電話する 134,135
calligraphy n shodō 書道 84
camera n kamera カメラ 124,125
camera case n kamera kēsu カメラケー
ス 125
camera shop n kameraya カメラ屋 98
camel-hair n kyameru キャメル 115
camping n kyanpu キャンプ 32

camp site n kyanpujō キャンプ場 32
can (of peaches) n kanzume 缶詰 120
can (to be able) dekiru できる 19,26
Canada n kanada カナダ 132,134,145
Canadian kanada (no) カナダ(の) 130 ;
(person) kanada jin カナダ人 94
cancel, to kyanseru suru キャンセルす
る 66
candy n kyandī キャンディー 126
candy store n kashiya 菓子屋 98
can opener n kankiri 缶切り 120
cap n bōshi 帽子 111
capital (finance) n shihon 資本 131
car n kuruma 車 20,26,76,79
carat n karatto カラット 121
carburet(t)or n kyaburetā キャブレタ
ー 79
card (business) n meishi 名刺 131
cardigan n kādegan カーデガン 111
car hire n renta kā レンタカー 20
carp n koi 鯉 45
car park n chūshajō 駐車場 78
car radio n kā rajio カーラジオ 119
car rental n renta kā レンタカー 20
carrot n ninjin 人参 54
cart n kāto カート 18,72
carton (of cigarettes) n kāton カートン
126
cartridge (camera) n kātorijji カートリ
ッジ 124
case (instance) n toki 時 142 ; (camera,
etc.) kēsu ケース 123,125
cash, to genkin ni kaeru 現金にかえる
130
cash desk n reji レジ 117
cassette n kasetto カセット 128
cassette player n kasetto purēyā カセッ
トプレーヤー 118
cassette recorder n kasetto rekōdā カ
セットレコーダー 118
castle n shiro 城 82
catalogue n katarogu カタログ 83
cathedral n daiseidō 大聖堂 82
catholic katorikku (no) カトリック(の)
85
cauliflower n karifurawā カリフラワー
54
caution n chūi 注意 154
cave n iwaya 岩屋 82
caviar n kyabia キャビア 45
cedar n seiyō sugi 西洋杉 86
celery n serori セロリ 45,54
cellophane tape n serotēpu セロテープ
105
cemetery n bochi 墓地 82
centre n chūshin 中心 19,21,77,82

century n seiki 世紀 149

ceramics n tōjiki 陶磁器 84,127

ceramics shop n tōkiya 陶器屋 98

cereal n serearu セレアル 43

chain (jewellery) n kusari 鎖 121

chair n isu 椅子 39

chamber music n shitsunai gaku 室内楽 128

champagne n shanpen シャンペン 59

change (money) n kozeni 小銭 78, 130

change, to kaeru かえる 63,123 ; tori-kaeru 取りかえる 76 ; (money) ryōgaesuru 両替する 18,129 ; (train) norikaeru 乗りかえる 69

change machine n ryōgaeki 両替機 68

charge n ryōkin 料金 20,28,135

charge, to kanjō ni ireru 勘定に入れる 24

cheap yasui 安い 14,24,101

check n kogitte 小切手 130,131 ; (res-taurant) kanjō 勘定 32,62

check, to shiraberu 調べる 76 ; (lug-gage) chikki ni suru チッキにする 72

check in, to chekku in suru チェックインする 65

check-up n kenshin 検診 141

cheers! kanpai 乾杯 58

cheese n chīzu チーズ 45

chemist's n kusuriya 薬屋 98 ; yakkyoku 薬局 106

cheque n kogitte 小切手 130,131

cherry n sakuranbo さくらんぼ 56

cherry tree n sakura (no ki) 桜（の木） 86

chess set n chesu setto チェスセット 128

chest n mune 胸 137

chestnut n kuri 栗 56

chewing gum n chūin gamu チューインガム 126

chicken n (niwa) tori （にわ）とり 40, 52

chiffon n kinu mosurin 絹モスリン ; shifon シフォン 115

child n kodomo 子供 24,63,83,95,117, 138

children's doctor n shōnika 小児科 136

China n chūgoku 中国 145

china n tōjiki 陶磁器 117

Chinese n chūgoku (no) 中国（の） 38

chips n poteto furai ポテトフライ 64

chocolate n chokorēto チョコレート 64,120,126 ; (drink) kokoa ココア 60

chop n honetsuki abaraniku 骨付あばら肉 51

chopsticks n hashi 箸 41,127

Christmas n kurisumasu クリスマス 153

church n kyōkai 教会 85

cigar n hamaki 葉巻 126

cigarette n tabako タバコ 17,126

cigarette holder n paipu パイプ 126

cigarette lighter n raitā ライター 121

cine camera n satsueiki 撮影機 124

cinema n eiga 映画 87,96

circle n nikai 二階 89

city machi 町 94

city air terminal n shiti eā tāminaru シティーエアーターミナル 21

city centre n machi no chūshin 町の中心 21,82

clam n hamaguri はまぐり 45,48

classical music n kurasshikku ongaku クラッシック音楽 128

clean kirei きれい 63

clean, to fuku 拭く 76 ; (clothes) kurīningu suru クリーニングする 30

cleansing cream n kurenjingu kurimu クレンジングクリーム 108

cloakroom n kurōku クローク 89

clock n oki dokei 置き時計 121,127 ; tokei 時計 152

clock-radio n tokei tsuki rajio 時計付ラジオ 118

close, to shimaru 締まる 11,83,106, 132

closed (shop) heiten 閉店 154

clothes (shop) n fuku 服 30 ; irui 衣類 111

clothes shop n yōsōten 洋装店 98

clothing n irui 衣類 117

club n kurabu クラブ 92

coach n chokutsū basu 直通バス 19,74

coat n uwagi 上着 111

coconut n yashi no mi やしの実 56

cod n tara たら 48

coffee n kōhi コーヒー 43,60,96

coin n kosen 古銭, kōka 硬貨 84

cold tsumetai 冷い 14,40,43 ; (weather) samui 寒い 14

cold (illness) n kaze 風邪 106,140

collar n eri 衿 112

colleague n dōryō 同僚 93

collect call n korekuto kōru コレクトコール 134

colour n iro 色 114 ; (photography) karā カラー 124,125

colour chart n karā mihon カラー見本 31

colourfast dasshoku bōshikakō (no) 脱色防止加工の 115

colour rinse n karā rinsu カラーリンス 31

DICTIONARY

colour shampoo n karā shanpū カラーシャンプー 109

colour slide n karā suraido カラースライド 124

colour television (set) n karā terebi カラーテレビ 119

comb n kushi くし 109

commission n tesūryō 手数料 130

compact disc n konpakuto disuku コンパクトディスク 128

compact disc player n konpakuto disuku purēyā コンパクトディスクプレーヤー 118

compartment n shindai 寝台 71

complaint n kujō 苦情 63

computer n konpūtā コンピューター 118

computer equipment store n konpūtā kikiten コンピューター機器店 98, 117

concert n konsāto コンサート 87

concert hall n konsāto hōru コンサートホール 87

conductor (orchestra) n shikisha 指揮者 87

confirm, to kakunin suru 確認する 66

confirmation n kakunin(sho) 確認（書）23

connection n renraku 連絡 68

constipated benpishiteiru 便秘している 139

constipation n benpi 便秘 106

consulate n ryōjikan 領事館 155

contact lens n kontakuto renzu コンタクトレンズ 123

contain, to hairu 入る 41

contraceptive n hiningu 避妊具；(pills) piru ピル 107

contract n keiyaku 契約 131

convent n shūdōin 修道院 82

cooked chōrishita 調理した 40

cookie n kukkī クッキー 64

copper n dō 銅 122

coral n sango さんご 122

corduroy n kōjuroi コージュロイ 115

cork n koruku コルク 63

corkscrew n korukunuki コルク抜き 120

corn (Am) n tōmorokoshi とうもろこし 54

corn plaster n uonomekōyaku 魚目膏薬 107

corner n sumi 隅 39；(street) magari-kado 曲り角 21

cost n kosuto コスト 131

cost, to kakaru かかる 81, 125

cot n kan-i beddo 簡易ベッド 24

cotton n momen 木綿 115

cotton wool n dasshimen 脱脂綿 107

cough n seki 咳 106, 140

cough, to seki o suru 咳をする 141

cough drops n sekidome gusuri 咳止め薬 107

counter n kauntā カウンター 39

country n kuni 国 94

countryside n kōgai 郊外 86

courgette n nagakabocho 長かぼちゃ 54

court house n saibansho 裁判所 82

cover charge n sekiryō 席料 62

crab n kani かに 45, 47

cramp n keiren けいれん 140

crayfish (river) n zarigani ざりがに 47

crayon n kureyon クレヨン 105

cream n kurimu クリーム 57, 60, 107, 108

crease resistant shiwa bōshikakō しわ防止加工 115

credit call n kurejitto kōru クレジットコール 134

credit card n kurejitto kādo クレジットカード 20, 32, 62, 102, 129, 130

cross n jūjika 十字架 121

crossroads n kōsaten 交差点 78

cruise n yūransen 遊覧船 75

crystal n suishō 水晶 122

cucumber n kyūri きゅうり 54

cuff link n kafusu botan カフスボタン 121

cultured pearl n yōshoku shinju 養殖真珠 122, 127

cup n koppu コップ 41

curler n kārā カーラー 109

currency n tsūka 通貨 129

currency exchange office n ryōgaejo 両替所 68, 129

curtain n kāten カーテン 29

customs n zeikan 税関 16, 102

customs office n zeikan jimusho 税関事務所 17

cut (wound) n kirikizu 切り傷 138

cut, to kiru 切る 135

cutlery n shokutaku yō naifu rui 食卓用ナイフ類 121

cutlet n honetsuki abaraniku 骨付あばら肉 54

cystitis n bōkō kataru 膀胱カタル 141

D

dance, to dansu suru ダンスする 90, 96

danger n kiken 危険 80, 154, 155

dark kurai 暗い 25, 114；iro no koi 色の濃い 101

辞書

date *(fruit)* n natsumeyashi なつめやし 56

daughter n musume むすめ 93

day n hi, nichi 日 16,20,25,81,150

day off n shigoto yasumi no hi 仕事休み の日 151

decaffeinated kafein nuki カフェイン抜き 43

December n jū-nigatsu 十二月 150

deck *(ship)* n dekki デッキ 75

declare,to *(customs)* shinkoku suru 申告する 17

degree *(temperature)* n do 度 139

delay n okure 遅れ 69

delicatessen n derikatessen デリカテッセン 98

delicious oishii おいしい 62

deliver, to todokeru 届ける 102

delivery n haitatsu 配達 102

demonstration n jitsuen 実演 91

denim n denimu デニム 115

Denmark n denmāku デンマーク 145

dentist n haisha 歯医者 144

denture n ireba 入歯 144

deodorant n deodoranto デオドラント 108

department n kōnā コーナー 117

department store n depāto デパート 98,100,117

departure n shuppatsu 出発 66,81

deposit n hoshōkin 保証金 130

deposit, to *(bank)* ireru 入れる 130

dessert n dezāto デザート 57

develop, to genzō suru 現像する 125

diabetic n tōnyōbyō 糖尿病 41,140

dial, to denwa o kakeru 電話をかける 134

diamond n daiyamondo ダイヤモンド 122

diaper n omutsu おむつ 109

diarrhoea n geri 下痢 106,139

dictating machine n kōjutsu rokuonki 口述録音機 118

dictionary n jisho 辞書 104

diesel n dizeru ディーゼル 78

different chigau 違う 25

difficult muzukashii 難しい 14

difficulty n mondai 問題 102 ; konnan 困難 140

digital dejitaru (no) デジタル (の) 122

dining car n shokudō sha 食堂車 69,72

dining room n shokudō 食堂 28

dinner n yūshoku 夕食 38,95

direct chokkō 直行 65

direct, to hōkō o shimesu 方向を示す 12

director *(theatre)* n kantoku 監督 88

disabled n shintai shōgaisha 身体障害者 83

discotheque n diskotekku ディスコ 90

discount n waribiki 割引 131

discount shop n yasuuri no mise 安売りの店 98

disembarkation n nyū koku 入国 16

dish n ryōri 料理 41

dish antenna n parabora antena パラボラアンテナ 118

disinfectant n shōdokuyaku 消毒薬 107

disk drive n disuku doraibu ディスクドライブ 118

dislocated dakkyū shiteiru 脱臼している 139

display case n shōkēsu ショーケース 100

disturb, to jama suru 邪魔する 154

dizzy memai めまい 139

doctor n isha 医者 80,136,143

doctor's office n shinsatsu shitsu 診察室 136

dog n inu 犬 154

doll n ningyō 人形 127,128

dollar n doru ドル 18,129

double daburu ダブル 60,75

double bed n daburu beddo ダブルベッド 23

double room n daburu rūmu ダブルルーム 19,23

down shita (ni) 下 (に) 15

downstairs kaika 階下 15

downtown area n hankagai 繁華街 82

dozen n dāsu ダース 120,148

drawing n dessan デッサン 84

drawing paper n gayōshi 画用紙 105

dress n doresu ドレス 111

dressing gown n basurōbu バスローブ 111

dressmaker's n yōfukuya 洋服屋 98

drink n nomimono 飲物 58

drink, to nomu 飲む 13,38,58

drip, to *(tap)* moreru 漏れる 29

drive, to unten suru 運転する 21

driver n untenshu 運転手 20

driving licence n untenmenkyo shō 運転免許証 20

drugstore n doraggusutoā ドラッグストアー 106 ; kusuriya 薬屋 98

dry dorai ドライ 59,109

dry cleaner's n dorai kuriningu ドライクリーニング 30

duck n ahiru あひる 52

duckling n ahiru no ko あひるの子 52

dummy n oshaburi おしゃぶり 109

during no aida の間 15,149;-chū -中 150

duty (customs) n zeikin 税金 17

dye (hair) n hea dai ヘアダイ 31

E

each -zutsu -ずつ 125

ear n mimi 耳 137

earache n mimi no itami 耳の痛み 140

ear drops n mimigusuri 耳薬 107

early hayai 早い 14

earring n iyaringu イヤリング 121

earth n daichi 大地 7

east n higashi 東 78

Easter n fukkatsusai 復活祭 153

easy yasashii 易しい 14

eat, to taberu 食べる 13,38,143

eel n unagi うなぎ 47

egg n tamago 卵 43,120

eggplant n nasu なす 54

eight hachi 八 146

eighteen jū-hachi 十八 146

eighth hachiban 八番 148

eighty hachi-jū 八十 147

elastic bandage n shinshukusei no aru hōtai 伸縮性のある包帯 107

Elastoplast n bansōkō 絆創膏 107

electric denki (no) 電気（の）118

electrical appliance n denki seihin 電気製品 118

electrical shop n denkiten 電気店 98

electronic denshi (no) 電子（の）118, 122,125,128

electronic game n denshi gēmu 電子ゲーム 118,128

electronics n erekutoronikusu エレクトロニクス 117

elevator n erebētā エレベーター 28, 117

eleven jū-ichi 十一 146

embankment (river) n teibō 堤防 82

embarkation n shutsu koku 出国 16;(boat) jōsen 乗船 75

embassy n taishikan 大使館 155

emerald n emerarudo エメラルド 122

emergency n kinkyū (no) 緊急（の）155

emergency exit n hijō guchi 非常口 28

emery board n tsumeyasuri 爪やすり 108

empty kara (no) 空（の）14

enamel n enameru エナメル 122

end (of month) n gejun 下旬 150

end, to owaru 終る 89

engine (car) n enjin エンジン 79

England n ingurando イングランド 145

English (language) eigo (no) 英語（の）11,16,40,83,89,104;(person) igirisu jin イギリス人 94

enjoy, to tanoshimu 楽しむ 62,96

enlarge, to hikinobasu 引伸す 125

enough jūbun (na) 充分（な）15,69

enquiry n annai 案内 68

entrance n iriguchi 入口 67,154

entrance fee n nyūjōryō 入場料 83

envelope n fūtō 封筒 27,105

equipment n yōgu 用具 92

eraser n keshi gomu 消しゴム 105

escalator n esukarētā エスカレーター 117

estimate (cost) n mitsumori 見積り 131

Europe n yōroppa ヨーロッパ 132,145

evening n ban 晩 32,89,151

everything zenbu 全部 62

exchange, to kōkan suru 交換する 103

exchange rate n kōkan rēto 交換レート 18,130

excursion n shō ryokō 小旅行 81

excuse me sumimasen すみません 11

exhaust pipe n mafurā マフラー 79

exhibition n tenrankai 展覧会 82

exit n deguchi 出口 67,73,154

expect, to matsu 待つ 130

expenses n shishutsu 支出 131

expensive takai 高い 14,19,24,101

export n yushutsu 輸出 131

exposure (photography) n -maidori -枚どり 124

exposure counter n roshutsukei 露出計 125

express (mail) sokutatsu 速達 132

expressway n kōsoku dōro 高速道路 77

extension cord/lead n tsugitashi kōdo 継ぎ足しコード 118

extra (additional) n mō hitotsu もう一つ 24

eye n me 目 137,138

eyebrow pencil n aipenshiru アイペンシル 108

eye drops n megusuri 目薬 107

eye liner n airainā アイライナー 108

eye shadow n aishadō アイシャドー 108

eyesight n shiryoku 視力 123

eye specialist n ganka 眼科 136

F

fabric (cloth) n orimono 織物 115,117

face n kao 顔 137

face pack n pakku パック 31

face powder n oshiroi おしろい 108

factory n kōjō 工場 82,95

fair n hakurankai 博覧会 82
fall (autumn) n aki 秋 149
fall, to ochiru 落ちる 138
family n kazoku 家族 94
fan n sensu 扇子 127; (electric) senpū-ki 扇風機 29
fan belt n fan beruto ファンベルト 76
far tōi 遠い 14,77,100
fare n ryōkin 料金 67,70; ikura いくら 21
farm n nōjō 農場 86
fast (film) hai supido ハイスピード 124
fat shibōbun 脂肪分 41
father n (your own) chichi 父 94; (someone else's) o-tō san お父さん
faucet n jaguchi 蛇口 29
February n nigatsu 二月 150
feeding bottle n honyū bin 哺乳びん 109
feel, to (physical state) kanjiru 感じる 139
felt-tip pen n fueruto pen フェルトペン 105
ferry n feri フェリー 75
fever n netsu 熱 139
few hotondo nai ほとんどない 14; (a) ni-san (no) 二三の 16,81; sukoshi 少し 14
field n nohara 野原 86
fifteen jūgo 十五 146
fifth goban 五番 148
fifty go-jū 五十 147
fig n ichijiku いちじく 56
fill in, to kakikomu 書き込む 143
fillet n hireniku ヒレ肉 51
filling (tooth) n tsumemono 詰め物 144
filling station n gasorin sutando ガソリンスタンド 76
film (cinema) n eiga 映画 87; (photography) firumu フィルム 124,125
filter n firutā フィルター 125,126
filter-tipped firutā tsuki フィルター付 126
find, to mitsukeru 見つける 18,27; aru ある 100
fine (ok) ii いい 25
fine grain biryūshi 微粒子 124
finger n yubi 指 137
Finland n finrando フィンランド 145
fire n hi 火 7; kaji 火事 155
first ichiban 一番 148; hajime 始め 94; (train, etc.) shihatsu (no) 始発 (の) 68,74
first class (green coach) n gurin sha グリーン車 70
first name n mei 名 26

fish n sakana 魚 40,47
fishing tackle n tsuri dōgu 釣り道具 127
fish market n uoichiba 魚市場 98
fishmonger's n sakanaya 魚屋 99
fit, to au 合う 113
fitting room n shichaku shitsu 試着室 113
five go 五 146
fix, to shochi o suru 処置をする 144
flannel n furanneru フランネル 115
flash (photography) n furasshu フラッシュ 125
flash attachment n furasshu no koteibu フラッシュの固定部 125
flat tyre n panku パンク 76,79
flea market nomi no ichi のみの市 82, 99
flight n bin 便 65
floor n -kai 一階 25
floor show n furoā shō フロアーショー 90
florist's n hanaya 花屋 99
flounder n hirame 平目 48
flour n komugiko 小麦粉 41
flower n hana 花 86
flower arranging n ikebana いけ花 84
flu n infuruenza インフルエンザ 141
fluid n eki 液 123
folk art n mingeihin 民芸品 84
folkcrafts n mingeihin 民芸品 127
folk music n min-yō 民謡 128
follow, to tsuiteiku ついて行く 78
food (meal) n tabemono 食物 94; (groceries) n shoku hin 食品 117
food poisoning n shoku chūdoku 食中毒 141
foot n ashi 足 116,137
football n sakkā サッカー 91
foot cream n ashi no kurīmu 足のクリーム 108
footpath n komichi 小道 86
for no tame ni のために; no kawari ni の代りに 154
forbid, to kinshi suru 禁止する 154
foreign gaikoku (no) 外国 (の) 58
forest n mori 森 86
fork n fōku フォーク 41,63
form (document) n yōshi 用紙 133,143
fortress n jōsai 城塞 82
forty yon-jū 四十 147
forward mae (ni) 前 (に) 89
foundation cream n fandēshon kurīmu ファンデーションクリーム 108
fountain n funsui 噴水 82
fountain pen n mannenhitsu 万年筆 105

four yon 四 146

fourteen jū-shi 十四 146

fourth yo(n)ban 四番 148

frame *(glasses)* n furēmu フレーム 123

France n furansu フランス 145

free *(vacant)* aki 突き 14；aiteiru 空いている 71

French furansu (no) フランス（の）38, 59；*(language)* furansugo 16, 104

French bean n sayaingen 莢いんげん 54

french fries n poteto furai ポテトフライ 64

fresh shinsen (na) 新鮮（な）63

Friday n kinyōbi 金曜日 150

fried ageta 揚げた 48, 51

fried egg n medama yaki 目玉焼 43

friend n tomodachi 友達 93

from kara から 15

front n mae (no) 前（の）144；omote 表 23

fruit n kudamono 果物 56

fruit cocktail n furūtsu sarada フルーツサラダ 57

fruit juice n furūtsu jūsu フルーツジュース 41, 43

full ippai (no) 一杯（の）14

full board san-shoku tsuki 三食付 24

full insurance n zenbu hoken 全部保険 20

furniture n kagu 家具 84, 117

furrier's n kegawaya 毛皮屋 99

G

game n gēmu ゲーム 128；*(food)* ryōchōjū no niku 猟鳥獣の肉 52

garage n shūrikōjō 修理工場 79

garden n niwa 庭 86

gardens n teien 庭園 82

garlic n ninniku にんにく 55

gas n gasu ガス 126, 155

gasoline n gasorin ガソリン 76, 79

gastritis n ien 胃炎 141

gate n mon 門 82

gauze n gāze ガーゼ 107

geisha n geisha 芸者 90

gem n hōseki 宝石 121

general delivery n kyokudome yūbin 局留郵便 133

general practitioner n ippan-i 一般医 136

genitals n seishokuki 生殖器 137

gentleman n shinshi 紳士 154

German *(language)* doitsugo ドイツ語 16, 104

Germany n doitsu ドイツ 145

get off, to oriru おりる 75

get up, to okiru 起る 143

gift n okurimono 贈物 17

gin n jin ジン 60

gin and tonic n jin tonikku ジントニック 60

ginger n shōga しょうが 55

girdle n gādoru ガードル 111

girl n onna no ko 女の子 110

girlfriend n gārufurendo ガールフレンド 94

give, to ataeru 与る 13

gland n sen 腺 137

glass n garasu ガラス 122；*(drinking)* koppu コップ, gurasu グラス 41, 63；hai, pai, bai 杯 59, 60

glasses n megane 眼鏡 123

glove n tebukuro 手袋 111

glue n nori 糊 105

go, to iku 行く 13, 21, 75

gold n kin 金 121, 122

golden kin iro 金色 114

gold plate n kin mekki 金めっき 122

golf n gorufu ゴルフ 92

golf course n gorufu kōsu ゴルフコース 92

good yoi 良い 14, 100, 101

good afternoon konnichiwa 今日は 10

good-bye sayōnara さようなら 10

good evening konbanwa 今晩は 10

good morning ohayō gozaimasu おはようございます 10

good night oyasumi nasai お休みなさい 10

go out, to dekakeru 出かける 29, 96

gram n guramu グラム 120

grammar n bunpō 文法 158

grape n budō ぶどう 56

grapefruit n gurēpu furūtsu グレープフルーツ 56

grapefruit juice n gurēpu furūtsu jūsu グレープフルーツジュース 43, 60

gray hai iro 灰色 114

graze n kasurikizu かすり傷 138

greasy yusei 油性 109

Great Britain n igirisu イギリス 134, 145；eikoku 英国 134

Greece n girisha ギリシア 145

green midori iro 緑色 114

green bean n sayaingen 莢いんげん 54

greengrocer's n yaoya 八百屋 99

green tea n ryoku cha 緑茶 61

grey hai iro 灰色 114

grilled yaita 焼いた 48, 51

grocery n shokuryōhinten 食料品店 99, 120

group n dantai 団体 83

guide n gaido ガイド 82

guidebook n annaisho 案内書 83 ; gaido bukku ガイドブック 104

gum (teeth) n haguki 歯茎 144

gurnet n hôbô ほうぼう 48

gynaecologist n fujinka 婦人科 136

H

hair n kami 髪 109

hairbrush n heâ burashi ヘアーブラシ 109

haircut n katto カット 31

hairdresser's n rihatsushitsu 理髪室 28, 31

hair dryer n heâ doraiyâ ヘアードライヤー 118

hairgrip n pin dome ピン止め 109

hair lotion n heâ rôshon ヘアーローション 109

hair slide n kamidome 髪止め 109

hairspray n heâ supurê ヘアースプレー 31, 109

half n hanbun 半分 148

half an hour sanju-ppun 三十分, hanji-kan 半時間 152

half board chôshoku to yûshoku tsuki 朝食と夕食付 24

half price (ticket) hangaku 半額 70

halibut n ohyô おひょう 47

hall porter n hôru pôtâ ホールポーター 26

ham n hamu ハム 43,45,50,120

ham and eggs n hamu eggu ハムエッグ 43

hand n te 手 137

handbag n handobaggu ハンドバッグ 111,155

hand cream n hando kurimu ハンドクリーム 108

handicrafts n shukôgeihin 手工芸品 84

handicrafts shop n shukôgeihinten 手工芸品店 99

handkerchief n hankachîfu ハンカチーフ 111

handmade tezukuri (no) 手作り (の) 110

hanger n hangâ ハンガー 27

harbour n minato 港 75,82

hard katai 固い 43 ; hâdo (na) ハード (な) 123

hard-boiled (egg) kata yude 固ゆで 43

hardware store n kanamonoya 金物屋 99

hat n bôshi 帽子 111

have, to motsu 持つ 130

hay fever n karekusa netsu 枯草熱 106 ; kafunshô 花粉症 106,140

hazelnut n hêzerunattsu ヘーゼルナッツ 56

head n atama 頭 137

headache n zutsû 頭痛 106,140

headphone n heddohôn ヘッドホーン 118

head waiter n chîfu チーフ 63

health food shop n kenkô shokuhinten 健康食品店 99

health insurance n kenkôhoken 健康保険 143

health insurance form n kenkôhoken no yôshi 健康保険の用紙 143

heart n shinzô 心臓 137

heart attack n shinzô hossa 心臓発作 140

heating n danbô sôchi 暖房装置 24,29

heavy omoi 重い 14,101

heel n hîru ヒール 116

helicopter n herikoputâ ヘリコプター 80

hello! (phone) moshi moshi もしもし 135

help n tasuke 助け 155

help! tasukete 助けて 155

help, to tetsudau 手伝う 12,72 ; (one-self) jibunde suru 自分でする 120

herbal remedies n kanpôyaku 漢方薬 106

herbal tea n hâbutî ハーブティー 107

here koko ここ 14,16

herring n nishin にしん 45,48

high ue (no) 上 (の) 25 ; takai 高い 140

hill n oka 丘 86

hire, to kariru 借りる 20,80,92 ; (per-son) tanomu 頼む 82

history n rekishi 歴史 84

hitchhiking n hitchi haiku ヒッチハイク 80

hole n ana 穴 30

holiday n kyûjitsu 休日 151

holidays n kyûka 休暇 16,93,151

holiday village n kyûka mura 休暇村 32

Holland n oranda オランダ 145

home address n genjûsho 現住所 26

homoeopathic remedies n doshuryô-hôyaku 同種療法薬 106

honey n hachimitsu 蜂蜜 43

hope, to nozomu 望む 95

hors d'oeuvre n ôdoburu オードブル 45

horse racing n keiba 競馬 91

hospital n byôin 病院 141,143

hot atsui 熱い 14,40,43 ; (weather) atsui 暑い 14

hotel n hoteru ホテル 19,21,22,66,81

DICTIONARY

hotel guide n hoteru gaido ホテルガイド 19

hotel reservation n hoteru (no) yoyaku ホテル（の）予約 19

hot spring n onsen 温泉 86

hot water n (o) yu （お）湯 24,29,43

hot-water bottle n yutanpo 湯たんぽ 27

hour n jikan 時間 29,81,152

house n ie 家 86

housewares n kateiyōhin 家庭用品 117

how dōyatte どうやって, dorekurai どれ位 11

how far dorekurai no kyori どれ位の距離 11

how long dorekurai no jikan どれ位の時間 11

how many ikutsu いくつ 11

how much dorehodo どれほど, ikura いくら 11

humid shikke ga aru 湿気がある 95

hundred hyaku 百 147

hungry, to be onaka ga suiteiru おなかがすいている 13,38

hurry (to be in a) isoideiru 急いでいる 21,40

hurt, to kega o suru けがをする 138 ; itamu 痛む 138,144

husband n (your own) shujin 主人 93,94,110 ; (someone else's) go-shujin 御主人

hydrofoil n suichūyokusen 水中翼船 77

I

ice n kōri 氷 27

ice cream n aisukurimu アイスクリーム 57

ill byōki de 病気で 13,155

illness n byōki 病気 139

Imperial palace n kōkyo 皇居 84

import n yunyū 輸入 131

important taisetsu (na) 大切（な）13

imported yunyū hin 輸入品 110

India n indo インド 145

India ink n sumi 墨 105

Indian indo (no) インド（の）38

indigestion n shōkafuryō 消化不良 140

Indonesia n indoneshia インドネシア 145

inexpensive yasui 安い 38,124

infect, to kanōsuru 化膿する 139

inflammation n enshō 炎症 141

inflation n infure インフレ 131

inflation rate n infure jōshōritsu インフレ上昇率 131

information n annai 案内 67

information desk n annai gakari 案内係 117

information office n annaijo 案内所 68,75

injection n chūsha 注射 141,143

injured kega o shiteiru けがをしている 138

ink n inku インク 105

inquiry n annai 案内 68

insect bite n mushi sasare 虫刺され 106,138

insect repellent n bōchūzai 防虫剤 107

insect spray n bōchū supurē 防虫スプレー 107

inside no naka ni の中に 15

instead kawari ni 代りに 42

instrumental music n kigaku 器楽 128

insurance n hoken 保険 20

interest (money) n rishi 利子 131

interested, to be kyōmi o motteiru 興味を持っている 84

interesting omoshiroi 面白い 85

international kokusai (teki) 国際（的）134

international call n kokusai tsūwa 国際通話 134

interpreter n tsūyaku 通訳 131

introduce, to shōkai suru 紹介する 93

introduction n shōkai(jō) 紹介（状）93,130

investment n tōshi 投資 131

invitation n shōtai 招待 95

invite, to shōtai suru 招待する 95

invoice n seikyūsho 請求書 131

iodine n yōdochinki ヨードチンキ 107

Ireland n airurando アイルランド 145

Irish (person) airurando jin アイルランド人 94

iron (laundry) n airon アイロン 118

iron, to airon o kakeru アイロンをかける 30

ironmonger's n kanamonoya 金物屋 99

island n shima 島 86

Israel n isuraeru イスラエル 145

Italian itaria (no) イタリア（の）38,59

Italy n itari イタリー 145

ivory n zōge 象牙 122

J

jacket n jaketto ジャケット 111

jade n hisui 翡翠 122

jam n jamu ジャム 43,120

jam, to ugokanai 動かない 29,125

January n ichigatsu 一月 150

Japan n nippon, nihon 日本 145
Japanese nihon (no) 日本 (の) 41,59;
  (language) nihongo (no) 日本語 (の)
  11,26,104
Japanese garden n nihon teien 日本庭
  園 84
Japanese-style wafū (no) 和風 (の) 43
jar n bin びん 120
jaundice n ōdan 黄胆 141
jaw n ago 顎 137
jazz n jazu ジャズ 128
jazz club n jazu kurabu ジャズクラブ
  90
jeans n jīpan ジーパン 111
jewel box n hōsekibako 宝石箱 121
jeweller's n hōsekiten 宝石店 98,121
jewellery n hōseki 宝石 117,121
joint n kansetsu 関節 137
journalist n jānarisuto ジャーナリスト
  95
journey n ryokō 旅行 153
judo n jūdō 柔道 91
juice n jūsu ジュース 41,43,61
July n shichigatsu 七月 150
June n rokugatsu 六月 150
just (only) chotto ちょっと 16

K

kabuki n kabuki 歌舞伎 88
kabuki theatre n kabukiza 歌舞伎座 82
karate n karate 空手 91
keep, to (store) azukaru 預かる 32
key n kagi 鍵 27
kidney n jinzō 腎臓 50,137
kilo(gram) n kiro(guramu) キロ (グラ
  ム) 120
kilometre n kiro(mētoru) キロ (メート
  ル) 20,79
kimono n kimono 着物 111,127
kind shinsetsu 親切 95
kind (type) n shurui 種類 122
kiosk n kiyosuku キヨスク 99,126
kite n tako たこ 127
knee n hiza 膝 137
knife n naifu ナイフ 41,63
know, to shiru 知る 112; wakaru わか
  る 16,25
Korea n kankoku 韓国 145
Korean kankoku (no) 韓国 (の) 38

L

label n fuda 符 105
lace n rēsu レース 115
lacquerware n shikki 塗器 85,127
lady n fujin 婦人 154
lake n mizuumi 湖 86

lamb n kohitsuji (no niku) 小羊 (の肉)
  50
lamp n ranpu ランプ 30,118
landscape n keshiki 景色 94
lantern n chōchin ちょうちん 127
lap computer n pōtaburu konpyūtā ポー
  タブルコンピューター 118
large ōkii 大きい 101,116
laser disc n rēzā disuku レーザーディ
  スク 118,128
last saigo (no) 最後(の) 14; (train,
  etc.) (sai) shū (最) 終 68,73,74;
  (week, etc.) sen- 先- 150,151
last, to kakaru かかる 88
late osoi 遅い 14
late, to be okureteiru 遅れている 73
launderette n koinrandori コインランド
  リー 99
laundry n (place) sentakuya 洗濯屋 30;
  (clothes) sentaku mono 洗濯物 30
laundry service n sentaku sābisu 洗濯サ
  ービス 24
laxative n gezai 下剤 107
leap year n urūdoshi 閏年 149
leather n kawa 皮, rezā レザー 115
leave, to deru 出る 69,75; tatsu たつ
  32; (deposit) azukeru 預ける 27,72
leek n negi ねぎ 54
left hidari 左 21
left-luggage office n (te)nimotsu ichiji
  azukarijo (手) 荷物一時預り所 68,
  72
leg n ashi 足 137
lemon n remon レモン 41,43,56,61
lemon juice n remon sukasshu レモンス
  カッシュ 61
lemonade n remonēdo レモネード 61
lend, to kasu 貸す 131
lens n renzu レンズ 123,125
lens cap n renzu kyappu レンズキャッ
  プ 125
lentil n renzumame レンズ豆 54
less motto sukunaku もっと少なく 14
letter n tegami 手紙 29,132
letter box n yūbinbako 郵便箱 132
letter of credit n shin-yōjō 信用状
  130
letter telegram n shoshin denpō 書信電
  報 133
library n toshokan 図書館 82,99
licence (permit) n menkyo 免許 20
lie down, to yoko ni naru 横になる 141
life belt n kyūmei beruto 救命ベルト
  75
life boat n kyūmei bōto 救命ボート 75
lift n erebētā エレベーター 28,117

light karui 軽い 14,101 ; *(colour)* iro no usui 色の薄い 101 ; akarui 明るい 114

light n *(electric)* dentō 電灯 29 ; *(cigarette)* hi 火 96

lighter n raitā ライター 121,126

lighter fluid n raitā yō oiru ライター用オイル 126

lighter gas n raitā yō gasu ライター用ガス 126

light meter n raito mētā ライトメーター 125

light music n kei ongaku 軽音楽 128

like, to suku 好く 94 ; kiniiru 気に入る 25,94 ; *(want)* hossuru 欲する 13, 20,23 ; *(ga)* iidesu (が) いいです 110

line n sen 線 73

linen (cloth) n rinneru リンネル, asa 麻 115

lingerie n shitagi 下着 111

lip n kuchibiru 唇 137

lipsalve n rippu kurimu リップクリーム 108

lipstick n kuchibeni 口紅 108

liqueur n rikyūru リキュール 60

liquor store n sakaya 酒屋 99

listen, to kiku 聞く 128

litre n rittoru リットル 76,120

little sukunai 少ない 77 ; *(a)* sukoshi (no) 少し (の) 14

live, to ikiru 生きる 85 ; *(reside)* sumu 住む 93

liver n kanzō 肝臓 50,137

loan n rōn ローン 131

lobster n ise-ebi 伊勢エビ 45,47

local train n futsū (ressha) 普通 (列車) 67

locker n rokkā ロッカー 18,68,72

long nagai 長い 63,113

long-sighted enshi 遠視 123

look, to miru 見る 100,138

look for, to sagasu 探す 13

look out! ki o tsukete 気をつけて 155

loose yurui ゆるい 113

lose, to nakusu なくす 123,144,155 ; *(one's way)* (michi ni) mayou (道に) 迷う 13,155

loss n songai 損害 131

lost and found office n ishitsubutsu toriatsukaijo 遺失物取扱い所 68,155

lost property n ishitsubutsu 遺失物 155

lost property office n ishitsubutsu toriatsukaijo 遺失物取扱い所 68,155

lot (a) takusan (no) 沢山 (の) 14

lotion n rōshon ローション 108

lotus n renkon れんこん 54

loud *(voice)* ōkii koe de 大きい声で 135

low hikui 低い 140 ; shita (no) 下 (の) 25

luck n kōun 幸運 153

luggage n (te)nimotsu (手) 荷物 18, 26,32,72

luggage claim n (te)nimotsu uketori (手) 荷物受取 18

luggage locker n (te)nimotsu yō rokkā (手) 荷物用ロッカー 18,68,72

luggage trolley n (te)nimotsu yō kāto (手) 荷物用カート 18,72

lump *(bump)* n kobu 138

lunch n chūshoku 昼食 38,81

lung n hai 肺 137

M

mackerel n saba さば 45,47

magazine n zasshi 雑誌 105

maid n meido メイド 26

mail n yūbin 郵便 133

mail, to yūsō suru 郵送する 28

mail box n yūbinbako 郵便箱 132

main shuyō na 主要な 100

make, to tsukuru 作る 107 ; yōi suru 用意する 71

make-up remover pad n keshōotoshi yō paddo 化粧落し用パッド 108

man n dansei 男性 110

manager n shihainin 支配人 26

manicure n manikyua マニキュア 31

many takusan (no) 沢山 (の) 14

map n chizu 地図 77,105

March n sangatsu 三月 150

marinated tsukejiru ni tsuketa 漬け汁に付けた 48

market n ichiba 市場 82,99

marmalade n māmarēdo マーマレード 43

married kekkon shiteiru 結婚している 95

mask n men 面 127

mass *(church)* n reihai 礼拝 85

massage n massāji マッサージ 31

match n matchi マッチ 120,126 ; *(sport)* shiai 試合 91

match, to au 合う 114

matinée n hiru no bu 昼の部 89

mauve fuji iro 藤色 114

May n gogatsu 五月 150

meadow n bokujō 牧場 86

meal n shokuji 食事 24

mean, to imi suru 意味する 11,26

measles n hashika はしか 141

measure, to hakaru 計る 112

meat n niku 肉 40,42,50

mechanic n shûrikô 修理工 79

mechanical pencil n shâpu penshiru シャープペンシル 105

medical certificate n shindan shômei(sho) 診断証明(書) 143

medicine n (drug) kusuri 薬 142

medium (meat) n futsû (no) 普通 (の), midiamu ミディアム 51

meet, to au 会う 96

melon n meron メロン 45,56

mend, to shûri suru 修理する 76; (clothes) tsukurou 繕う 30

menthol (cigarettes)n hakka ハッカ, mensôru メンソール 126

menu n menyû メニュー 40,44

message n kotozuke 言付 29; dengon 伝言 135

metre n mêtoru メートル 115

mezzanine (theatre) n nikai 二階 89

middle mannaka (no) 真中 (の) 89

middle (of month) chûjun 中旬 150

midnight n gozen reiji 午前零時 151

milk n miruku ミルク 43,60,61

milkshake n miruku sêki ミルクセーキ 61

milliard n jû-oku 十億 148

million n hyaku-man 百万 148

mind, to kamau かまう 96

mineral water n mineraru wôtâ ミネラルウォーター 61

miniature television (set) n chôkogata terebi 超小型テレビ 119

minute n fun, pun 分 152

mirror n kagami 鏡 113,123

Miss n san さん 10,93

missing (to be) (tari)nai (足り)ない 30,63

mistake n machigai 間違い 62,102

moccasin n mokashin モカシン 116

modern kindai (teki) 近代 (的) 84; gendai 現代 128

modified American plan n chôshoku to yûshoku tsuki 朝食と夕食付 24

moisturizing cream n moisuchâraijingu kurîmu モイスチャーライジングクリーム 108

monastery n sôin 僧院 82

Monday n getsuyôbi 月曜日 150

money n (o)kane (お)金 18,129,130

month n tsuki, gatsu, getsu 月 16,149, 150

monument n kinenhi 記念碑 82

moon n tsuki 月 7

moped n môtâ tsuki jitensha モーター付自転車 80

more motto (ôku) もっと (多く) 14

morning n asa 朝 151

mortgage n tanpo 担保 131

mosque n kaikyô jiin 回教寺院 85

mother n (your own) haha 母 94; (someone else's) o-kâ san お母さん

motorbike n môtâ baiku モーターバイク 80

motorway n kôsoku dôro 高速道路 77

mountain n yama 山 7,23,86

moustache n kuchi hige 口ひげ 31

mouth n kuchi 口 137

mouthwash n ugaigusuri うがい薬 107

move, to ugoku 動く 138

movie camera n satsueiki 撮影機 124

movie n eiga 映画 87,96

Mr./Mrs. n san さん 10,93

much takusan (no) 沢山 (の) 14

mullet n bora ぼら 48

muscle n kinniku 筋肉 137

museum n hakubutsukan 博物館, bijutsukan 美術館 82

mushroom n masshurûmu マッシュルーム 45,54

music n ongaku 音楽 128

music box n orugôru オルゴール 127

must (have to) nakute wa ikenai なくてはいけない 17,24

mustard n karashi 辛子 120

mutton n maton マトン 50

my wata(ku)shi no 私の 16,18,20,26

N

nail (human) n tsume 爪 108

nail brush n tsume burashi 爪ブラシ 108

nail clippers n tsumekiri 爪切り 108

nail file n tsumeyasuri 爪やすり 108

nail polish n manikyua マニキア 108

nail scissors n tsumekiribasami 爪切りばさみ 108

name n namae 名前 23,26,93

napkinn napukin ナプキン 41,105, 120

nappy n omutsu おむつ 109

narrow kitsui きつい 116

national kokuritsu 国立 83,84,87

nationality n kokuseki 国籍 26,94

National Museum n kokuritsu bijutsukan 国立美術館 84

National Theatre n kokuritsu gekijô 国立劇場 83,87

nauseous hakike 吐気 139

near chikai 近い 14; chikaku 近く 19

nearby chikaku ni 近くに 78,85

nearest moyori no 最寄りの 79,98,104

neat (drink) sutorêto ストレート 60

neck n kubi 首 50,137 ; (nape) erikubi えり首 31
necklace n nekkuresu ネックレス 121
nectarine n nekutarin ネクタリン 56
need, to iru 要る 13,30
needle n hari 針 27
negative n nega ネガ 125
nerve n shinkei 神経 137
nervous system n shinkei keitō 神経系統 137
never kesshite...nai 決して…ない 15
new atarashii 新しい 14
newspaper n shinbun 新聞 104
newsstand n shinbun uriba 新聞売場 68,99,104
New Zealand n nyūjirando ニュージーランド 145
next tsugi no 次の 14,65,68,73,74 ; (week, etc.) rai- 来- 150,151
next to (no) tonari (ni) (の)となり(に) 15,78
nice (beautiful) ii いい 95
night n yoru 夜 151
nightclub n naito kurabu ナイトクラブ 89,90
night cream n naito kurimu ナイトクリーム 108
nightdress n nemaki 寝間着 111
nine kyū, ku 九 146
nineteen jū-kyū 十九 146
ninety kyū-jū 九十 147
ninth kyūban 九番 148
no iie いいえ 10
noh n nō 能 88
noisy urusai うるさい 25
nonalcoholic arukōru no hairanai アルコールの入らない 58,60
none hitotsu mo nai 一つもない 15
nonsmoker n kin-en sha 禁煙者 70
nonsmoking kin-en 禁煙 39,70
noodle n men めん 40,53
noon hiru 昼 32 ; (12 a.m.) shōgo 正午 151
north n kita 北 78
North America n hokubei 北米 145
Norway n noruē ノルウェー 145
nose n hana 鼻 137
nosebleed n hanaji 鼻血 140
nose drops n hanagusuri 鼻薬 107
not nai ない 15
note (banknote) n shihei 紙幣 130
notebook n nōto ノート 105
nothing nani mo nai なにもない 15,17
notice (sign) n hyōji 標示 154
novel n shōsetsu 小説 104
November n jū-ichigatsu 十一月 150

now ima 今 15
number n bangō 番号 26,134,135 ; (numeral) sūji 数字 146
nurse n kangofu 看護婦 143

O

observatory n tenmondai 天文台 82
occupied shiyōchū 使用中 14,154
o'clock ji 時 39,71,151
October n jūgatsu 十月 150
octopus n tako たこ 48
off-licence n sakaya 酒屋 99
office n ofuisu オフィス 95
oil n oiru オイル 41,76,109
oily (greasy) yusei 油性 109
old furui 古い 14 ; (person) toshitotteiru 年とっている 14
olive n oribu オリーブ 45
omelet n omuretsu オムレツ 46
on no ue (ni) の上(に) 15
once ichido 一度 148
one ichi 一 146
oneway (ticket) katamichi 片道 65,70 ; (street) ippō tsūkō 一方通行 78,80
on foot aruite 歩いて 77
onion n tamanegi 玉ねぎ 54
only dake だけ 15,25
onyx n onikkusu オニックス 122
open aiteiru 開いている 14,83,106
open, to aku 開く 11,83,106,132 ; (account) hiraku 開く 130
open-air museum n yagai bijutsukan 野外美術館 82
opera n opera オペラ 87
operation n shujutsu 手術 143
operator n kōkanshu 交換手 26,134,135
opposite hantai (no) 反対 (の) 78
optician n meganeya 眼鏡屋 99,123
or aruiwa あるいは 15
orange orenji (iro) オレンジ (色) 114
orange n orenji オレンジ 56
orange juice n orenji jūsu オレンジジュース 43,61
orchestra n ōkesutora オーケストラ 87 ; (seats) ōkesutora bokkusu オーケストラボックス 89
orchestral music n kangen gaku 管弦楽 128
order, to chūmon suru 注文する 42,63,102
ordinary futsū (no) 普通 (の) 133
origami paper n origami 折り紙 105,127
original genkei (no) 原形 (の) 85
ornithology n chōruigaku 鳥類学 84

other hoka (no) 他 (の) 101
outlet (electric) n soketto ソケット 27
outside (no) soto (ni) (の) 外 (に) 15
oval daenkei no だ円形の 101
overalls n ōbāōru オーバーオール 111
overdone yakesugi 焼けすぎ 63
overheat, to (engine) ōbāhīto suru オーバーヒートする 78
overnight (stay) hitoban 一晩 25
overtake, to oikosu 追い越す 80
owe, to ikura いくら 143
oxtail n okkusutēru オックステール 50
oyster n kaki かき 45,47

P

pacifier n oshaburi おしゃぶり 109
packet n pakku パック 120 ; hako 箱 126
pad n paddo パッド 108
page (hotel) n bōi ボーイ 26
pagoda n tō 塔 84
pain n itami 痛み 140,143
painkiller n chintsūzai 鎮痛剤 107,143
paint n penki ペンキ 154
paint, to kaku 描く 85
paintbox n enogu 絵具 105
paintbrush n efude 絵筆 105
painted screen n byōbu 屏風 127
painter n gaka 画家 85
painting n kaiga 絵画 84
pair n kumi 組 148 ; tsui 対 111
palace n kyūden 宮殿 83
palpitation n dōki 動悸 140
pancake n pankēki パンケーキ 64
panties n panti パンティー 111
pants (trousers) n zubon ズボン 111
panty hose n panti sutokkingu パンティーストッキング 111
paper n kami 紙 105
paperback n bunko-bon 文庫本 104
paperclip n kamibasami 紙ばさみ 105
paper napkin n kami napukin 紙ナプキン 105
paper products n kamiseihin 紙製品 127
parcel n kozutsumi 小包 29, 133
park n kōen 公園 83
park, to chūsha suru 駐車する 26,78
parking meter n pākingu mētā パーキングメーター 78
parliament building n kokkai gijidō 国会議事堂 83
party (social gathering) n pātī パーティー 95
pass, to (car) oikosu 追い越す 80
passport n pasupōto パスポート 16, 155

passport number n pasupōto bangō パスポート番号 26
passport photo n pasupōto yō no shashin パスポート用の写真 124
pass through, to tachiyoru 立ち寄る 16
paste (glue) n nori 糊 105
pastry n pesutorī ペストリー 64
pastry shop n kēkiya ケーキ屋 99
patch, to (clothes) tsugiate suru つぎあてする 30
path n komichi 小道 86
patient n kanja 患者 143
pay, to harau 払う 17,62,102,135
payment n shiharai 支払い 131
pea n endōmame えんどう豆 54
peach n momo 桃 56,120
peak n mine 峰 86
peanut n pīnattsu ピーナッツ 56
pear n nashi なし 55
pearl n shinju 真珠 121,122,127
pedestrian n hokōsha 歩行者 80
pen n pen ペン 105
pencil n enpitsu 鉛筆 105
pencil sharpener n enpitsu kezuri 鉛筆けずり 105
pendant n pendanto ペンダント 121
penicillin n penishirin ペニシリン 142
people (inhabitants) n hitobito 人々 94
pepper n koshō 胡椒 41,43
per cent n pāsento パーセント 148
percentage n ritsu 率 131
per day ichi-nichi 一日 20,92
performance n kōen 公演 88
perfume n kōsui 香水 108
perhaps tabun たぶん 15
per hour ichi-jikan 一時間 78,92
period (monthly) n seiri 生理 140
period pains n seiritsū 生理痛 140
permanent wave n pāma パーマ 31
per night i-ppaku 一泊 24
personal call n shimei tsūwa 指名通話 134
personal cheque n ginkō kogitte 銀行小切手 130
person-to-person call n shimei tsūwa 指名通話 134
per week isshū kan 一週間 20,24
petrol n gasorin ガソリン 76,79
pewter n pyūtā ピューター 122
pharmacy n kusuriya 薬屋 99 ; yakkyoku 薬局 106
pheasant n kiji きじ 52
Philippines n firipin フィリピン 145
photo n shashin 写真 83,124
photocopy n kopī コピー 28

photographer n shashinya 写真屋, kamera man カメラマン 99

photogenic equipment n shashin yōhin 写真用品 117

photography n shashin (jutsu) 写真 (術) 124

phrase n iimawashi 言いまわし 12

pick up, to (person) mukae ni yuku 迎えに行く 81

picnic n pikunikku ピクニック 64

picture n e 絵 85 ; (photo) shashin 写真 83

picture postcard n ehagaki 絵葉書 105

pier n futō 埠頭 75

pigeon n hato はと 52

pike n kamasu かます 47

pill (contraceptive) n hinin yaku 避妊薬 107,140

pillow n makura 枕 27

pin n pin ピン 122

pine n matsu 松 86

pineapple n painappuru パイナップル 56

pink pinku ピンク 114

pipe n paipu パイプ 126

pipe cleaner n paipu kurinā パイプクリーナー 126

pipe tobacco n paipu tabako パイプタバコ 126

pipe tool n paipu yō kigu パイプ用器具 126

place n basho 場所, tokoro 所 77

place of birth n shusshōchi 出生地 26

plane n hikōki 飛行機 65

plaster (cast) n gibusu ギプス 139

plate n sara 皿 41,63

platform (station) n (puratto)hōmu (プラット) ホーム 68,69,71

platinum n purachina プラチナ 122

play (theatre) n shibai 芝居 87

play, to yaru やる 87,88 ; (music) ensō suru 演奏する 87

playing cards n toranpu トランプ 105

please dōzo どうぞ, o-negai shimasu お願いします 10 ; kudasai 下さい 12

Plimsolls n sunikā スニーカー 118

plug (electric) n sashikomi 差し込み 30 ; puragu プラグ 119

plum n puramu プラム 56

pneumonia n haien 肺炎 141

poached karuku yudeta 軽くゆでた 48

pocket n poketto ポケット 112

pocket calculator n poketto keisanki ポケット計算機 119

pocket copier n poketto kopī ポケットコピー 119

pocket dictonary n poketto jisho ポケット辞書 104

point, to (show) yubisasu 指さす 12

poison n doku 毒 107,155

police n keisatsu 警察 79,155

police station n kōban 交番 155

pond n ike 池 86

pop music n poppu myūjikku ポップミュージック 128

poplin n popurin ポプリン 115

porcelain n jiki 磁器 127

pork n butaniku 豚肉 40,50,51

port n minato 港 75 ; (wine) pōtowain ポートワイン 60

portable pōtaburu ポータブル 119

porter n pōtā ポーター 18,26,72 ; akabō 赤帽 18,72

Portugal n porutogaru ポルトガル 145

possible dekiru 出来る 136

post (letters) n yūbin 郵便 133

post, to yūsō suru 郵送する 28

postage stamp n kitte 切手 28,132

postcard n hagaki 葉書 105,132

poste restante n kyokudome yūbin 局留郵便 133

post office n yūbin kyoku 郵便局 132

potato n jagaimo じゃがいも 54

pottery n tōki 陶器 85,127

poultry n kakin 家禽 52

pound (money) n pondo ポンド 18,102, 129,130

powder n oshiroi おしろい 108

prawn n kuruma-ebi 車エビ 45,47

pregnant ninshin 妊娠 140

premium (gasoline) sūpā スーパー 76

prepare, to yōi suru 用意する 29

prescribe, to shohō suru 処方する 142

prescription n shohōsen 処方箋 107, 142

present n okurimono 贈物 17,121

press, to (iron) puresu suru プレスする 30

press stud n sunappu スナップ 112

pressure (tyre) n kūkiatsu 空気圧 76

price n nedan 値段 24,40 ; kakaku 価格 131

print (photo) n purinto プリント 125

printer (computer) n purintā プリンター 119

private kojin (no) 個人 (の) 24,82

private property n shiyūchi 私有地 154

product n seihin 製品 106

profession n shokugyō 職業 26

profit n rieki 利益 131

programme n puroguramu プログラム 89

pronunciation n hatsuon 発音 8
propelling pencil n shāpu penshiru シャープペンシル 105
Protestant purotesutanto プロテスタント 85
provide, to tsukeru 付ける 131
prune n hoshi sumomo 干すも 56
public paburikku パブリック 92
public holiday n shukusai jitsu 祝祭日 153
public lodge n kokumin shukusha 国民宿舎 32
pull, to hiku 引く 154
pullover n puru ōbā プルオーバー 111
pumpkin n kabocha かぼちゃ 54
puncture n panku パンク 76
purchase n kōnyū 購入 131
pure jun (sui na) 純 (粋な) 115
purple murasaki iro 紫色 114
push, to osu 押す 154
put, to ireru 入れる 24
pyjamas n pajama パジャマ 111

Q

quail n uzura うずら 52
quality n (hin)shitsu (品)質 101, 115
quantity n ryō 量 14
quarter n yonbun no ichi 四分の一 148
question n shitsumon 質問 11
quick hayai 速い 14
quickly hayaku 速く 40, 80, 155
quiet shizuka (na) 静か (な) 24, 25

R

racket (sport) n raketto ラケット 92
radiator (car) n rajiētā ラジエーター 79
radio n rajio ラジオ 24, 29, 119
radio cassette recorder n rajio kasetto kōdā ラジオカセットコーダー 119
radish n radisshu ラディッシュ 45, 54
railway n tetsudō 鉄道 67
railway station n (tetsudō no) eki (鉄道の) 駅 67, 71
rain n ame 雨 95
rain, to ame ga furu 雨が降る 95
rainboot n reinbūtsu レインブーツ 116
raincoat n reinkōto レインコート 111
raisin n hoshi budō 干しぶどう 56
rangefinder n renji faindā レンジファインダー 125
rare (meat) nama yake (no) 生焼け (の) 51, 63 ; reā レアー 51
rash n hasshin 発疹 143
raspberry n kiichigo 木いちご, razuberī ラズベリー 56
rate (price) n ryōkin 料金 20

raw (uncooked) nama (no) 生 (の) 40, 45, 48
razor n kamisori かみそり 109
razor blade n kamisori no ha かみそりの刃 109
read, to yomu 読む 26
reading-lamp n sutando スタンド 27
ready, to be deki(aga)ru でき (あが)る 30, 40, 116, 119, 123, 144
real hontō (no) 本当 (の) 121
receipt n ryōshūsho 領収書 102, 143
reception n furonto フロント 23
receptionist n furonto gakari フロント係 26
recommend, to susumeru 勧める 40, 45 ; oshieru 教える 38, 90 ; shōkai suru 紹介する 136, 144
record (disc) n rekōdo レコード 117, 128
record player n rekōdo purēyā レコードプレーヤー 119
record shop n rekōdoten レコード店 99
rectangular chōhōkei (no) 長方形 (の) 101
red aka (i) 赤 (い) 59, 114
reduction n waribiki 割引 24, 83
refill (cartridge) n kātorijji カートリッジ 105
refund n harai modoshi 払い戻し 103
register, to (luggage) chikki ni suru チッキにする 72
registered mail n kakitome 書留 132
registration n tōroku 登録 26
regular (petrol) regyurā レギュラー 76
religion n shūkyō 宗教 85
religious shūkyō (no) 宗教 (の) 84
rent, to kariru 借りる 20, 80, 92
repair, to naosu 直す 30, 116, 123, 144 ; shūri suru 修理する 119, 121, 125
repeat, to mō ichido iu もう一度言う 12, 135
report, to (a theft) (tōnan) todoke o dasu (盗難) 届けを出す 155
reservation n yoyaku 予約 19, 23, 66, 70
reservations office n yoyaku madoguchi 予約窓口 19, 68
reserve, to yoyaku suru 予約する 19, 39, 70, 89
restaurant n resutoran レストラン 33, 38, 39 ; shokudō 食堂 68
return (ticket) ōfuku 往復 65, 70
return, to (give back) kaesu 返す 103
reversed charge call n korekuto kōru コレクトコール 134
rheumatism n ryūmachi リューマチ 140

DICTIONARY

rib n rokkotsu 肋骨 137

rice n gohan ごはん 40,53

right migi 右 21 ; (correct) tadashii 正しい 14

ring (on finger) n yubiwa 指輪 122

ring, to (doorbell) beru o osu ベルを押す 154 ; (phone) denwa (o) suru 電話（を）する 134

river n kawa 川 7,86

road n michi 道 77,86

road map n dōro chizu 道路地図 105

road sign n dōro hyōshiki 道路標識 80

roast beef n rōsuto bīfu ローストビーフ 51

roasted rōsutoshita ローストした 51

rock n iwa 岩 86

rock garden n sekitei 石庭 84

roll n rōru pan ロールパン 43

roll film n maki firumu 巻フィルム 124

roller skate n rōrā sukēto ローラースケート 128

roll-neck tātoru nekku タートルネック 111

room n heya 部屋 19,23,24,25,27,29 ; -shitsu -室 27

room number n heya bangō 部屋番号 26

room service n rūmu sābisu ルームサービス 24

rosary n rozario ロザリオ 121

rosé (wine) rōze ローゼ 59

rouge n kuchibeni 口紅 109

round marui 丸い 101

round (golf) n raundo ラウンド 92

round-neck maru kubi 丸首 111

roundtrip (ticket) ōfuku 往復 65,70

route n kōsu コース 86

rubber (material) gomu ゴム 115 ; (eraser) keshi gomu 消しゴム 105

ruby n rubī ルビー 122

rugby n ragubī ラグビー 91

ruin n iseki 遺跡 83

rum n ramu ラム 60

S

safe n kinko 金庫 27

safety pin n anzenpin 安全ピン 109

sake n sake 酒 41,58

sake cup n shuhai 酒盃 127

salad n sarada サラダ 46,54

salami n sarami サラミ 45

sale n hanbai 販売 131

salmon n sake 鮭 45,47

salt n shio 塩 41,43

salty shio no kiita 塩のきいた 40 ; (shio) karai (塩) 辛い 63

same onaji (no) 同じ（の）116

sandal n sandaru サンダル 116

sandwich n sandoitchi サンドイッチ 64,72

sanitary towel/napkin n seiriyō napukin 生理用ナプキン 107

sapphire n safaia サファイア 122

sardine n iwashi いわし 45,47

satin n saten サテン 115

Saturday n doyōbi 土曜日 150

sauna n sauna サウナ 24

sausage n sōsēji ソーセージ 45,50

scallop n hotate-gai 帆立貝 48

scarf n sukāfu スカーフ 111

scarlet hi iro 緋色 114

scenic keshiki no yoi 景色の良い 86

scissors n hasami はさみ 108,120

scooter n sukūtā スクーター 80

Scotland n sukottorando スコットランド 145

Scottish (person) sukottorando jin スコットランド人 94

scrambled egg n iri tamago いり卵 43

sculptor n chōkokuka 彫刻家 85

sculpture n chōkoku 彫刻 84

sea n umi 海 23,86

sea bass n suzuki すずき 47

sea bream n tai 鯛 48

seafood n gyokai rui 魚介類 40,47

season n kisetsu 季節 149

seasoning n chōmiryō 調味料 55

seat n seki 席 70,71,89

seaweed n nori のり 55

second niban 二番 148

second n byō 秒 152

second-hand book n furu hon 古本 104

secretary n hisho 秘書 27,95,131

see, to miru 見る 12,25,84 ; (meet) au 会う 96

self-service n serufu sābisu セルフサービス 38

sell, to uru 売る 100

send up, to ageru 上げる 26

send, to okuru 送る 29,102,132 ; (telegram) utsu 打つ 133 ; (dispatch) yo-kosu よこす 79

sentence n bun 文 12

separately betsubetsu ni 別々に 62

September n kugatsu 九月 150

service n (charge) sābisuryō サービス料 62 ; (religion) reihai 礼拝 85

serviette n napukin ナプキン 41

set menu n teishoku 定食 40

setting lotion n setto rōshon セットローション 31,109

seven shichi 七 146

seventeen jū-shichi 十七 146

seventh shichiban 七十番 148
seventy nana-jū 七十 147
sew, to nuu 縫う 30
shade *(colour)* n iro 色 114
shampoo n shanpū シャンプー 109
shampoo and set n shanpū setto シャンプーセット 31
share *(finance)* n kabu 株 131
shave, to hige o soru ひげをする 31
shaver n (denki) kamisori （電気）かみそり 27,109,119
shaving cream n higesori yō kurīmu ひげそり用クリーム 109
shelf n tana 棚 120
sherry n sheri シェリー 60
ship n fune 船 75
shirt n waishatsu ワイシャツ 111
shiver n samuke 寒気 39
shoe n kutsu 靴 116,117
shoelace n kutsu himo 靴ひも 116
shoe polish n kutsu migaki 靴みがき 116
shoe repairs n kutsushūri 靴修理 116
shoe shop n kutsuya 靴屋 99
shop n mise 店 99
shopping area n shoppingu gai ショッピング街 83,100
shopping centre n shoppingu sentā ショッピングセンター 99
shop window n (shō)uindō （ショー）ウインドー 100,110
short mijikai 短い 31,113
shorts n shōto pantsu ショートパンツ 111
short-sighted kinshi 近視 123
short story n tanpen shōsetsu 短編小説 104
shoulder n kata 肩 137
show n shō ショー 89
show, to miseru 見せる 12,13,100, 101,103,124 ; shimesu 示す 77
shower n shawā シャワー 23
shrimp n ko-ebi 小エビ 45,47
shrine *(Shintō)* n jinja 神社 83,84
shrink, to chijimu 縮む 115
shut shimatteiru 締っている 14
shutter n *(window)* yoroido よろい戸 30 ; *(camera)* shattā シャッター 125
sick *(ill)* byōki de 病気で 13,155
sickness n byōki 病気 139
side n gawa 側 31
sideboards/burns n hoo hige 頬ひげ 31
sightseeing n kankō 観光 16,81
sightseeing tour n kankō tsuā 観光ツアー 81
sign *(notice)* n hyōji 標示 154
sign, to sain suru サインをする 130

silk n kinu 絹 115,127
silver n gin 銀 121,122
silver *(colour)* gin iro 銀色 114
silver plate n gin mekki 銀めっき 122
silverware n ginki 銀器 122
simple kantan (na) 簡単（な）124
since irai 以来 15 ; kara から 150
single *(not married)* dokushin (no) 独身（の）95 ; *(ticket)* katamichi 片道 65, 70
single room n shinguru rūmu シングルルーム 19,23
sister n shimai 姉妹 94
sit, to suwaru 座る 39,96
six roku 六 146
sixteen jū-roku 十六 146
sixth rokuban 六番 148
sixty roku-jū 六十 147
size n saizu サイズ 112,113,124
ski n suki スキー 92
ski, to suki suru スキーする 92
ski boot n suki gutsu スキー靴 92
skiing n suki スキー 91,92
skiing equipment n suki yōgu スキー用具 92
skin n hifu 皮膚, hada 肌 137
skirt n sukāto スカート 111
sleep, to nemuru 眠る 143
sleeping car n shindai sha 寝台車 69,71
sleeping pill n suimin yaku 睡眠薬 107, 142,143
sleeve n sode 袖 111
slide *(photo)* n suraido スライド 124
slip n surippu スリップ 111
slipper n surippa スリッパ 116
slow osoi 遅い 14
slowly yukkuri (to) ゆっくり（と）12, 21,135
small chīsai 小さい 14,25,101,116
small change n kozeni 小銭 78,130
smoke, to tabako o suu たばこを吸う 96
smoked kunsei ni shita くん製にした 48 ; kunsei no くん製の 45
smoked salmon n sumōku sāmon スモークサーモン 45
smoker n kitsuen sha 喫煙者 70
smoking kitsuen 喫煙 70
snack n sunakku スナック 64
snack bar n sunakku bā スナックバー 34,38,68
snail n katatsumuri かたつむり 45
snap fastener n sunappu スナップ 112
sneakers n sunikā スニーカー 116
snow n yuki 雪 95
snow, to yuki ga furu 雪が降る 95

DICTIONARY

soap *n* sekken 石けん 27,109
soccer *n* sakkā サッカー 91
sock *n* kutsushita 靴下 111
socket *(outlet) n* sokettto ソケット 27
soda water *n* haibōru ハイボール 60
soft-boiled *(egg)* hanjuku 半じゅく 43
sole *n* kutsuzoko 靴底 116；*(fish)* shitabirame 舌平目 47
soloist *n* dokusōsha 独奏者 87
someone dareka 誰か 32,96
something nanika 何か 38,125,138
son *n* musuko むすこ 93
soon sugu ni すぐに 15
sore throat *n* nodo no itami のどの痛み 140
sorry! gomennasai ごめんなさい 11
sort *(kind)* shurui 種類 120
soup *n* sūpu スープ 40,46
south *n* minami 南 78
South Africa *n* minami afurika 南アフリカ 145
South America *n* nan bei 南米 145
souvenir *n* (o) miyage （お）みやげ 127
souvenir shop *n* miyagemonoya みやげ物屋 99
Soviet Union *n* soren ソ連 145
soy sauce *n* shōyu しょう油 41,55
Spain *n* supein スペイン 145
spare tyre supea taiya スペアタイヤ 76
spark(ing) plug *n* tenka puragu 点火プラグ 76
sparrow *n* suzume すずめ 52
speak, to hanasu 話す 11,12,16,135
speaker *(loudspeaker) n* supīkā スピーカー 119
special tokubetsu (na) 特別（な） 20, 41
special delivery sokutatsu 速達 132
specimen *(medical) n* mihon 見本 141
spectacles *n* megane 眼鏡 123
spectacle case *n* megane kēsu 眼鏡ケース 123
spend, to tsukau 使う 101
spice *n* supaisu スパイス 55
spicy kōshinryō ga kiiteiru 香辛料がきいている 40
spinach *n* hōrensō ほうれん草 54
spine *n* sebone 背骨 137
sponge *n* suponji スポンジ 109
spoon *n* supūn スプーン 41,63
sport *n* supōtsu スポーツ 91
sporting goods shop *n* supōtsuyōhinten スポーツ用品店 99
sprain, to kujiku 挫く 139
spring *(season) n* haru 春 149
squab *n* hinabato ひなばと 52

square shikakui 四角い 101
square *(open space) n* hiroba 広場 83
stadium *n* kyōgijō 競技場 83
stain *n* shimi しみ 30
stainless steel *n* sutenresu ステンレス 122
staircase *n* kaidan 階段 117
stalls *(theatre) n* ōkesutora bokkusu オーケストラボックス 89
stamp *(postage) n* kitte 切手 28,132
star *n* hoshi 星 7
start, to hajimeru 始める 89；deru 出る 81；*(engine)* kakaru かかる 79
starter *(appetizer) n* zensai 前菜, ōdoburu オードブル 45
station *(train) n* eki 駅 67,71,73
stationer's *n* bunbōguten 文房具店 99, 104
stationery *n* bunbōgu 文房具 117
statue *n* zō 像 83
stay, to taizai suru 滞在する 16,25, 94；tomaru 泊る 32
steak *n* sutēki ステーキ 50
steal, to nusumu 盗む 155
steamed mushita 蒸した 48
stereo system *n* sutereo sōchi ステレオ装置 119
stew *n* shichū niku シチュー肉 50
stewed shichūnishita シチューにした 51
stiff neck *n* mageru to itai kubi 曲げると痛い首 140
sting *n* sashikizu 刺し傷 138
sting, to sasu 刺す 138
stitch, to *(clothes)* kagaru かがる 30
stock exchange *n* shōken torihikijo 証券取引所 83
stocking *n* sutokkingu ストッキング 111
stomach *n* i 胃 137
stomach ache *n* i no itami 胃の痛み 140
stone *n* ishi 石 86,122
stools *n* ben 便 141
stop *(shop)* store *n* mise 店 99
stop, to tomaru 止まる 21,69；teisha suru 停車する 71；*(arrest)* tsukamaeru つかまえる 155
store *(shop) n* mise 店 99
straight *(drink)* sutorēto ストレート 60
straight ahead massugu 真すぐ 21
strange kimyō (na) 奇妙（な） 85
strawberry *n* ichigo いちご 56
street *n* tōri 通り 21
streetcar *n* shiden 市電 74
street level *n* chijō 地上 73
street map *n* kuwashii chizu 詳しい地図 19

辞書

string *n* himo 紐 105
strong tsuyoi 強い 142
student *n* gakusei 学生 83,95
stuffed tsumemono o shita 詰め物をした 51
subway *(rail)* *n* chikatetsu 地下鉄 73
suede suēdo スエード 115
sufficient jūbun 十分 69
sugar *n* satō 砂糖 41,43
suit *(man)* *n* sebiro 背広 111 ; *(woman)* sūtsu スーツ 112
suitcase *n* sūtsukēsu スーツケース 18
summer *n* natsu 夏 149
sumo *n* sumō 相撲 91
sun *n* taiyō 太陽 7
sunburn *n* hiyake 日焼け 107
Sunday *n* nichiyōbi 日曜日 150
sunglasses *n* sangurasu サングラス 123
sunny hareru 晴れる 95
sunstroke *n* nisshabyō 日射病 140
sun-tan cream *n* santan kurīmu サンタンクリーム 109
sun-tan oil *n* santan oiru サンタンオイル 109
super *(petrol)* sūpā スーパー 76
supermarket *n* sūpāmāketto スーパーマーケット 99,120
suppository *n* zayaku 座薬 108
surgeon *n* gekai 外科医 143
surgery *(consulting room)* shinsatsu shitsu 診察室 136
surname *n* sei 姓 26
suspenders *(Am.)* *n* zubon tsuri ずぼんつり 112
swallow, to nomikomu 飲み込む 107, 142
sweater *n* sētā セーター 112
sweatshirt *n* torēnā トレーナー 112
Sweden *n* suēden スウェーデン 145
sweet amai 甘い 57,59
sweet corn *n* tōmorokoshi とうもろこし 54
sweet shop *n* kashiya 菓子屋 99
swell, to hareru 腫れる 138
swelling *n* haremono 腫物 138
swimming *n* suiei 水泳 91
swimming pool *n* pūru プール 24,92
swimming trunks *n* kaisui pantsu 海水パンツ 112
swimsuit *n* mizugi 水着 112
switch *n* suitchi スイッチ 30
switchboard operator *n* kōkanshu 交換手 26
Switzerland *n* suisu スイス 145
swollen hareteiru 腫れている 138
sword *n* tōken 刀剣 127

swordfish *n* makajiki まかじき 48
synagogue *n* yudaya kyōkai ユダヤ教会 85
synthetic gōsen (no) 合繊 (の) 115

T

table *n* tēburu テーブル 39
tablet *n* jōzai 錠剤 108
tailor's *n* yōfukuya 洋服屋 99
Taiwan *n* taiwan 台湾 145
take, to motsu 持つ 18,102 ; *(bus, etc.)* noru 乗る 73,74
take away, to *(carry)* motte kaeru 持って帰る 64
talcum powder *n* tarukamu paudā タルカムパウダー 109
talk, to hanasu 話す 95
tampon *n* tanpon タンポン 108
tangerine *n* mikan みかん 56
tap *(water)* *n* jaguchi 蛇口 29
tape *n* tēpu テープ 105
tape recorder *n* tēpu rekōdā テープレコーダー 119
taste, to aji ga suru 味がする 63
tax-free menzei 免税 102,117
taxi *n* takushī タクシー 18,21
tea *n* (o)cha (お) 茶 41,61,61 ; *(Indian)* kōcha 紅茶 43,61 ; *(Japanese)* nihon cha 日本茶 41,61
tea bowl/cup *n* chawan 茶碗 127
tea ceremony *n* cha no yu 茶の湯 61
teacher *n* kyōshi 教師 95
teahouse *n* chashitsu 茶室 84
tea pot *n* kyūsu きゅうす 127
telegram *n* denpō 電報 133
telephone *n* denwa 電話 28,79,134
telephone, to denwa suru 電話する 134,135
telephone booth *n* kōshū denwa 公衆電話 134
telephone call *n* denwa 電話 135
telephone card *n* terehon kādo テレホンカード 135
telephone number *n* denwa bangō 電話番号 134
telephoto lens *n* bōen renzu 望遠レンズ 125
television *n* terebi テレビ 24,119
telex *n* terekkusu テレックス 133
telex, to terekkusu o utsu テレックスを打つ 130
tell, to oshieru 教える 12,74,77 ; tsutaeru 伝える 135
temperature *n* *(water)* suion 水温 92 ; *(body)* taion 体温 139,141
temple *(Buddhist)* *n* tera 寺 83,85

ten *n* jū 十 146
tendon *n* ken 腱 137
tennis *n* tenisu テニス 91,92
tennis court *n* tenisu kōto テニスコート 92
tennis racket *n* tenisu raketto ラケット 92
tenth *n* jūban 十番 148
terrace *n* terasu テラス 39
terrifying osoroshii 恐しい 85
tetanus *n* hashōfū 破傷風 139
textile *n* orimono 織物 84
textile shop *n* kijiya 生地屋 99
Thailand *n* taikoku タイ国 145
thank you arigatō gozaimasu ありがとうございます 10
that are あれ 11,100
theatre *n* gekijō 劇場 83,87
theft *n* tōnan 盗難 155
then sonotoki その時, *(after that)* sorekara それから 15
there (a)soko （あ）そこ 14,100
thermometer *n* taionkei 体温計 108,143
thief *n* dorobō 泥棒 155
thigh *n* momo 腿 137
thin usui 薄い 115
think, to omou 思う 102
third sanban 三番 148
third *n* sanbun no ichi 三分の一 148
thirsty nodo ga kawaiteiru のどが乾いている 13,38
thirteen jū-san 十三 146
thirty san-jū 三十 147
this kore これ 11,100
thousand sen 千 147
thread *n* ito 糸 27
three san 三 146
throat *n* nodo 喉 137
throat lozenge *n* nodogusuri 喉薬 108
through o tōshite を通して 15
through train *n* chokutsū ressha 直通列車 68
Thursday *n* mokuyōbi 木曜日 150
ticket *n* kippu 切符 19,65,70,74,89,91
ticket machine *n* kippu hanbaiki 切符販売機 68,70,73
ticket office *n* kippu uriba 切符売場 68
tie *n* nekutai ネクタイ 112
tie clip *n* nekutai dome ネクタイ止め 122
tie pin *n* nekutai pin ネクタイピン 122
tight *(clothes)* kitsui きつい 113
tights *n* panti sutokkingu パンティーストッキング 112
time *n* jikan 時間 69,151; *(occasion)* kai 回 142

timetable *n* jikokuhyō 時刻表 68
tin *(can)* *n* kanzume 缶詰 120
tin opener *n* kankiri 缶切り 120
tinted iro no haitta 色の入った 123
tire *n* taiya タイヤ 76,77,79
tired tsukareteiru 疲れている 13
tire pressure *n* taiya no kūkiatsu タイヤの空気圧 76
tissue *(handkerchief)* *n* tisshu pēpā ティッシュペーパー 109
title *n* taitoru タイトル 104
to *(direction)* e へ 15,18
toast *n* tōsuto トースト 43
tobacco *n* tabako タバコ 126
tobacconist's *n* tabakoya タバコ屋 99,126
today kyō 今日 151
toe *n* ashi no yubi 足の指 137
tofu *n* tōfu 豆腐 55
toilet *(lavatory)* *n* tearai 手洗 24,28; senmenjo 洗面所 28
toilet bag *n* keshōbukuro 化粧袋 109
toilet paper *n* toiretto pēpā トイレットペーパー 109
toiletry *n* keshōhin 化粧品 108
toilet water *n* ōdotoware オードトワレ 109
tomato *n* tomato トマト 54
tomato juice *n* tomato jūsu トマトジュース 61
tomb *n* haka 墓 83
tomorrow asu 明日 30,95,151
tongue *n* shita 舌 50,137
tonic water *n* tonikku wōtā トニックウォーター 61
tonight kon-ya 今夜 30,88,89
tonsil *n* hentōsen 扁桃腺 137
too sugi すぎ 15,113; amari あまり 101; *(also)* mo (mata) も（又）15
tool *n* kigu 器具 126
tooth *n* ha 歯 144
toothache *n* haita 歯痛 107,144
toothbrush *n* haburashi 歯ブラシ 109
toothpaste *n* nerihamigaki ねり歯みがき 109
topaz *n* topāzu トパーズ 122
torn saketeiru 裂けている 139
touch, to fureru 触れる 154
tough *(meat)* katai 固い 63
tour *n* tsuā ツアー 81
tourist information centre *n* kankō annaijo 観光案内所 19,81
tournament *n* kyōgi 競技 91
towards ni (mukatte) に（向って）15
towel *n* taoru タオル 109
towelling *n* taoruji タオル地 115

tower n tō 塔 83

town n machi 町 38,77

town centre n chūshin gai 中心街 21 ; shinai 市内 66

town hall n shiyakusho 市役所 83

tow truck n ken-insha けん引車 79

toy n omocha おもちゃ 128

toy shop n omochaya おもちゃ屋 99

tracksuit n torēnā トレーナー 112

traditional dentō(teki na) 伝統 (的な) 84,110

traffic n kuruma no tōri 車の通り 77

traffic light n shingō 信号 78

train n ressha 列車 66,67,68,69,71, 72 ; densha 電車 19,73

tram n shiden 市電 74

tranquillizer n chinseizai 鎮静剤 108, 142

transfer (bank) n sōkin 送金 131

transformer n toransu トランス 119

translate, to yakusu 訳す 12

translation n (hon-)yaku （翻）訳 104

translator n (hon-)yakusha （翻）訳者 131

travel, to ryokō suru 旅行する 94

travel agency n ryokō dairiten 旅行代理 店 99

travel guide n ryokō annaisho 旅行案内 書 104

traveller's cheque n toraberā chekku ト ラベラーチェック 18,62,102,130

travel sickness norimono yoi 乗り物酔 い 107

treatment n chiryō 治療 142

tree n ki 木 86

trim, to (beard) totonoeru ととのえる 31

trip n ryokō 旅行 153

tripod n sankyaku 三脚 125

trolley n kāto カート 19,72

trousers n zubon ズボン 112

trout n masu ます 48

try, to tamesu 試す 113 ; (sample) aj-iwattemiru 味わってみる 60

T-shirt n tīshatsu Tシャツ 112

tube n chūbu チューブ 120

Tuesday n kayōbi 火曜日 150

tuna/tunny n maguro まぐろ 45,48

tuner n chūnā チューナー 119

turbot n karei かれい 47

turkey n shichimenchō 七面鳥 52

turn, to (change direction) magaru 曲る

turquoise toruko burū トルコブルー 114

turquoise n toruko ishi トルコ石 122

turtleneck tātoru nekku タートルネッ ク 111

tweezers n kenuki 毛抜き 109

twelve jū-ni 十二 146

twenty ni-jū 二十 146

twice nido 二度 148

twin bed n tsuin beddo ツインベッド 23

two ni 二 146

typewriter n taipuraitā タイプライター 27

tyre n taiya タイヤ 76,79

U

ugly minikui みにくい 14

umbrella n kasa 傘 112

unconscious ishiki fumei (no) 意識不明 （の）138

under no shita ni の下に 15

underdone (meat) namayake 生焼け 51, 63 ; reā レアー 51

underground (railway) n chikatetsu 地下 鉄 73

underpants n pantsu パンツ 112

undershirt n shatsu シャツ 112

understand, to wakaru わかる 12,16

undress, to fuku o nugu 服を脱ぐ 141

United States n amerika(gasshū koku) アメリカ（合衆国）132,145

university n daigaku 大学 83

unleaded muen 無鉛 76

until made (ni) まで（に）15

up ue (ni) 上（に）15

upset stomach n i no motare 胃のもた れ 107

upstairs kaijō 階上 15

urgent kyūyō 急用 13

urgent telegram n shikyū denpō 至急電 報 133

urine n nyō 尿 141

use, to tsukau 使う 70,79,134

usual itsumo (no) いつも（の）95,142

V

vacancy n aki 空き 154

vacation n kyūka 休暇 16,93,151

vacation village n kyūka mura 休暇村 32

vaccinate, to yobō chūsha o suru 予防注 射をする 139

vaginal infection n chitsuen 膣炎 140

valley n tani 谷 81

value n kachi 価値 131

veal n koushi(niku) 仔牛（肉）40,50

vegetable n yasai 野菜 40,54,64

vegetable store n yaoya 八百屋 99

vegetarian saishoku (shugi no) 菜食（主 義の）38,42

vegetarian n saishokushugi sha 菜食主義者 42

vein n kekkan 血管 137

velvet n birōdo ビロード 115

velveteen n men birōdo 綿ビロード, betchin 別珍 115

venereal disease n seibyō 性病 141

vermouth n berumotto ベルモット 60

very taihen (ni) 大変 (に) 15

vest n shatsu シャツ 112 ; (Am.) chokki チョッキ 112

video cassette n bideo kasetto ビデオカセット 128

video recorder n bideo rekōdā ビデオレコーダー 119

video shop n bideo yōhinten ビデオ用品店 99

view n keshiki 景色 23,25

village n mura 村 86

vinegar n su 酢 41

visit n hōmon 訪問 94

visit, to tazuneru 尋ねる 85

visiting hours n menkai jikan 面会時間 143

visitor n hōmonsha 訪問者 85

vitamin pill n bitaminzai ビタミン剤 108

V-neck bui nekku Vネック 111

vodka n uokka ウォッカ 60

volleyball n barēbōru バレーボール 91

voltage n boruto ボルト 27,119

vomit, to modosu もどす 139

W

waistcoat n chokki チョッキ 112

wait, to matsu 待つ 21,69,96,106

waiter n uētā ウエイター 40

waiting room n machiai shitsu 待合室 68

waitress n uetoresu ウエイトレス 40

wake, to okosu 起こす 27,71

walk n sanpo 散歩 96

walk, to aruku 歩く 80,86

wall n kabe 壁, hei へい 86

wallet n satsuire 札入れ 155

walnut n kurumi くるみ 56

want, to (wish) hossuru 欲する 13, 101 ; (to do) (shi)tai (し)たい 13, 18,20,26,30

warning n keikoku 警告 154

wash, to arau 洗う 30

washable araeru 洗える 115

wash basin n senmendai 洗面台 29

watch n tokei 時計 121,122,127

watchmaker's n tokeiya 時計屋 99,121

watchstrap n tokei bando 時計バンド 122

water n mizu 水 7,41,43,76

waterfall n taki 滝 86

watermelon n suika すいか 56

watermill n suisha 水車 86

waterproof bōsui (no) 防水 (の) 122

way (road) n michi 道 21,77

weather n tenki 天気 95

weather forecast n tenki yohō 天気予報 95

Wednesday n suiyōbi 水曜日 150

week n shū 週 16,20,24,25,81,151

weekend n shūmatsu 週末 151

well yoku よく 113

well-done (meat) n yoku yaku よく焼く, werudan ウエルダン 51

west n nishi 西 78

Western-style yōfū (no) 洋風 (の) 43

what nani 何 11

wheel n sharin 車輪 79

when itsu いつ 11

where doko どこ 11

which dochira どちら, dore どれ 11

whipped cream n hoippu kuīmu ホイップクリーム 57

whisky n uisuki ウイスキー 17,60

white shiro 白 59,114

whitebait n shirauo しらうお 47

who dare 誰 11

why naze 何故, dōshite どうして 11

wick n shin 芯 126

wide (clothes) yurui ゆるい 116

wide-angle lens n kōkaku renzu 拡角レンズ 125

wife n (your own) kanai 家内 93,95 ; (someone else's) oku san 奥さん

wild boar n inoshishi いのしし 52

wind n kaze 風 95

window n mado 窓 29,39,70 ; (shop) uindō ウインドー 100,110

windscreen/shield n furonto garasu フロントガラス 76

windy kaze ga tsuyoi 風が強い 95

wine n wain ワイン 17,41,59

wine list n wain risuto ワインリスト 59

wine merchant's n sakaya 酒屋 99

winter n fuyu 冬 149

winter sports n uintā supōtsu ウインタースポーツ 92

wiper n waipā ワイパー 76

with to tomo ni 共に 15

withdraw, to (bank) hikidasu 引き出す 130

without nashi de なしで 15

woman n josei 女性 110

wood n ki 木 84 ; (forest) hayashi 林 86

DICTIONARY

woodblock print n mokuhanga 木版画 127

woodblock print shop n mokuhanga ten 木版画店 99

woodcraft n kibori 木彫 84

wool n yōmō 羊毛, ūru ウール 115

word n (tan) go （単）語 12,133

word processor n wāpuro ワープロ 119

work n shigato 仕事 95

work, to hataraku 働く 95 ; *(function)* ugoku 動く 29

working day n heijitsu 平日 151

worse yori warui より悪い 14

worsted n ūsuteddo ウーステッド 115

wound n kizu 傷 138

wrap, to tsutsumu 包む 103

wrapping paper n hōsōshi 包装紙 105

wrinkle resistant shiwa bōshikakō しわ防止加工 115

write, to kaku 書く 12,101

writing paper n binsen 便箋 27,105

wrong machigai 間違い 14

X

X-ray *(photo)* n rentogen レントゲン 139

Y

year n toshi, nen 年 149

yellow ki iro 黄色 114

yes hai はい 10

yesterday sakujitsu, kinō 昨日 151

yet mada まだ 15,16

yoghurt n yōguruto ヨーグルト 43,64

young wakai 若い 14

youth hostel n yūsu hosuteru ユースホステル 32

Z

Zen temple n zendera 禅寺 84

zip(per) n chakku チャック 112

zoo n dōbutsuen 動物園 83

zoom lens n zūmu renzu ズームレンズ 125

zucchini n nagakabocha 長かぼちゃ 54

日本語索引

あ

赤帽（ポーター）	18, 72
遺失物	155
医者	136
衣料品	111
色	114
映画	87
駅	67, 71
織物	115
音楽	128
おしぼり	38

か

海水浴場	92
買物（案内）	98
貸自転車	80
カセット	128
ガソリンスタンド	76
歌舞伎	82, 88
（お）金	18, 129
体（の部分）	137
観光	81
観光所内所	19, 81
喫茶店	33
季節（四季）	149
切手	28, 132
切符	
コンサート，劇場	89
サッカー	91
列車	70
美術館	83
教会	85
魚介類	40, 47
キヨスク	99, 126
緊急	155
銀行	129
空港	16, 65
果物	56
靴	116, 117
国（の名前）	145
車	76
故障	79
事故	79
駐車	78
レンタカー	20
警察	79, 155

劇場	87
化粧品	108
郊外	86
交通	
案内	68
切符	70
バス	74
飛行機	65
船	75
列車	66
交番	155
娯楽	87

さ

菜食主義者	42
サイズ	113
魚	40, 47
酒	58
事故	79, 138
時間	151, 152
神社	83, 84
新聞	104
紹介	93
招待	95
写真（屋）	124
しゃぶしゃぶ	35, 51
宗教（礼拝）	85
祝祭日	153
祝辞	153
宿泊	22, 23
食料品	99, 120
食料品店（スーパーマーケット）	120
食器	41
すき焼き	35, 52
数字	146
寿司（すし）	35, 49
スパイス（香辛料）	55
スープ	40, 46
スポーツ	91
相撲	91
税関	16, 102
洗濯屋	30
そば／うどん	35, 53

た

タクシー	21
タバコ屋	126

単位（度量衡）
　温度　　　　　　　　　　　157
　体積　　　　　　　　　　　156
　距離　　　　　　　　　　　156
　サイズ（体の）　　　　　　113
地下鉄　　　　　　　　　　　73
地図　　　　　　　　　　77, 105
茶碗蒸　　　　　　　　　　　46
駐車　　　　　　　　　　　　78
朝食　　　　　　　　　　　　42
月（十二箇月）　　　　　　　150
庭園　　　　　　　　　　82, 84
ディスコ　　　　　　　　　　90
デート　　　　　　　　　　　96
デパート　　　　　98, 100, 117
寺　　　　　　　　　　　83, 84
天気　　　　　　　　　　　　95
電気器具　　　　　　　　　　118
電気店　　　　　　　　　　　118
電報、テレックス　　　　　　133
電話　　　　　　　　　　　　134
とうふ　　　　　　　　　　　55
糖尿病　　　　　　　　　41, 140
道路標識　　　　　　　　　　80
時計　　　　　　　　　　　　121
年　　　　　　　　　　　　　149
鳥肉類　　　　　　　　　　　52
泥棒　　　　　　　　　　　　155
とんかつ　　　　　　　　　　51

な
ナイトクラブ　　　　　　89, 90
肉類　　　　　　　　　　　　50
荷物　　　　　　　　　　18, 72
能　　　　　　　　　　　　　88
飲物　　　　　　　　　　　　58
　アルコール抜き　　　　　　60

は
歯医者　　　　　　　　　　　144
箸　　　　　　　　　　　36, 41
バス　　　　　　　　　　　　74
パスポート　　　　　　　　　16
バレー　　　　　　　　　　　87
繁華街　　　　　　　　　　　82
飛行機　　　　　　　　　　　65
ピクニック　　　　　　　　　64
ビジネス　　　　　　　　　　131
日付　　　　　　　　　　　　150
病院　　　　　　　　　　　　143

美容院，理容院　　　　　　　31
病気　　　　　　　　　　　　139
表現（基礎）　　　　　　　　10
標示　　　　　　　　　　　　154
フィルム　　　　　　　124, 125
船　　　　　　　　　　　　　75
文法　　　　　　　　　　　　158
文房具店　　　　　　　　　　105
方向（東西南北）　　　　　　77
宝石店　　　　　　　　　　　121
ホテル　　　　　　　　　　　22
　困り事　　　　　　　　　　29
　出発（チェックアウト）　　32
　フロント　　　　　　　　　23
　郵便物　　　　　　　　　　28
　予約　　　　　　　　　　　19
ホテルスタッフ　　　　　　　26
本屋　　　　　　　　　　　　104

ま
店（のリスト）　　　　　　　98
道を尋ねる　　　　　　　　　77
みやげ　　　　　　　　　　　127
名刺　　　　　　　　　　　　131
眼鏡屋　　　　　　　　　　　123
メニュー　　　　　　　　　　44
免税店　　　　　　　　102, 117

や
焼き鳥　　　　　　　　　35, 52
焼肉　　　　　　　　　　　　51
野菜　　　　　　　　　　　　54
屋台　　　　　　　　　　　　34
薬局，薬屋　　　　　　　　　106
郵便局　　　　　　　　　　　132
曜日　　　　　　　　　　　　150

ら
ラーメン　　　　　　　　　　53
両替　　　　　　　　　　18, 129
猟鳥獣の肉　　　　　　　　　52
旅館　　　　　　　　　　　　22
レコード　　　　　　　　　　128
レストラン　　　　　　　　　33
　勘定　　　　　　　　　　　62
　苦情　　　　　　　　　　　63
　注文　　　　　　　　　　　40
　メニュー　　　　　　　　　44

わ
ワイン　　　　　　　　　　　59

Say BERLITZ®

... and most people think of outstanding language schools. But Berlitz has also become the world's leading publisher of books for travellers – Travel Guides, Phrase Books, Dictionaries – plus Cassettes and Self-teaching courses.

Informative, accurate, up-to-date, Books from Berlitz are written with freshness and style. They also slip easily into pocket or purse – no need for bulky, old-fashioned volumes.

Join the millions who know how to travel. Whether for fun or business, put Berlitz in your pocket.

BERLITZ®

Leader in
Books and Cassettes
for Travellers

A division of Macmillan, Inc.

BERLITZ® Books for travellers

TRAVEL GUIDES

They fit your pocket in both size and price. Modern, up-to-date, Berlitz gets all the information you need into 128 lively pages with colour maps and photos throughout. What to see and do, where to shop, what to eat and drink, how to save.

ASIA, MIDDLE EAST	China (256 pages)
	Hong Kong
	India (256 pages)
	Japan (256 pages)
	Singapore
	Sri Lanka
	Thailand
	Egypt
	Jerusalem and the Holy Land
	Saudi Arabia
AUSTRAL-ASIA	Australia (256 pages)*
	New Zealand
BRITISH ISLES	Channel Islands
	London
	Ireland
	Oxford and Stratford
	Scotland
BELGIUM	Brussels

AFRICA	Kenya
	Morocco
	South Africa
	Tunisia

*in preparation

PHRASE BOOKS

World's bestselling phrase books feature all the expressions and vocabulary you'll need, and pronunciation throughout. 192 pages, 2 colours.

Arabic	Hebrew	Serbo-Croatian
Chinese	Hungarian	Spanish (Castilian)
Danish	Italian	Spanish (Lat. Am.)
Dutch	Japanese	Swahili
Finnish	Norwegian	Swedish
French	Polish	Turkish
German	Portuguese	European Phrase Book
Greek	Russian	European Menu Reader

FRANCE	Brittany			Costa Blanca
	France (256 pages)			Costa Brava
	French Riviera			Costa del Sol and Andalusia
	Loire Valley			Ibiza and Formentera
	Normandy*			Madrid
	Paris			Majorca and Minorca
GERMANY	Berlin		EASTERN	Budapest
	Munich		EUROPE	Dubrovnik and Southern
	The Rhine Valley			Dalmatia
AUSTRIA	Tyrol			Hungary (192 pages)
and	Vienna			Istria and Croatian Coast
SWITZER-	Switzerland (192 pages)			Moscow & Leningrad
LAND				Split and Dalmatia
GREECE,	Athens		NORTH	U.S.A. (256 pages)
CYPRUS &	Corfu		AMERICA	California
TURKEY	Crete			Florida
	Rhodes			Hawaii
	Greek Islands of the Aegean			New York
	Peloponnese			Toronto
	Salonica and Northern Greece			Montreal
	Cyprus			
	Istanbul/Aegean Coast		CARIBBEAN,	Puerto Rico
			LATIN	Virgin Islands
ITALY and	Florence		AMERICA	Bahamas
MALTA	Italian Adriatic			Bermuda
	Italian Riviera			French West Indies
	Italy (256 pages)*			Jamaica
	Rome			Southern Caribbean
	Sicily			Mexico City
	Venice			Rio de Janeiro
	Malta			
			EUROPE	Business Travel Guide –
NETHER-	Amsterdam			Europe (368 pages)
LANDS and	Copenhagen			Pocket guide to Europe
SCANDI-	Helsinki			(480 pages)
NAVIA	Oslo and Bergen			Cities of Europe (504 pages)
	Stockholm		CRUISE	Caribbean cruise guide
PORTUGAL	Algarve		GUIDES	(368 pages)
	Lisbon			Alaska cruise guide
	Madeira			(168 pages)
				Handbook to Cruising
SPAIN	Barcelona and Costa Dorada			(240 pages)
	Canary Islands			

in preparation

**Most titles with British and U.S. destinations are available
in French, German, Spanish and as many as 7 other languages.**

DICTIONARIES

Bilingual with 12,500 concepts each way. Highly practical for travellers,
with pronunciation shown plus menu reader, basic expressions and useful
information. Over 330 pages.

| Danish | Finnish | German | Norwegian | Spanish |
| Dutch | French | Italian | Portuguese | Swedish |

**Berlitz Books, a world of information in your pocket!
At all leading bookshops and airport newsstands.**

Finally... a fast, fun, and affordable way to learn a foreign language...

INTRODUCING THE BERLITZ EXPRESS PROGRAMS

Self-study programs for beginners

Available in:
- Spanish
- French
- German
- Italian

THE TEN COMMANDMENTS OF GOD
God's Law of Love, Grace and Freedom

X. You shall not covet your neighbor's goods.

We should desire the things of God, like grace and virtue. We should not wish for things that do not belong to us. We must be willing to share our things. Jesus, help me not to be selfish with my things or envious of what others have.

A LITTLE LITANY OF THANKSGIVING

For this Happy Day,
Jesus, I thank You.

For being my sweet Guest,
Jesus, I thank You.

For giving me good parents,
Jesus, I thank You.

For the grace of a good Confession,
Jesus, I thank You.

For this Holy Communion,
Jesus, I thank You.

For my many graces and blessings,
Jesus, I thank You.

For my joy and happiness,
Jesus, I thank You.

For my troubles and sadness,
Jesus, I thank You.

For giving me a Holy Guardian Angel,
Jesus, I thank You.

For staying with us Yourself,
Jesus, I thank You.

Imagine, in a short time from now, being able to speak an entirely new language. French, perhaps. Or Spanish. German. Or Italian.

Berlitz, the world-renowned language instruction institution, has developed these self-study programs *expressly* for those people who want to learn to speak a foreign language *fast*. And without going through the tedious, repetitive drills and grammar rule memorization that are featured in other courses.

Instead, with the Berlitz Express programs, you learn to speak *naturally,* by listening to—and then joining in on—"real-life" dialogue on cassette tapes. This helps you *absorb* correct grammar and vocabulary almost unconsciously. And because the tapes use *sound effects* to convey meaning, you can learn your new language while you're driving, biking, walking, or doing just about anything.

Each Express Program Contains:

- TWO CASSETTES TOTALLING 100 minutes of instruction and using lively *sound effects* to identify objects, actions, and situations in your new language.

- LESSON TEXT explains new words and grammar variations as you encounter them.

- BERLITZ ROTARY VERB FINDER. How do you change the expression "I go" to "I will go" or "I went" in the language you're learning? Just spin the dial and you'll have your answer for a wide variety of common verbs.

- CONVENIENT STORAGE ALBUM protects tapes, book, and Verb Finder from damage.

Dial (no charge, USA)
24 hours, 7 days a week.

In the U.S.A.   **In Great Britain**

1-800-431-9003   **0323-638221**

Refer to Dept. No. 11604. Why not give us a ring – right now!

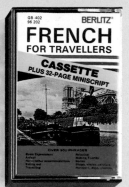

Treat yourself to an hour with BERLITZ®

Just listen and repeat

It's fun, not work. And you'll surprise your friends and yourself: it's so easy to pick up some basic expressions in the foreign language of your choice. These cassettes are recorded in hi-fi with four voices. Bringing native speakers into your home, they permit you to improve your accent and learn the basic phrases before you depart.

With each cassette is a helpful 32-page script, containing pronunciation tips, plus complete text of the dual-language recording.

An ideal companion for your Berlitz phrase book, pocket dictionary or travel guide. Order now!

$9.95/£5.95 (incl. VAT)

use convenient envelope attached.